IMAGES
of America

The Chinese Community of Stockton

IMAGES
of America

THE CHINESE COMMUNITY OF STOCKTON

Sylvia Sun Minnick

ARCADIA
PUBLISHING

ISBN 978-0-7385-2053-7

Published by Arcadia Publishing
Charleston, South Carolina

Printed in the United States of America

Library of Congress Catalog Card Number: 2001098834

For all general information contact Arcadia Publishing at:
Telephone 843-853-2070
Fax 843-853-0044
E-Mail sales@arcadiapublishing.com
For customer service and orders:
Toll-Free 1-888-313-2665

Visit us on the Internet at www.arcadiapublishing.com

Contents

Acknowledgments 6

Introduction 7

1. Early History 9

2. Chinese Cultural Ties 19

3. Economic Energy 29

4. Families, Friends, and Events 61

5. Spirited Renewal 93

ACKNOWLEDGMENTS

Fourteen years ago I wrote *SAMFOW: The San Joaquin Chinese Legacy*, a scholarly history of the Chinese using a breadth of modern research and archival material including cemetery and marriage records, Sanborn maps, and census information. *SAMFOW* covered the period from the California Gold Rush to the traumatic disruption of the cultural practice of returning interred Chinese remains to their native village for final rest. The venue of *SAMFOW* did not totally describe through photographs and text the total social dynamics of the people.

In this sequel, the people are the author. Casual requests for photographs turned into an unexpected, but extremely exciting, wealth of family albums. Seniors scoured their attics, garages and overstuffed closets to find a particular album or boxes of pictures. When memories of specific dates faded, they called siblings or friends for specificity. Valuable, and at times scratched and torn personal photos of grandparents' weddings and youthful club activities of 80 years past as well as streetscapes of businesses just prior to demolition fell into my hands rather quickly. I was humbled. Although I have lived in Stockton for over 40 years after arriving at the age of 20, the photos provided a clearer understanding of familial relationships and business partners, *Raison d'Être*.

My apologies to those whose pictures were not all used. The constraints of this publication kept the number of photos in line and kept the story in focus. So many people participated in this effort, I am doing an injustice by not naming them all and I apologize. Some provided family photos or images of themselves. Others, however, provided many, many photos of the community and also data that made writing easier. These wonderful friends need to be acknowledged, and they are: Doug and Violet Jann, Violet Chan, Norman Lew, Jimmy Lam, Freeman Chang, Frank Kim, Dun Fong, Val Acoba, Wing Chan, Keith Wong, Leona Wong, Mary Huey, Esther Chan, Bonnie Lew, Conrad Mar, Chance Wong, Margo Chin Mah, Shu-Lin Duan, Gladys Ikeda, Robert Wong, Kathy Meissner, Lois Yee, Jun Wang, and Rose Yip. I am also indebted to Bob Price for excellent reproduction efforts and Derald Smith for researching and interpreting several of the World War II photos. Lastly, but more importantly, I need to acknowledge my husband, Richard—he was patient and understanding, *God bless him*.

INTRODUCTION

The Chinese from Kwangtung, China, looked forward to arriving in San Francisco, the main port of entry to the California gold fields. To them the "big" city was called Dai Fow. Hurrying to try their luck in the goldfields, they headed for the next largest city, Sacramento, entry to the Northern Mother Lode mines. Based on her size, that city was commonly known as Yee Fow, or City #2. And, in sequential order, the third metropolitan area was Sam Fow, referring to Stockton, lying on the San Joaquin River and serving as the gateway to the Southern Mother Lode.

The macro history of the Chinese experience from the Gold Rush period of 1849 to the mid-20th century is pockmarked with anti-Chinese sentiments and ensuing negative legislation at the national, state, and local levels. The Foreign Miners Tax in 1852 and the 1882 Chinese Exclusion Law are two major examples in the 19th Century. Even in the last century, passage of the California Alien Land Act of 1913 demonstrated efforts to block Chinese as well as other Asians from owning property. Local laws stymied the Chinese from becoming equal participants in the larger community life. Ordinances constraining activities in laundry, fishing, peddling goods, and even having sufficient air space in bedrooms were directly enacted to make life difficult for the Chinese. It is not until more recent times that scholars, economists, and policy makers have come to realize that in spite of the active anti-Chinese movements and legislation, the Chinese were major contributors to California's economy. From gold mining to building the transcontinental railroad and feeder lines, to reclaiming delta islands and utilizing their fertile land for agriculture, time and time again, the Chinese displayed their skills and perseverance.

The Chinese appeared so different in culture and society that they were considered a disadvantaged group. Their strong ethnic ties, sense of familial obligations, and the psychological drive to preserve "face" assured their survival, appearance and physical description notwithstanding. Wisely, strong religious influences and personal convictions that instilled emotional and spiritual strength helped to meet and strengthen their resolve. The added critical psychological attachment to "face," the absolute necessity of maintaining, at all costs, one's esteem, image, and family honor before the world bonded families and community into a singular vision—that of being Chinese in heritage and American in citizenship.

The Stockton Chinese, not unlike other Chinese Americans, evolved through their parents' old world upbringing to utilizing modern medical recommendations. As children they balanced Chinese school with that of western education and activities. They trekked to the cemetery and paid homage to deceased relatives during Ching Ming and Cheung Yeung, the bi-annual Chinese memorial days. Many became devout Christians and married in the western style in churches and white wedding gowns but later celebrated the occasion with traditional Chinese banquets. As early as World War I, the Stockton Chinese joined the war efforts. Fundraising to help Chinese in China during the Japanese invasion in the 1930s brought forth outstanding patriotic efforts. Stockton Chinese alone raised over $400,000 for the China effort. Their energy was boundless.

In time, most communities paid tribute to their pioneers and leaders. Certainly, the individuals thus recognized were praised for their keen sense of business, their ability to establish and shape local societies, and their desire to build charitable and fellowship organizations so that their community survived and thrived. It is in this context that this story of the Chinese in Stockton is told. One that demonstrates the achievement of sojourners turned immigrant entrepreneurs; of pioneers and their legacy; of illiterates whose descendants became civic leaders and policymakers.

The Stockton Chinese story goes beyond the expected. It chronicles a group whose geographic home in Chinatown was physically ripped apart under the guise of redevelopment and the construction of the Crosstown Freeway. It was a pogrom that dislocated a people. The literal foundation of their homes, businesses, association headquarters, hangouts, playgrounds, and churches gave way to bulldozers in the late 1960s and early '70s.

Some 30-plus years have passed. Gloriously, the people's resilience and optimism gave purpose to the second and third generations to rebuild—concentrating less on physical structures or relocation and focusing instead on the internal needs of the community at large. With advanced education many became professionals or entered careers in upper management. Some became civic leaders and even founded new organizations to serve the senior population. Still others promoted a renewal of interest in Chinese song and dance and other forms of physical therapy and entertainment. Some left the confines of Stockton and made their way into other communities, including the entertainment field. Reunions brought them back, time and time again, knowing that the early familial and community bonds were still strong.

The Stockton Chinese Community, small in comparison to major cities, is similar to other Chinese community valley towns. Jimmy Lam, a well-respected business leader and known for his love of football, once was asked the secret to his success. He replied with his motto, "Forward, Ever; Backward, Never." This same sense of purpose holds true for his fellow Stocktonians.

One

Early History

The push-pull factors that drew the Chinese from Kwangtung Province to California's gold hills included natural, economic, and social upheavals coupled with the dreams of gold and increased family fortune. In March of 1850, a newspaper article mentioned that 100 Chinese passed through Stockton headed for the gold fields. The 1850 census data for San Joaquin County listed 53 Chinese men, but no Chinese women, in the population.

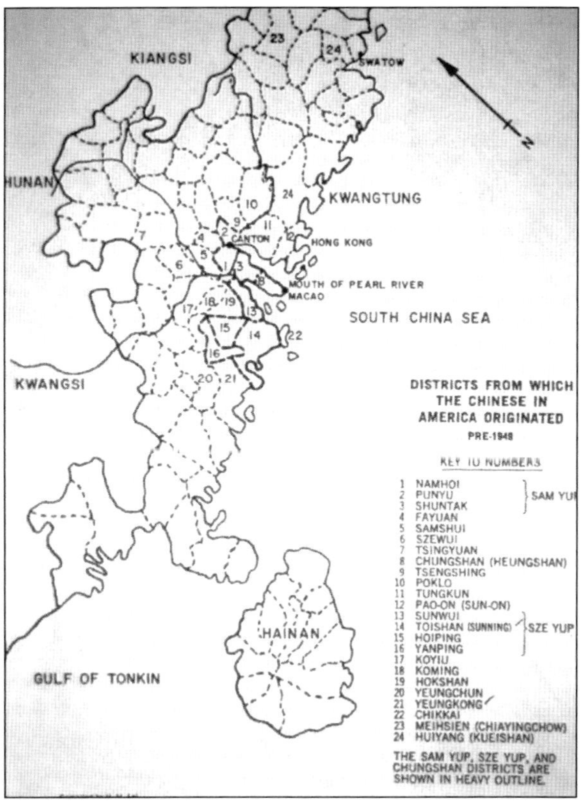

This map shows the major provinces of China and selected districts within Guangdong Province.

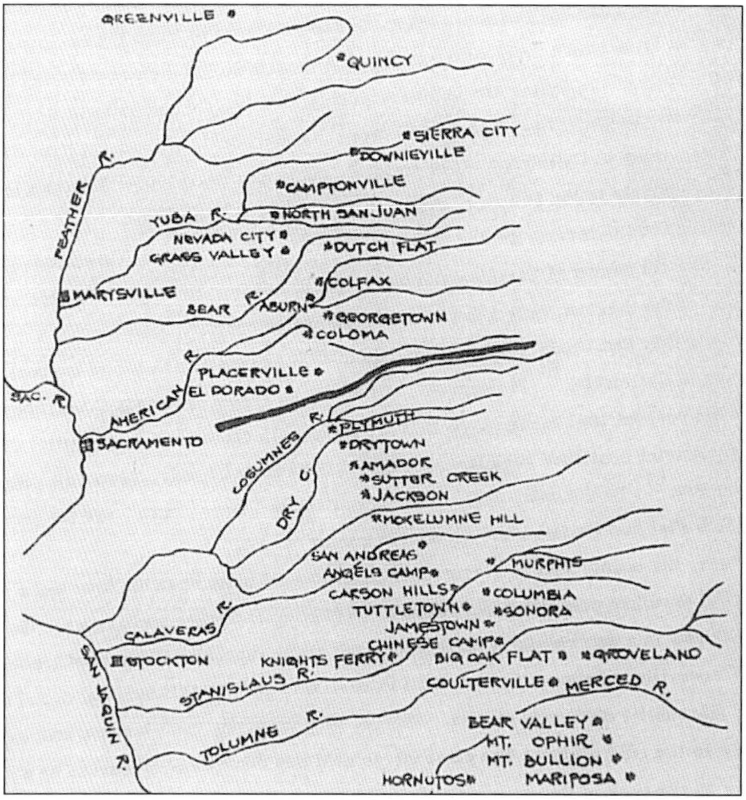

From San Francisco the gold miner chose Sacramento or Stockton as his inland port city, depending on his choice of the northern or southern mines. Both cities served as the supply centers between the gold mining foothill communities and the Bay Area metropolis.

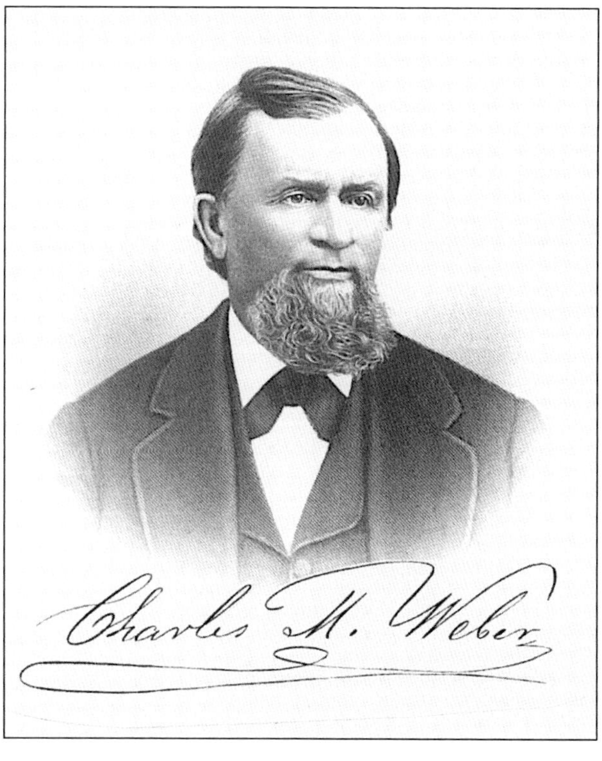

German immigrant and Stockton founder Charles M. Weber played a benefactor's role in the development of Chinese legacy in this city, including allowing the Chinese fishermen to squat on his Mormon Slough property. At his death in 1881, 200 Chinese mourners participated in his funeral procession.

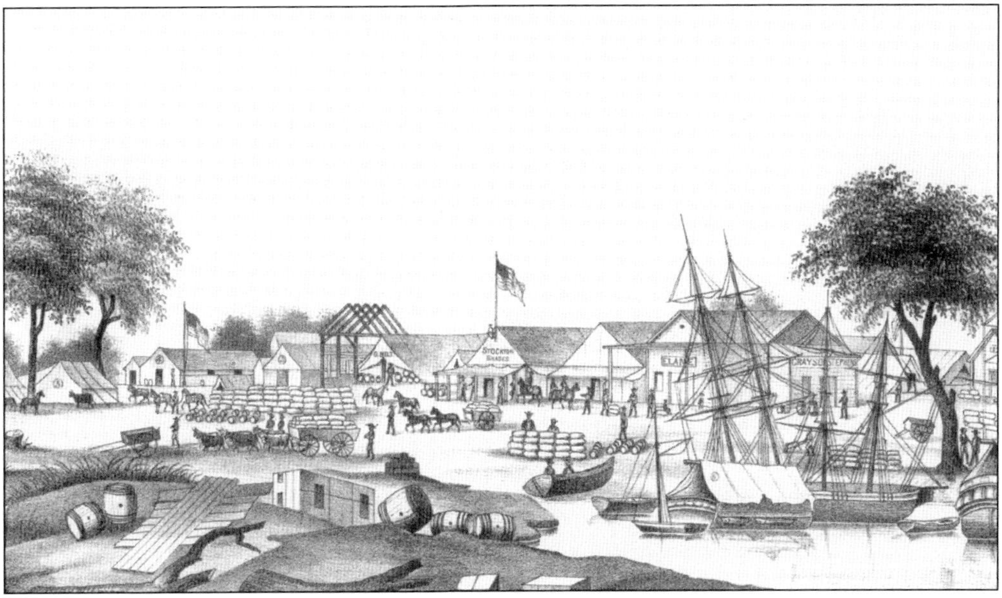

This painting by W.H. Creasy shows the early port and budding town of Stockton in 1849.

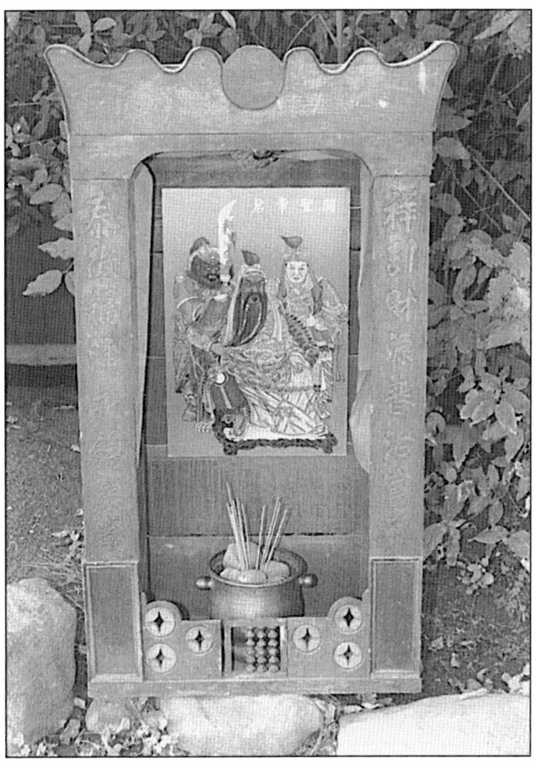

This abandoned wayside shrine was found strapped to an oak tree in the Southern Mother Lode. Chinese miners offered incense, joss candles, and simple offerings to their gods; their prayers asked for safety and success in their venture.

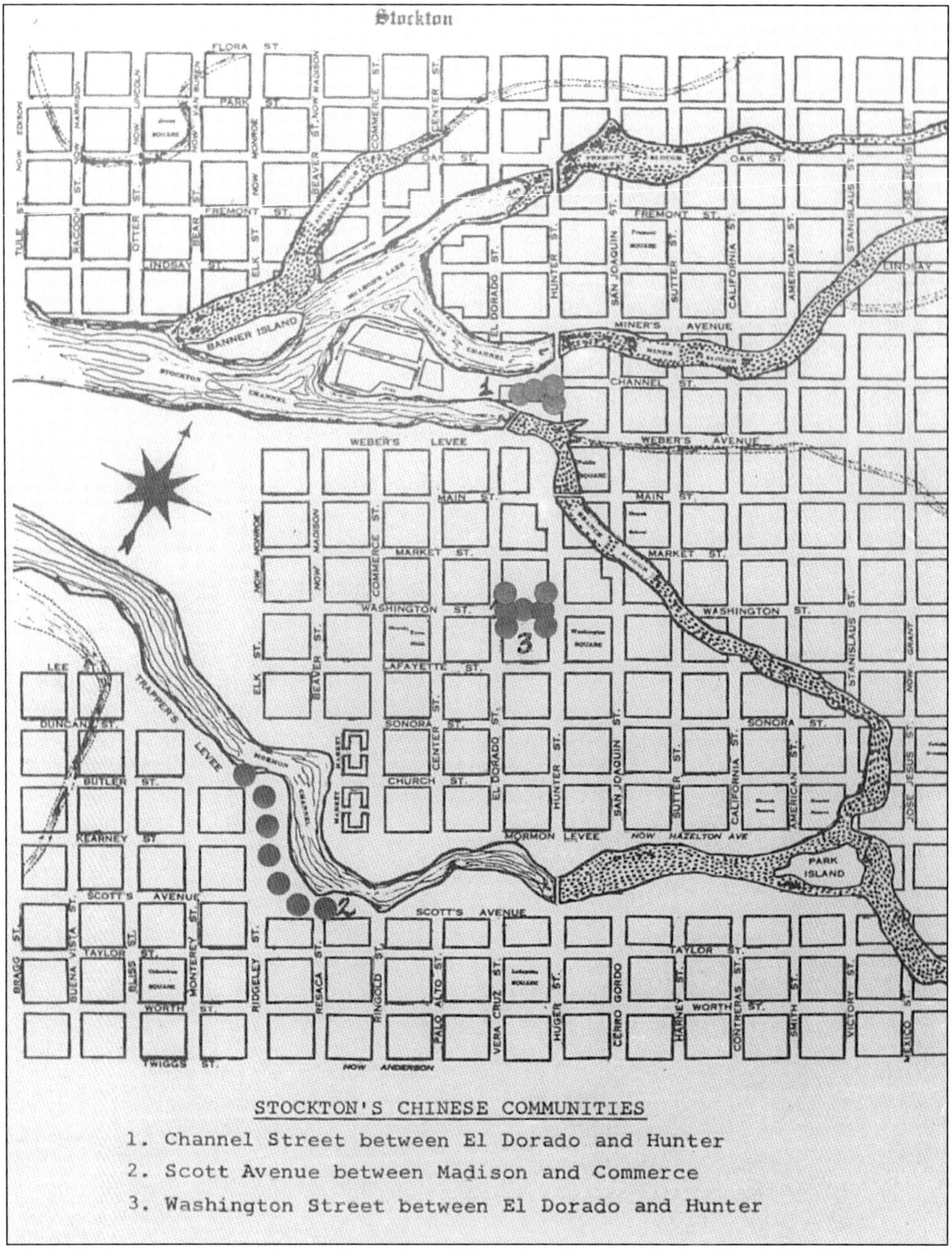

STOCKTON'S CHINESE COMMUNITIES

1. Channel Street between El Dorado and Hunter
2. Scott Avenue between Madison and Commerce
3. Washington Street between El Dorado and Hunter

These are locations of the Chinese communities in Stockton prior to the 1890s. Also visible are the many sloughs and inlets that cut through the city. At one period all three settlements existed simultaneously. The Channel Street settlement closed in the early 1920s; Scott Avenue ended when Capt. Weber's family sold the land in 1893; and Washington Street underwent urban renewal in the late 1960s and '70s.

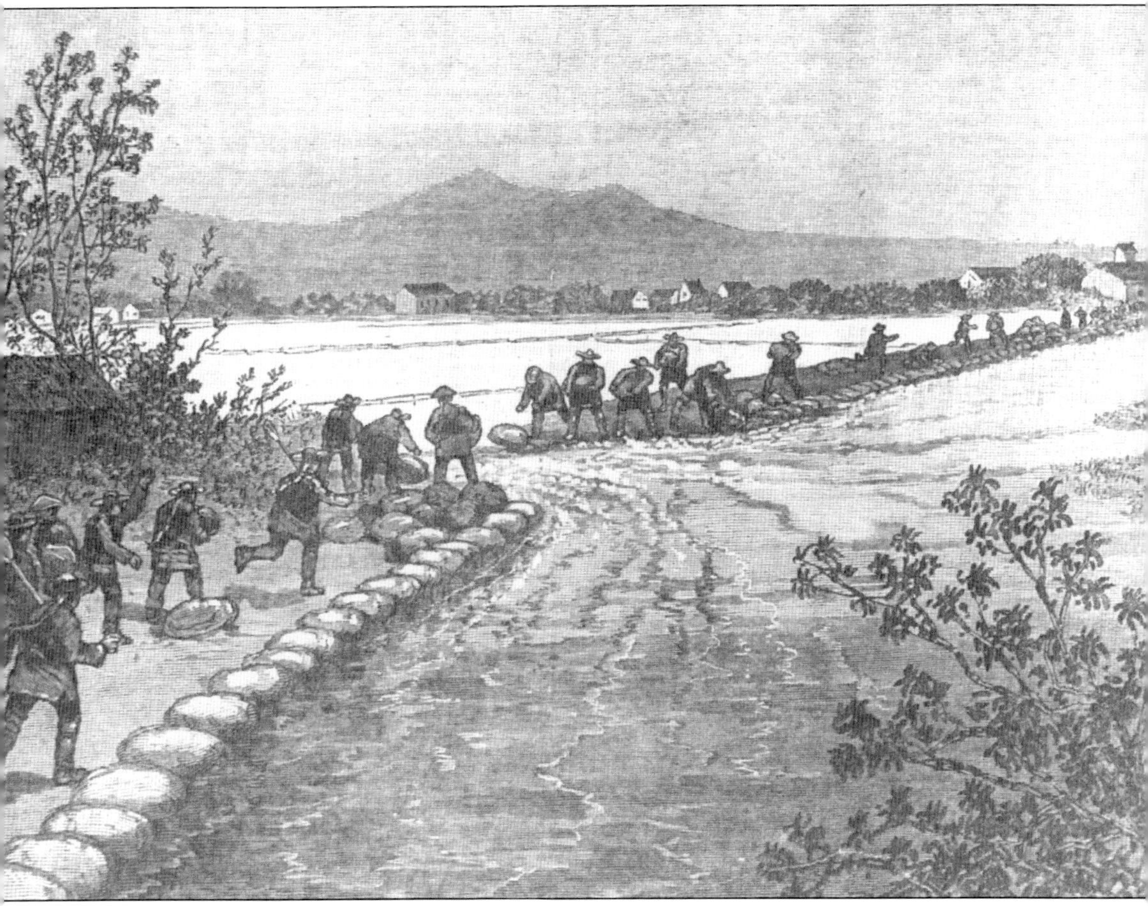

An unknown artist in 1884 captured Chinese reclamation workers closing a foot levee break on the San Joaquin River, 4 miles south of Stockton. The Mount Diablo range is silhouetted in the background. *(Courtesy of the Haggin Museum)*

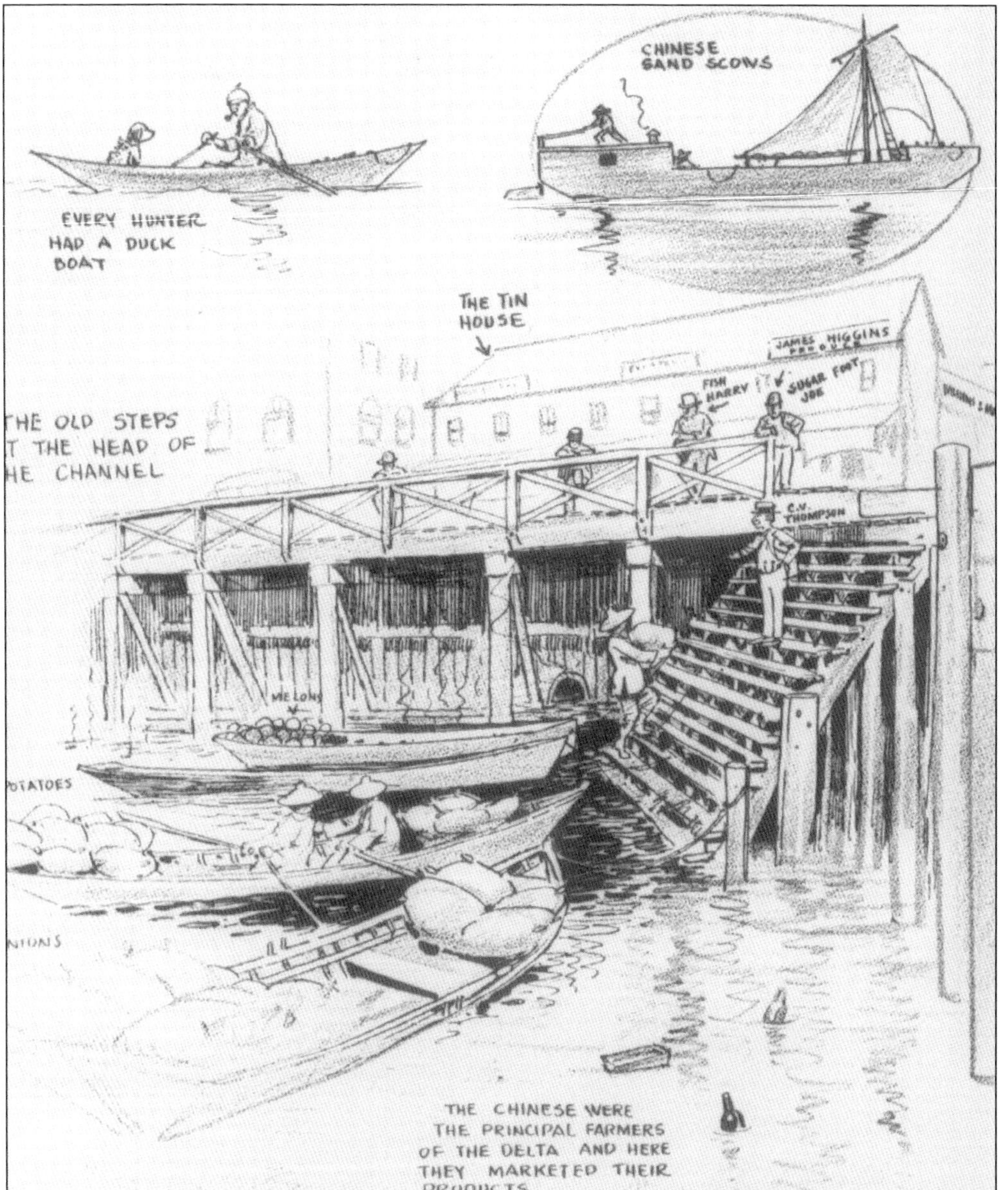

Ralph Yardley, a local cartoonist at the turn of the century, incorporated much of the Chinese activities and locations in his works. Chinese Delta farmers used the waterway and Stockton's inland port to ship their produce to market via rail and steamer connections ideally located at the head of the Stockton channel. *(Courtesy of the Haggin Museum)*

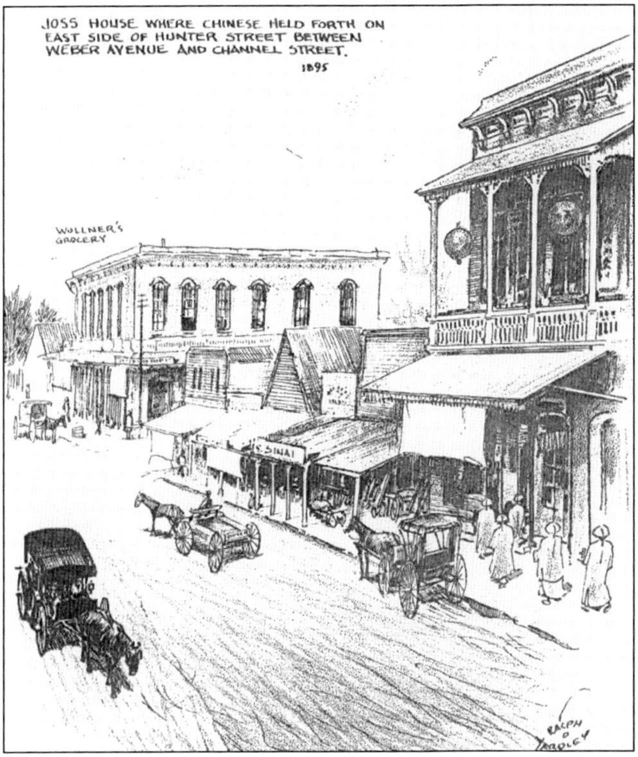

This is a Ralph Yardley sketch of the two-story, brick Heungshan Joss Temple on Hunter Street built in 1882. This building abutted the Turnverian Hall, a social gathering place for the local German population. The Chinese, predominately from the Heungshan district of Guangdong Province, lived around the temple and used it for both worship and as an area to house the sick and dying, as there were no medical facilities available to the early Chinese. By the 1950s many of the temple artifacts were moved to Washington Street. The building, while no longer a house of worship, still stands and is used today as a professional building. *(Courtesy of the Haggin Museum)*

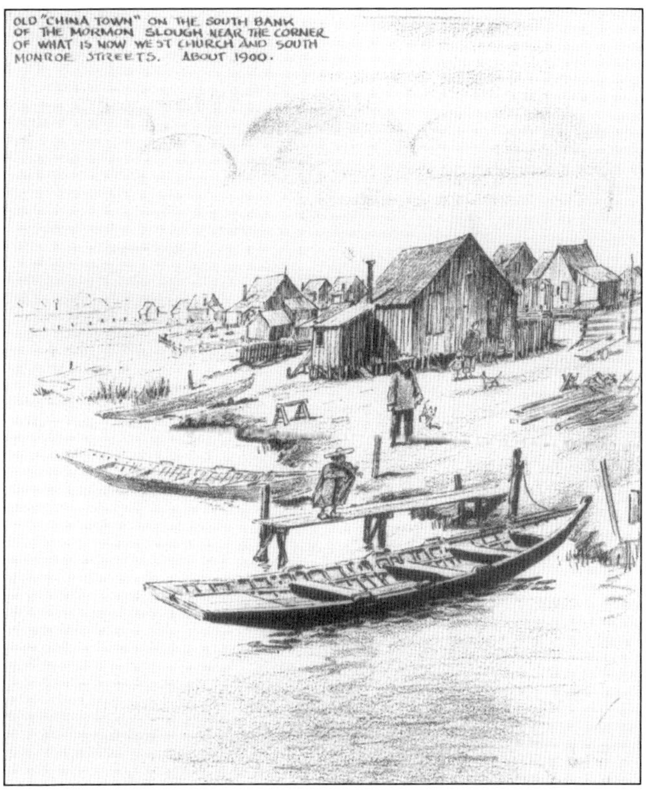

Yardley sketched the Chinese fishing village at Mormon Slough. He drew upon his memories of several decades; however, in this case, his date was not accurate. The little fishing settlement ended in the early 1890s, not at the turn of the century as indicated. The Charles Weber's family sold the land to the Buel Land and Lumber Company in 1894. *(Courtesy of the Haggin Museum)*

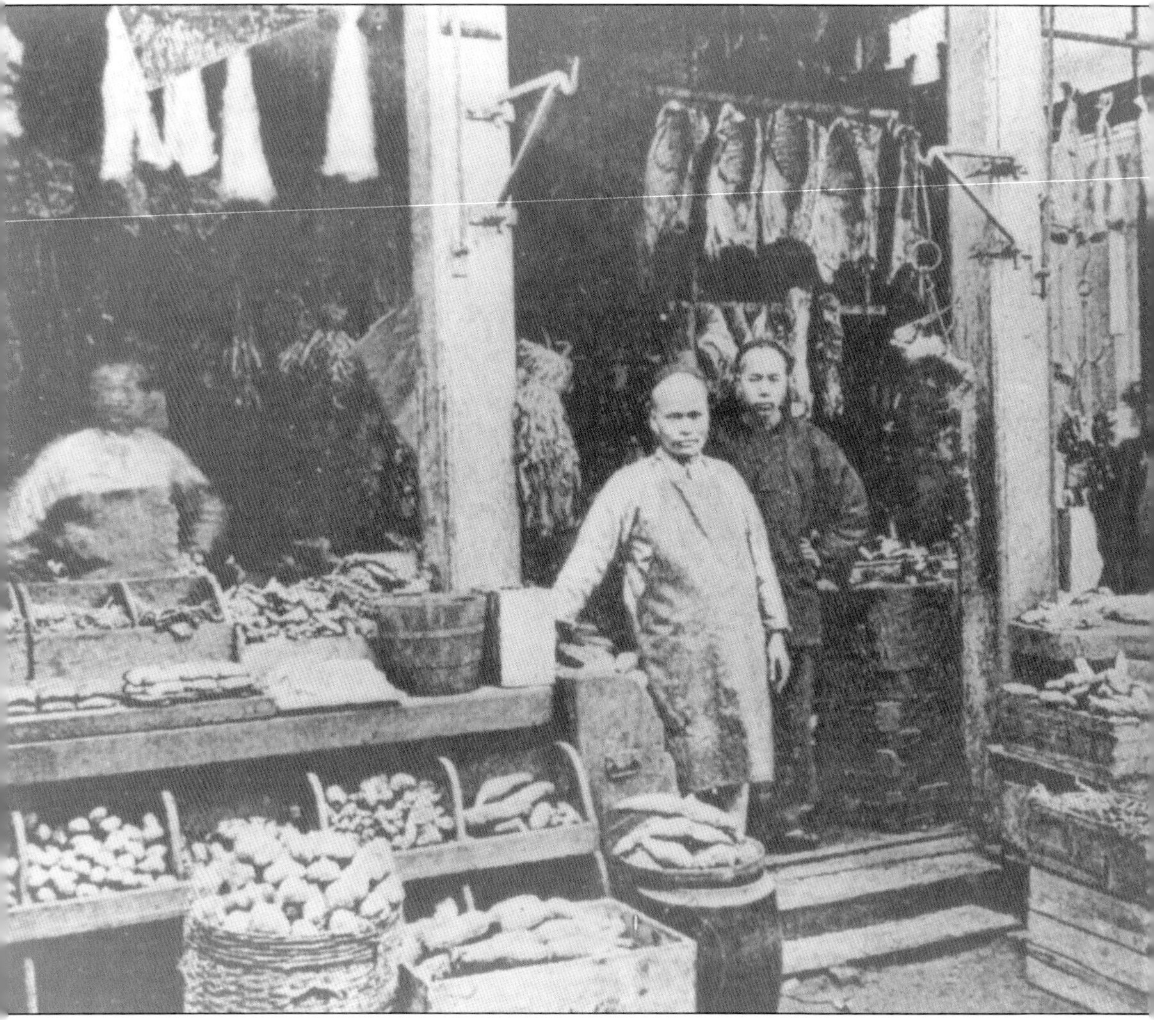

Astute merchants, knowing their countrymen's needs, stocked their stores amply with imported native food products, clothing, medicines, herbs, and fresh produce.

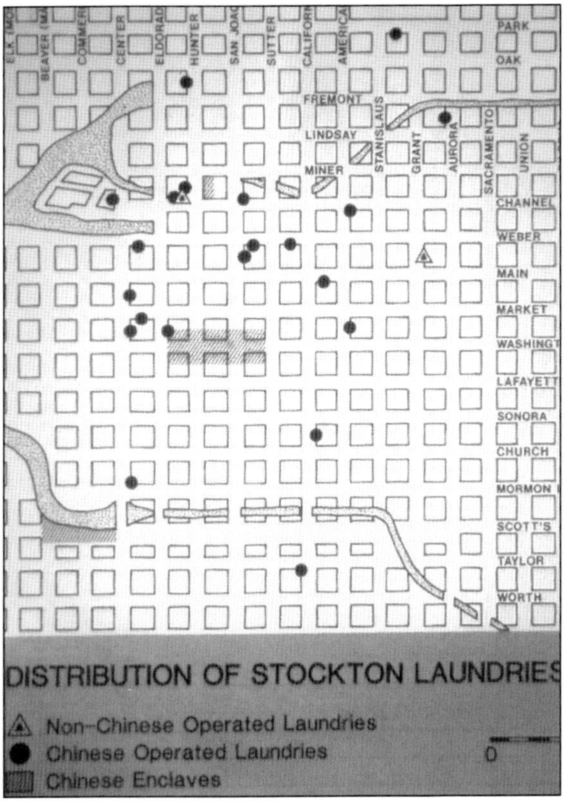

Chinese laundries dotted the inner core of Stockton except for the Chinatown areas. These laundries depended on the Caucasian community for their business and, as a convenience for their customers, were near boardinghouses and within walking distance of downtown and manufacturing companies.

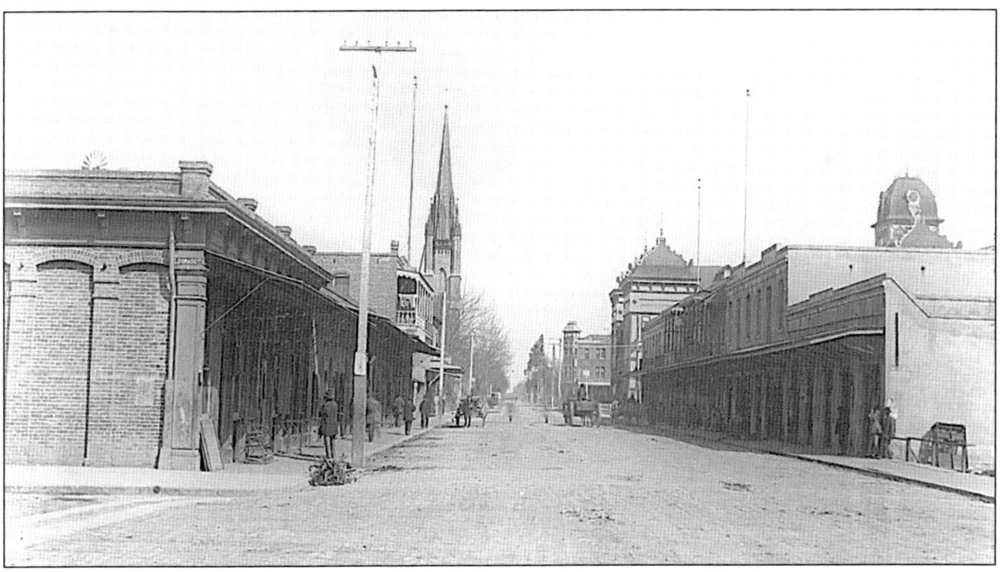

Washington Street Chinatown was the heart and soul of the community with restaurants, family association buildings, herb shops, stores, and gambling houses. Other Chinese businesses extended one block north and one block south from the main street. This 1895 picture of Washington Street shows the steeple of St. Mary's Catholic Church built in 1861 (left side), and on the right the Agricultural Pavilion, an enormous glass exhibit hall built in 1887 and destroyed by fire in 1902. The land reverted back to being Washington Park.

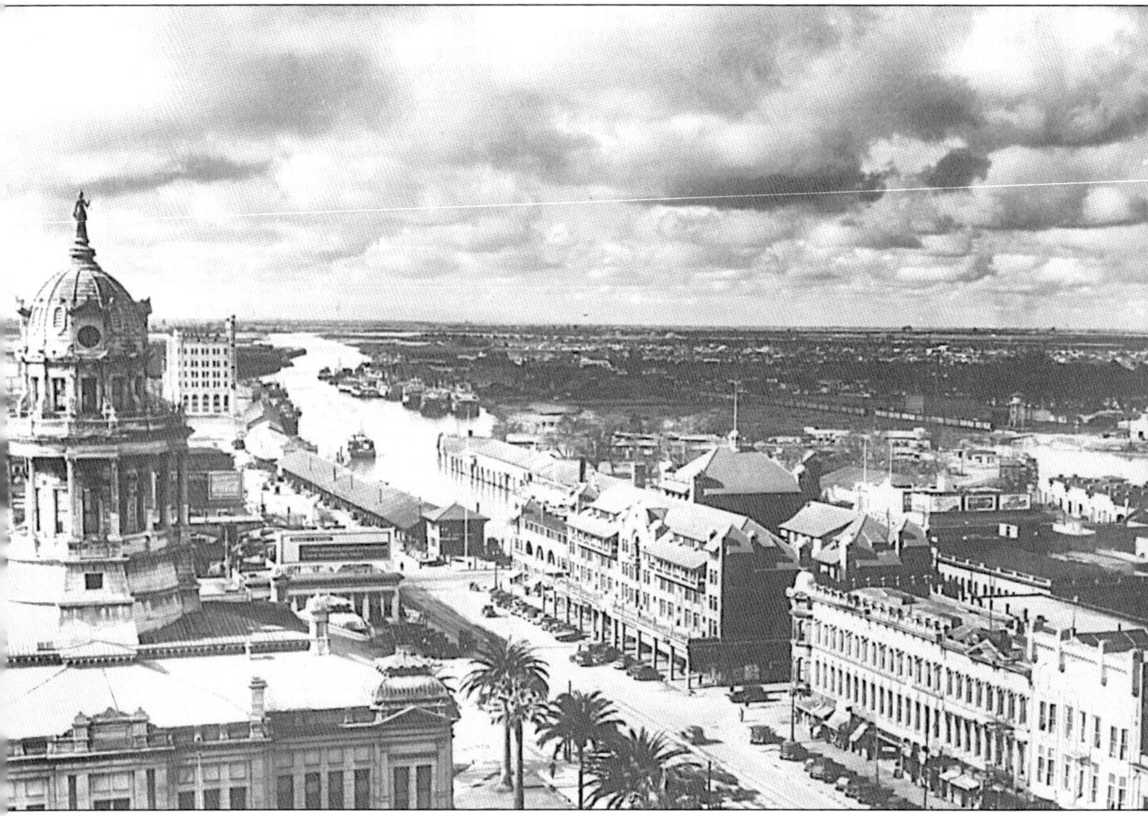

A skyline view, looking west over the Delta, gives a good view of the Stockton Channel and the second courthouse in the left foreground, *c.* 1925.

Two

CHINESE CULTURAL TIES

Ethnic groups and immigrants bring to a new land cultural traditions and customs as part of their heritage. Continual use of the mother tongue, native diet and medicine, and adherence to religious and secular holidays provide a sense of continuity and emotional security for many newcomers. Of added importance to the Chinese are the familial and village ties in the form of clan (same surname) associations and regional dialect organizations. These networks established themselves in sizeable Chinese communities and provided members the camaraderie and social needs such as entertainment, advice, and temporary aid. Regional differences among the Chinese resulted in subtle variations in the holidays celebrated and foods associated with each. Some of their customs commonly practiced had universal significance, as do the incense sticks, candles, and firecrackers.

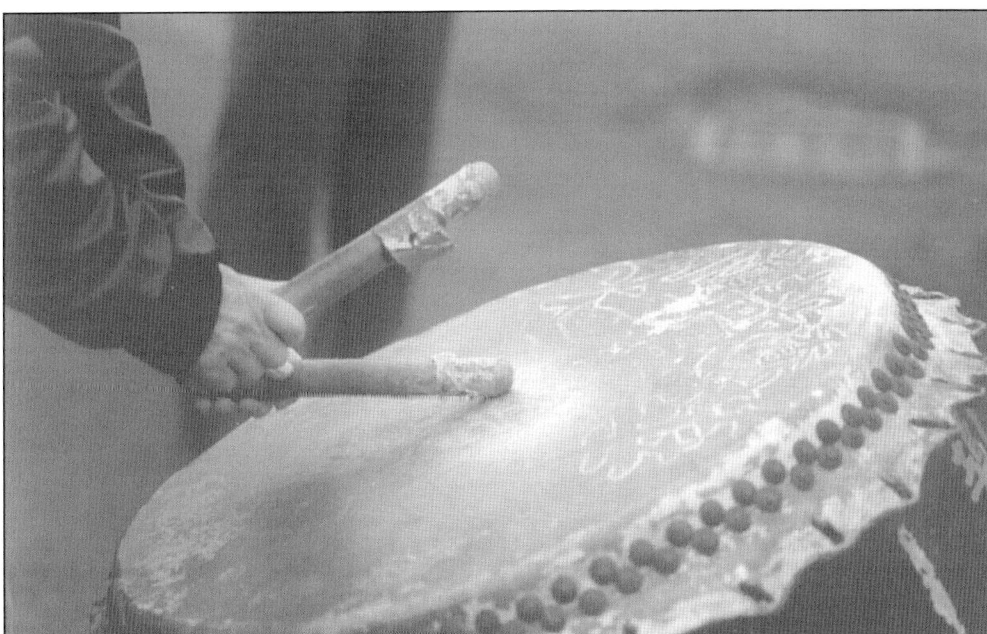

Drums, cymbals, and gongs are used frequently in celebrations. The noise purportedly woke up the gods and got their attention, and firecrackers chased away the evil spirits. The current use of drums provides the rhythm for the lion dance. *(Courtesy of Jene Wah, Inc.)*

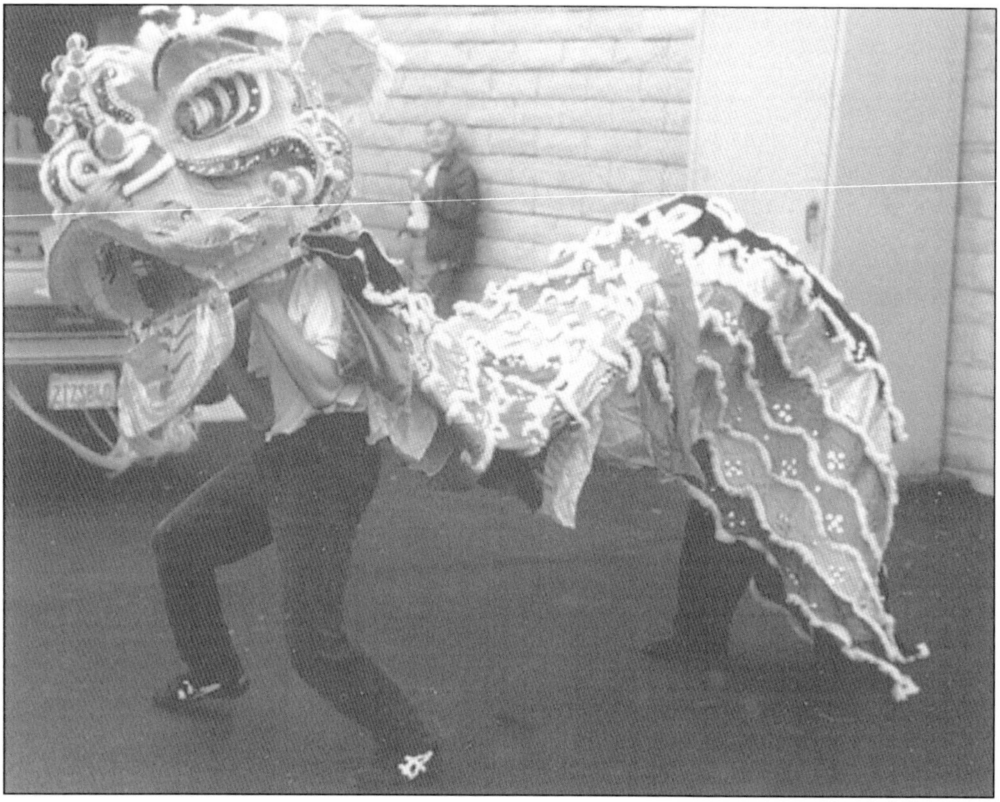

The lion symbolizes goodness and connotes characteristics of courage, energy, wisdom, and strength. In ancient days the Buddhist sect used the lion dance as a form of exorcism. In the Stockton community it is employed for festive occasions, including the opening of new businesses and Chinese New Year. Dancers are especially trained in acrobatic movements and require great stamina. *(Courtesy of Jene Wah, Inc.)*

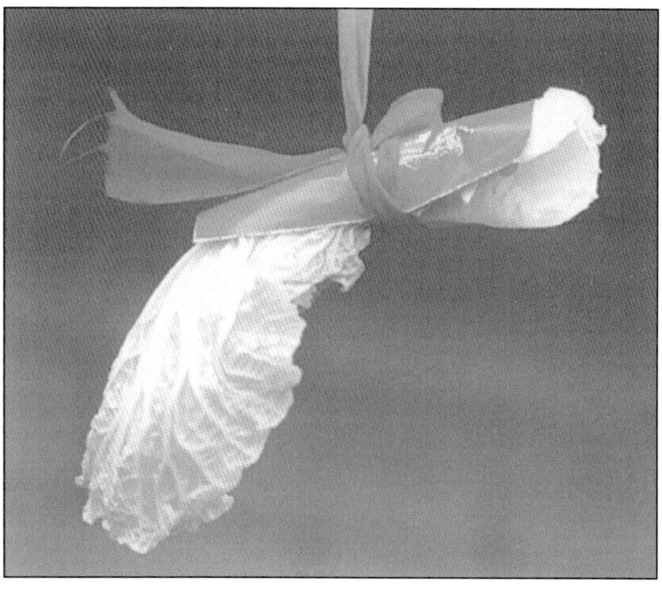

Lettuce is associated with the Lion Dance and represents food or "green" (wealth). In the form of a narrative, gongs and drums wake the Lion, and as he shakes away sleep he experiences hunger. The dance consists of foraging movements. The lettuce, extended much higher than the Lion, becomes the goal. The animal's success quest is synonymous with one's acquisition of wealth. *(Courtesy of Jene Wah, Inc.)*

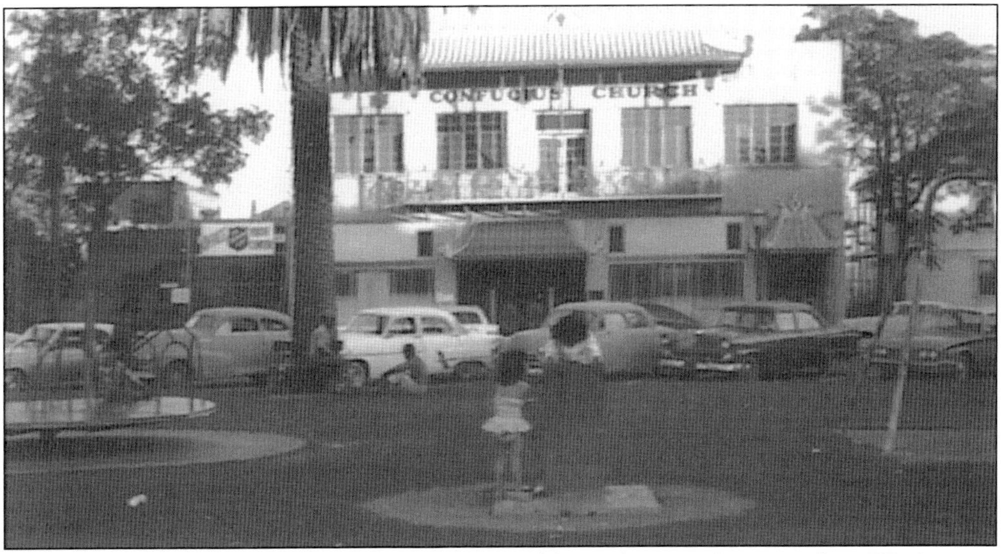

The Confucius Church Building, built in 1924 and located across the street from Washington Park on Lafayette Street, serves as the headquarters of the Chinese Benevolent Association, also commonly called *Chung Wah* in Cantonese. This is the umbrella organization representing all the clan, regional dialect, and tong associations. Chung Wah's duties include promoting goodwill, adjudicating disputes between various groups, serving as a unified voice of the community, operating the Chinese Language School, and maintaining the Chinese cemetery. The name Confucius Church, itself, is not a religious unit in the western concept, but named to suggest the espousing of the teaching of Confucius and his precepts. *(Courtesy of the Norman Lew Collection)*

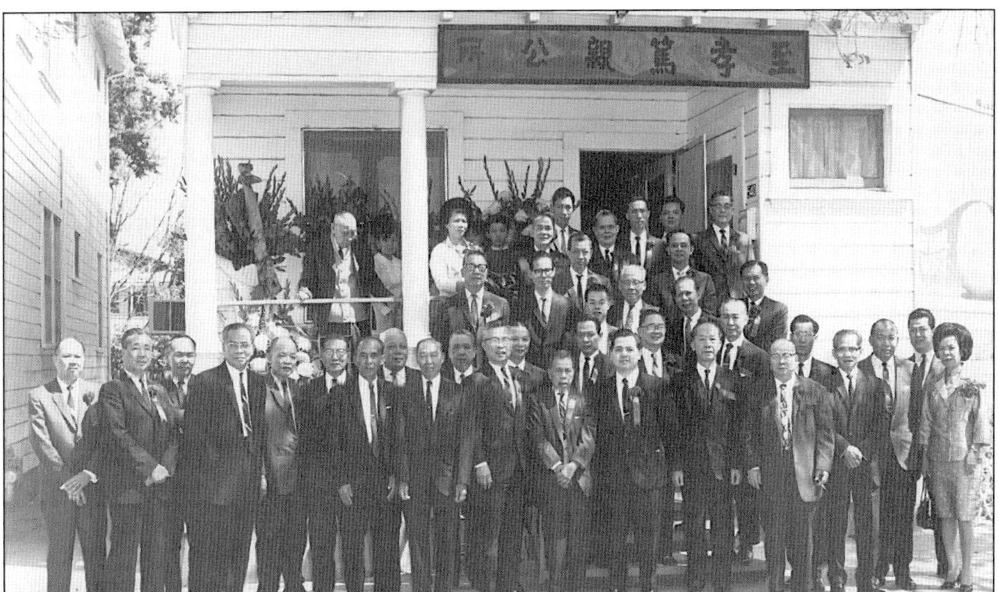

The Gee How Oak Tin Association celebrated its grand opening on South San Joaquin Street in 1968. A clan organization, its members are direct descendants of the Chan, Chen, Chin, and Chinn Families. Regardless of the different English spelling, the Chinese character for *Chan* is the same. Also in the picture are representatives of other associations. *(Courtesy of Wing Chan)*

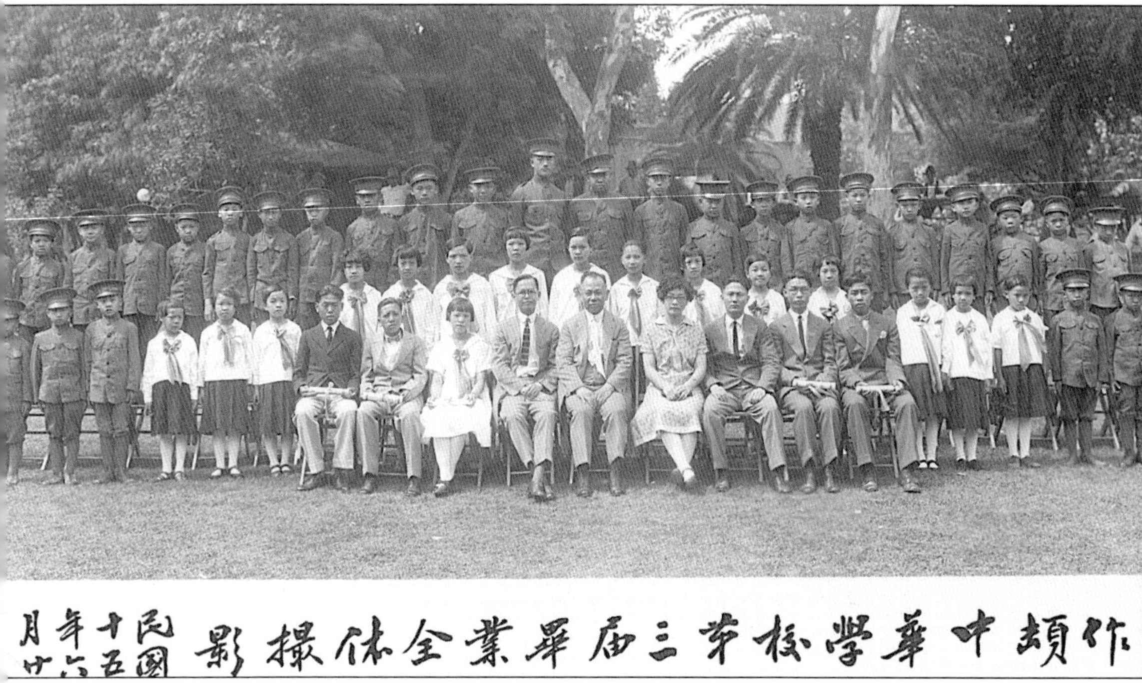

This 1926 picture shows the entire student body of 49 students and 3 faculty members taken at Washington Park. Young male students wore military style uniforms to suggest that discipline in school was strictly enforced. The Chinese words indicate this was the third full graduating class since the school began. *(Courtesy of the Freeman Chang Collection)*

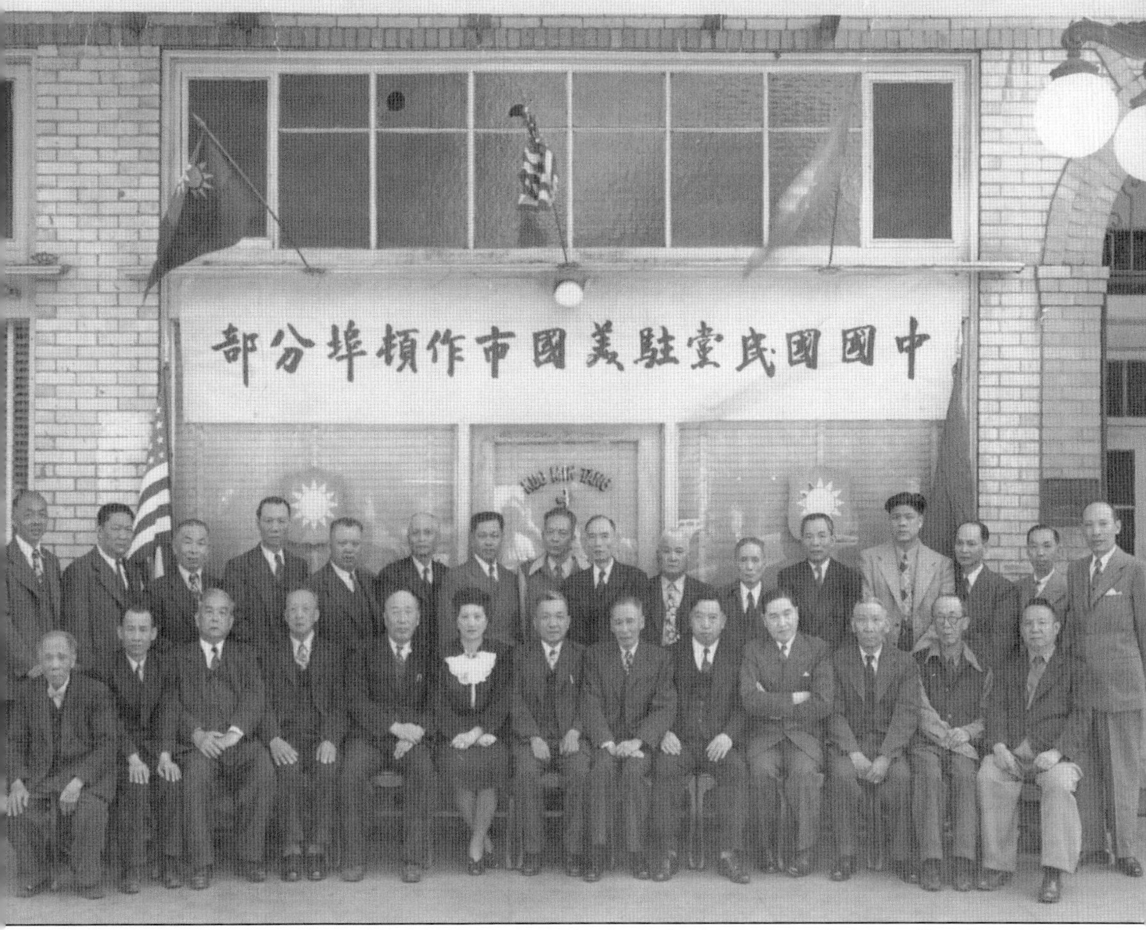

Leaders and members of the Kuomingtang are photographed in front of their office located within the Chinese Benevolent Association building in this late 1930s photograph. At the turn of the century, Dr. Sun Yat Sen created the revolutionary party to overthrow the decadent Ching government. The local Kuomingtang, formed in 1924, raised substantial amounts of money for the war effort and its members were the *crème de la crème* of the business community. The lady pictured in the center is Julia Wong, an early activist. *(Courtesy of Violet Chan)*

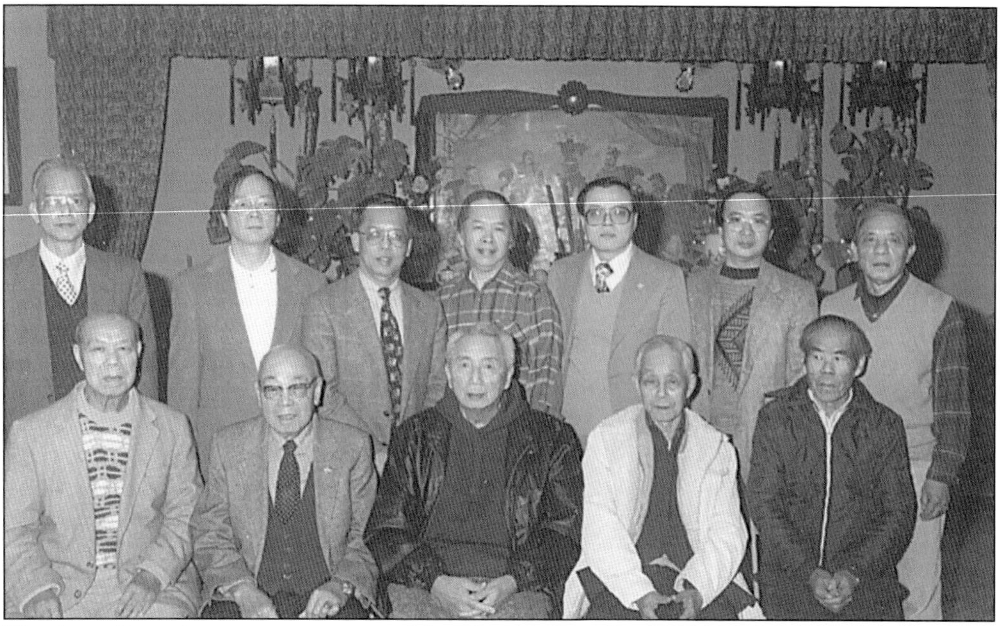

The Lung Kong Association consists of four family clans: Low (Liu), Quan (Kwan), Chang (or Cheung) and Chew (Chu, Chiu). According to ancient Chinese legends, these smaller family clans united in a brotherhood to increase their numbers against the much larger clans. This is a 1983 official photograph of the Lung Kong Association along with the officers of each of the four families. Paul Lew, the presiding chairman/president, sits in the traditional center. Lew came to America in 1919, was a lumberjack in Seattle, came to Stockton to farm potatoes, and started a freight line hauling his produce to Los Angeles. During World War II he served in the 5th Army Air Corps. Upon his return home he worked in a cannery and later became a real estate agent before retirement. *(Courtesy of the Freeman Chang Collection)*

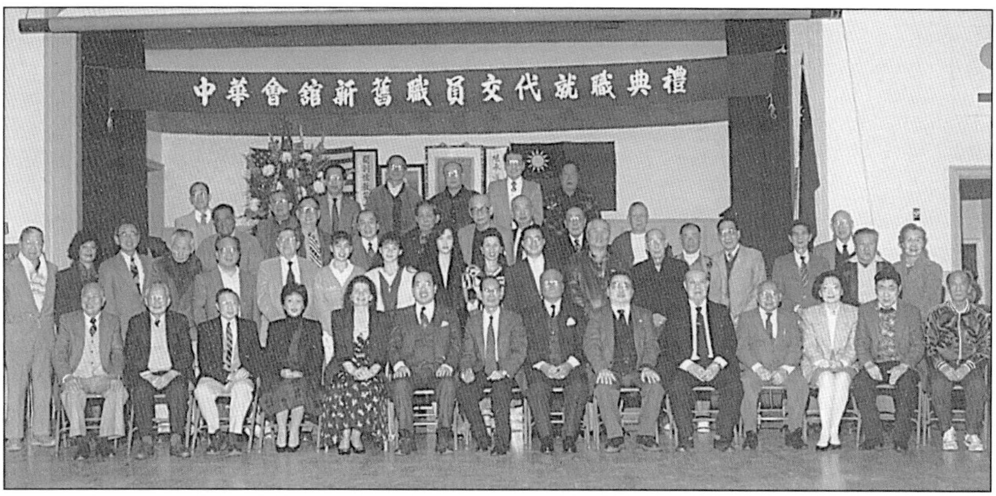

Seated around the 1993 Chung Wah president Louis Chu are members of the board and their families. During this fairly modern period and under Chu's leadership the association thrived and its language school boasted of over 125 students. Women began to serve on the board of directors. There were approximately 17 active organizations at that time. *(Courtesy of the Freeman Chang Collection)*

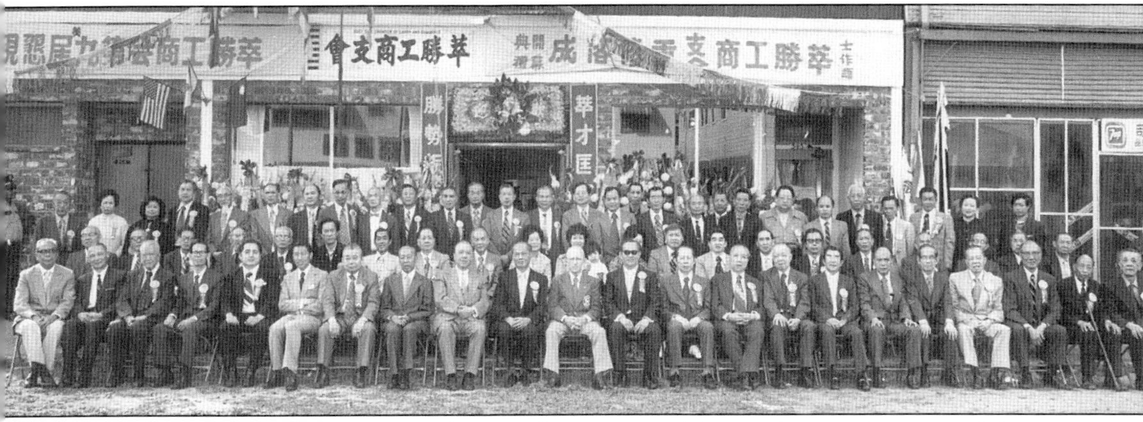

In 1974, the Suey Sing Chamber of Labor and Commerce celebrated the grand opening of their headquarters on the corner of San Joaquin and Sonora Street. Once an active organization, its members numbered almost 400 in the early 1900s. Many pictured here include community leaders. *(Courtesy of Wing Chan)*

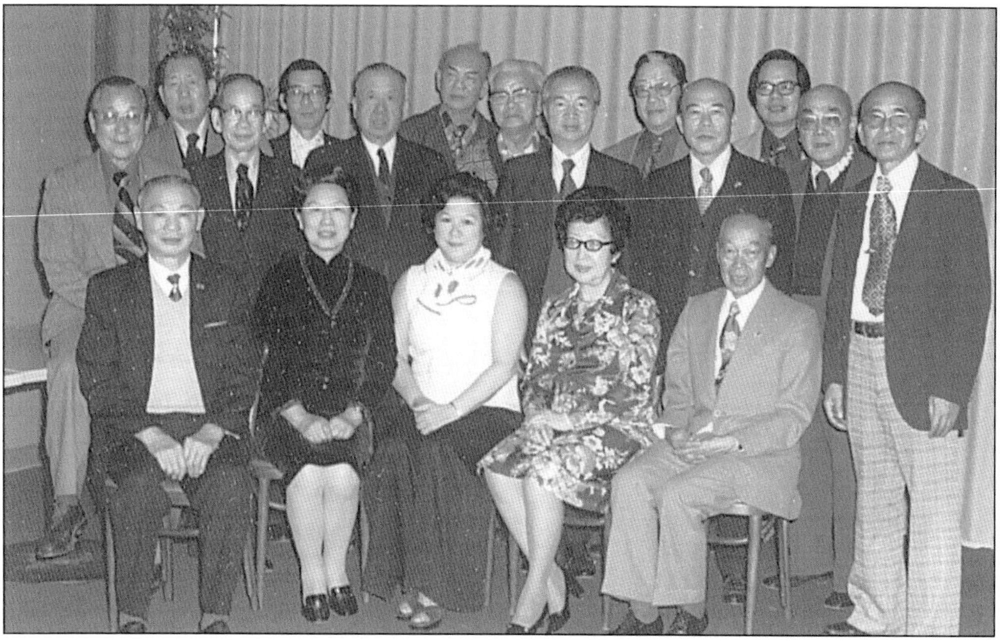

This is a 1970s picture of community leaders with their wives. Many in this group were graduates of western colleges and had professional careers such as a science teacher, chiropractor, insurance agent, and a plethora of other business occupations. Thus, this generation achieved the transition from immigrant sojourners to citizens. *(Courtesy of Margo Chin Mah)*

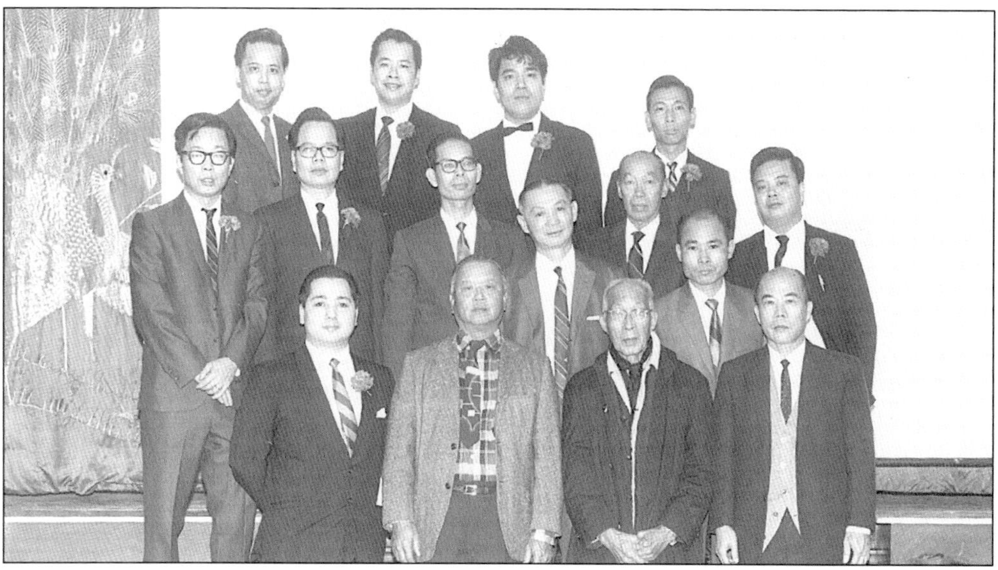

The Chinese Youth Club, a social organization founded in 1957, is still active. Core officers and board of directors are shown in this 12th anniversary photo. Originally the club was formed to preserve the art of Lion Dancing and provide the Lion Dance on request. Years ago during Chinese New Year the benevolent Lion visited the Chinese businesses to solicit donations to help augment Chung Wah's operations. Formerly an all-male organization, the Chinese Youth Club now admits women as members. *(Courtesy of Wing Chan)*

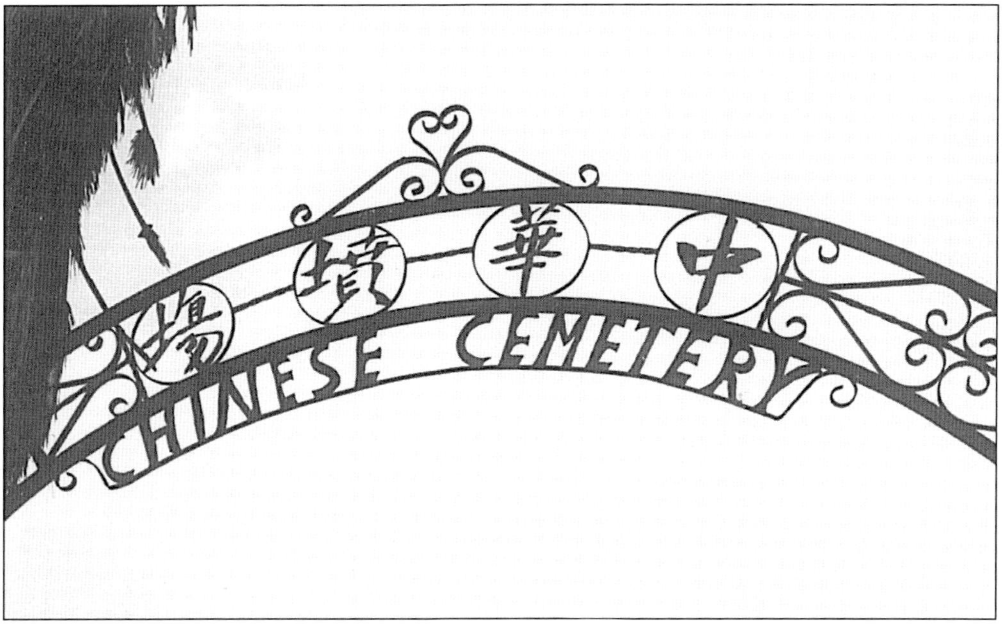

The Chinese Cemetery is located just off of Interstate 5 and Matthews Road in French Camp. The 10-acre cemetery started in the late 1920s and its location was selected because the sandy soil was conducive to speeding up the interment process of returning bones to China. Though this practice ended in 1936, most Chinese still use this cemetery. *(Courtesy of Margo Chin Mah)*

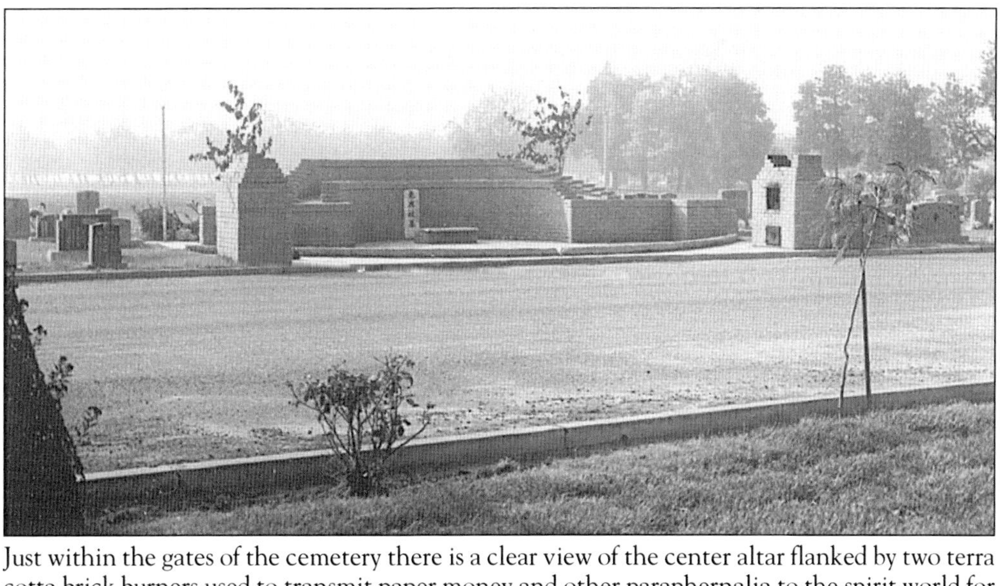

Just within the gates of the cemetery there is a clear view of the center altar flanked by two terra cotta brick burners used to transmit paper money and other paraphernalia to the spirit world for ancestors' use. *(Courtesy of Margo Chin Mah)*

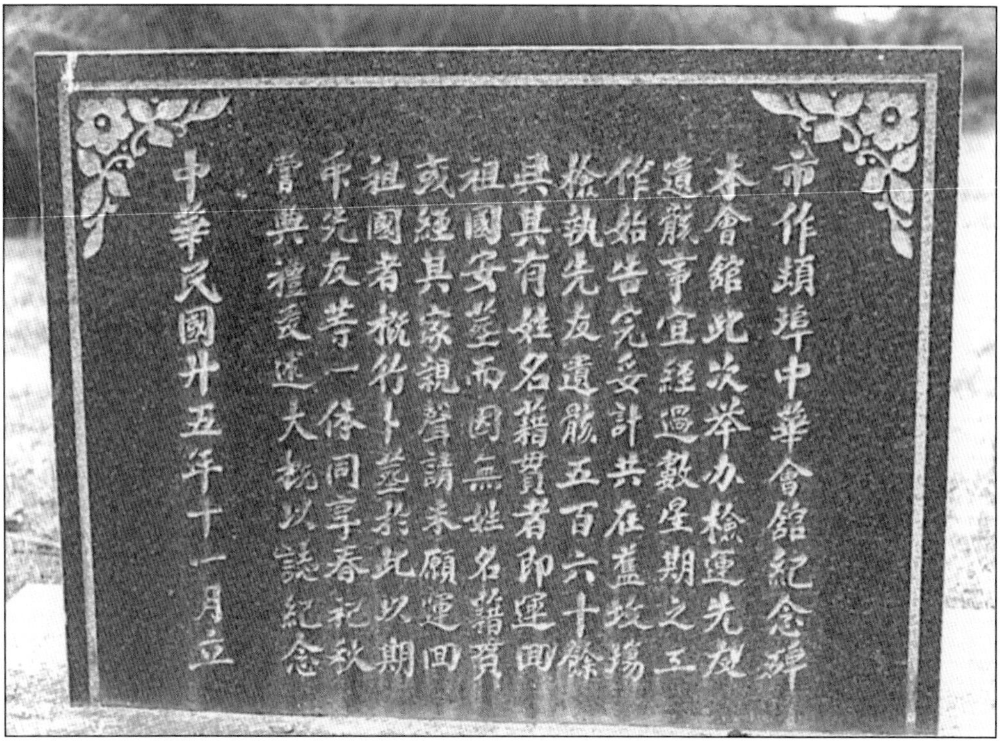

Located in the rear section of the Chinese cemetery, this marble tombstone marks a large common grave of 560 boxes of individuals' bones laid to rest on November 6, 1936. The Japanese invasion of China in 1934–37 prevented these bones from being returned to the villages and family graves, as was the tradition. This traumatic change in the burial practice also added a dramatic change in the Chinese psyche in that the sojourner mentality transformed into that of permanent residents.

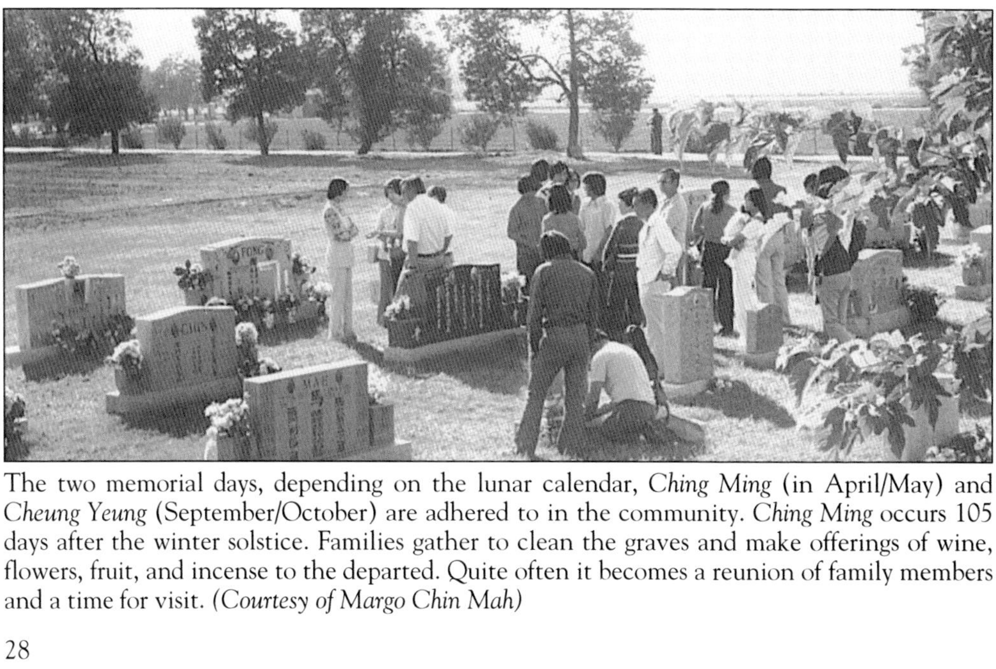

The two memorial days, depending on the lunar calendar, *Ching Ming* (in April/May) and *Cheung Yeung* (September/October) are adhered to in the community. *Ching Ming* occurs 105 days after the winter solstice. Families gather to clean the graves and make offerings of wine, flowers, fruit, and incense to the departed. Quite often it becomes a reunion of family members and a time for visit. *(Courtesy of Margo Chin Mah)*

Three

ECONOMIC ENERGY

The news of California's golden opportunities reverberated many leagues and for many decades in Guangdong, China. From the early gold-seeking sojourners and even through to the 1950s and beyond, dreams of betterment based on hard but honest work drew thousands upon thousands of Chinese to California. Mostly illiterate, but strong and endowed with that positive "can do" attitude, the Chinese worked at every job that came along. Nothing was too menial, nothing was too difficult, and every work experience added another building block to economic betterment for themselves and their families.

When placer mining played out, building railways and byways led to building the Delta levees. And the levees provided an opportunity to farm. Other labor-intensive endeavors included woodcutters, lumberjacks, cooks, and ranch hands. Cities and towns provided other opportunities: cooks, waiters, houseboys, peddlers, gardeners, and laundrymen. Chinatown was the employment and social center. With a little education and a little luck, Chinese residents there became herbalists, merchants, and restaurateurs.

Stockton's Chinatown businesses literally disappeared in the late 1960s and early 1970s due to two major construction projects that worked with simultaneous deadlines. The north side of Washington Street gave way to a city redevelopment and the state of California's freeway construction acquired all the land on the south side of the street.

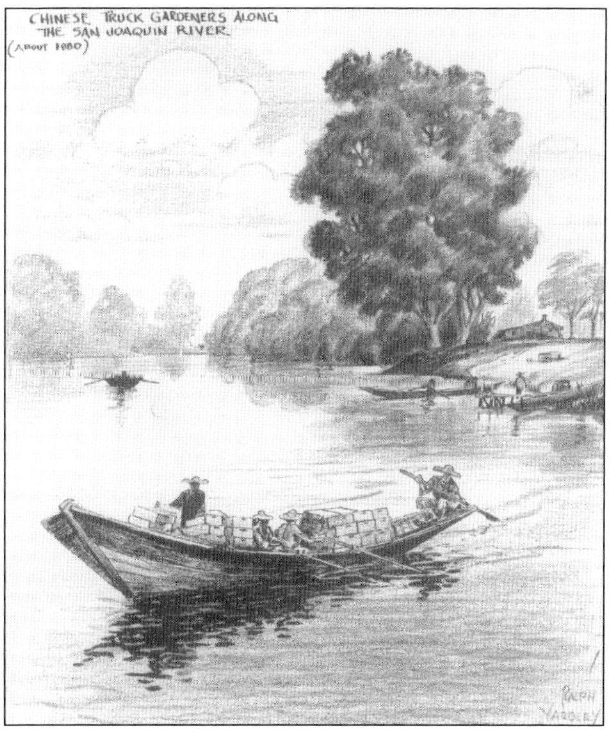

The Delta itself is composed of 1,000 miles of waterway. While Chinese fishermen paddled up the Mormon Slough to deeper waters for their catch, other Chinese took full advantage of water transport to farm the delta islands. These farmers grew mostly "stoop labor" products such as potatoes, onions, and asparagus. *(Courtesy of the Haggin Museum)*

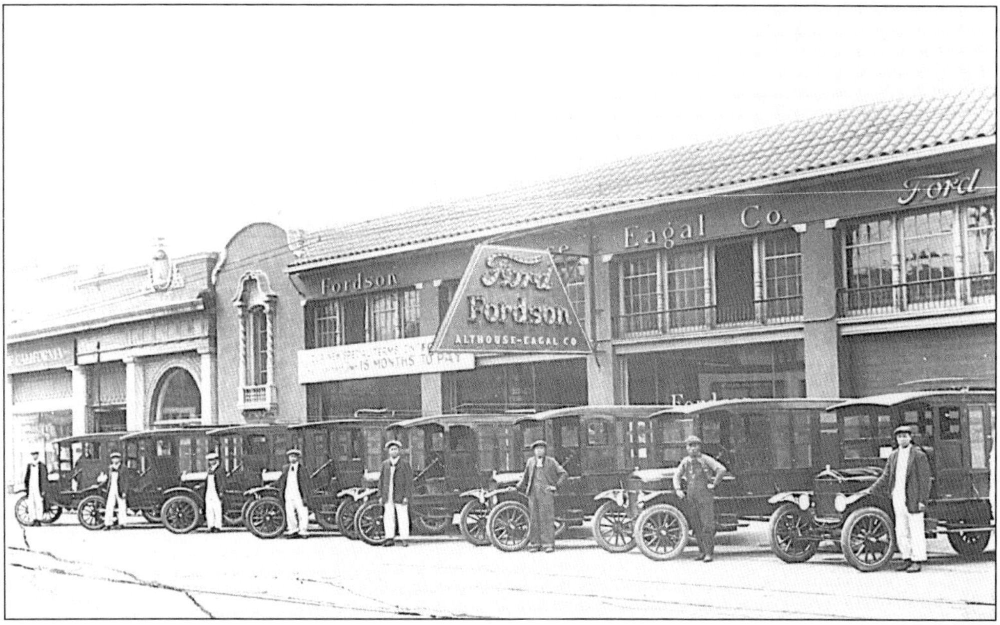

At the turn of the century the river towns of Isleton, Walnut Grove, and Courtland attracted canneries. In the 1920s two Chinese-owned companies, Bayside Canning Company and National Cannery, specialized in canning asparagus, tomatoes, and fruit. In later years, Bayside remained administratively Chinese but augmented its work force with Mexican, Italian, Portuguese, and Japanese workers. This photo is of Bayside Cannery's fleet of Model-T trucks purchased from a Stockton dealer in 1927 to transport workers and produce.

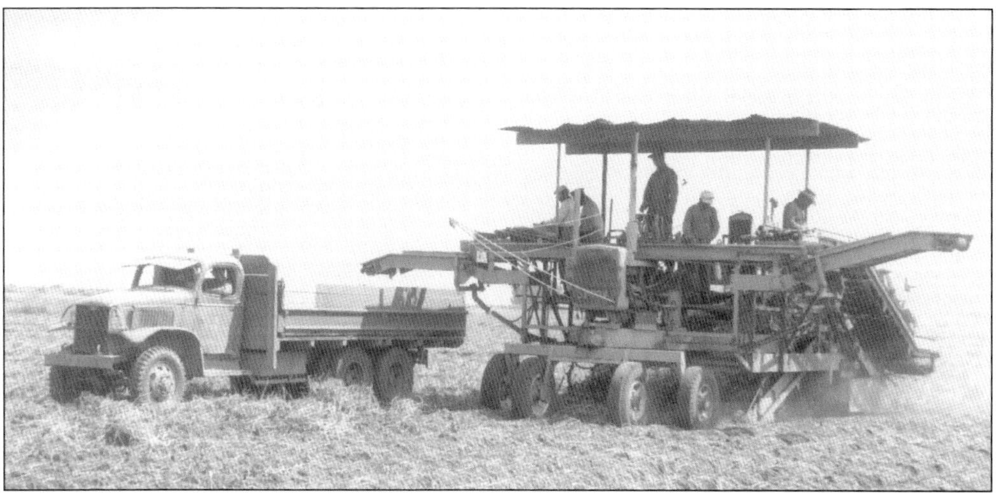

Known as the Chinese Potato King, young immigrant Huey Tai Soon arrived in Walla Walla, Washington, in 1915. By 1932 he started producing potatoes on Roberts' Island. For over 60-plus years the Huey family farmed and marketed their produce under the JHJ label. The J.J. Milano Co. custom built for the Huey Farm the first self-propelled, four-row potato digger that was capable of digging 6,000 sacks of potatoes a day. Family members dubbed it "the monster." *(Courtesy of Hong and Mary Huey)*

The Quan Yak store, in the heart of the business community, was just on the outskirts of the Chinatown area. Its goods were much appreciated as curio pieces by the Caucasian community. The storeowner, conversant in English, served as an interpreter and a resource for those seeking laborers—a conduit between the dominant Caucasian society and the Chinese-speaking community. The caption showed this particular store moved three times, not unusual as the Chinese willingly relocated when markets and rental rates dictated. *(Courtesy of the Haggin Museum)*

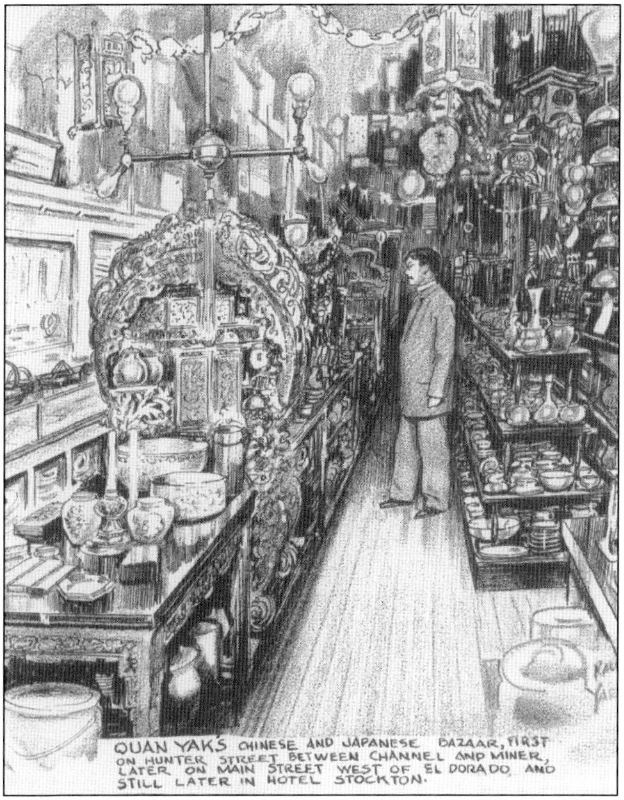

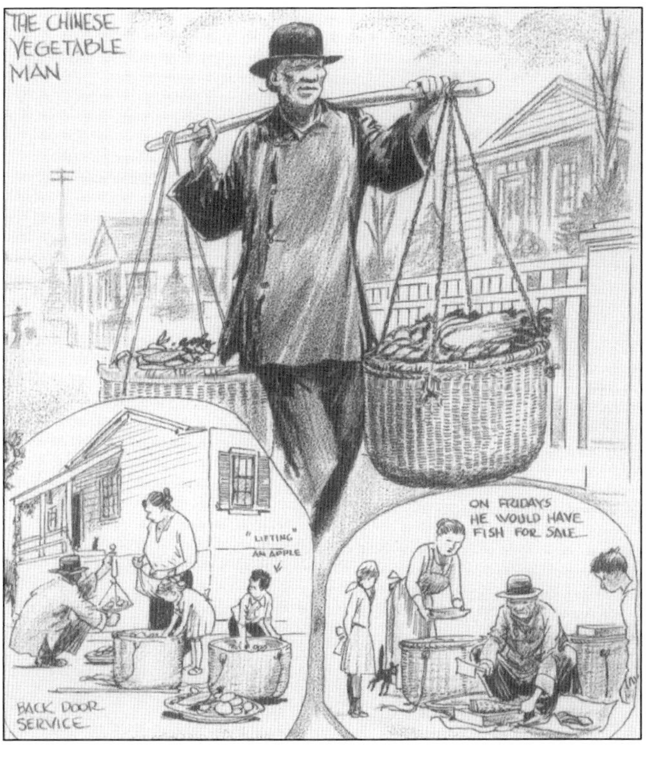

Chinese vegetable peddlers also were communicators between Caucasians and Chinese. They developed faithful customers along their routes and often knew of employment opportunities that they would relay to those seeking work. *(Courtesy of the Haggin Museum)*

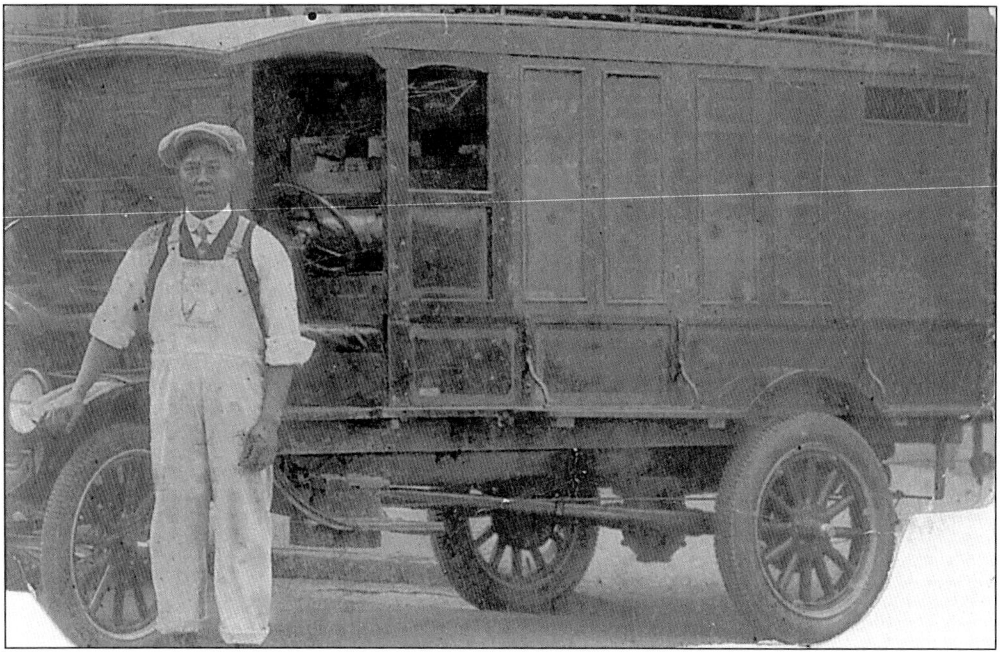

The vegetable peddling business evolved from foot transportation to horse-drawn wagons and finally to motor transport, like this 1922 Model-T produce truck. One now had the ability to travel farther, carry more produce and increase one's income. The proud gentleman by his vehicle is Go Mon Game, whose descendants still live in Stockton. *(Courtesy of Mabel Jue Morodomi)*

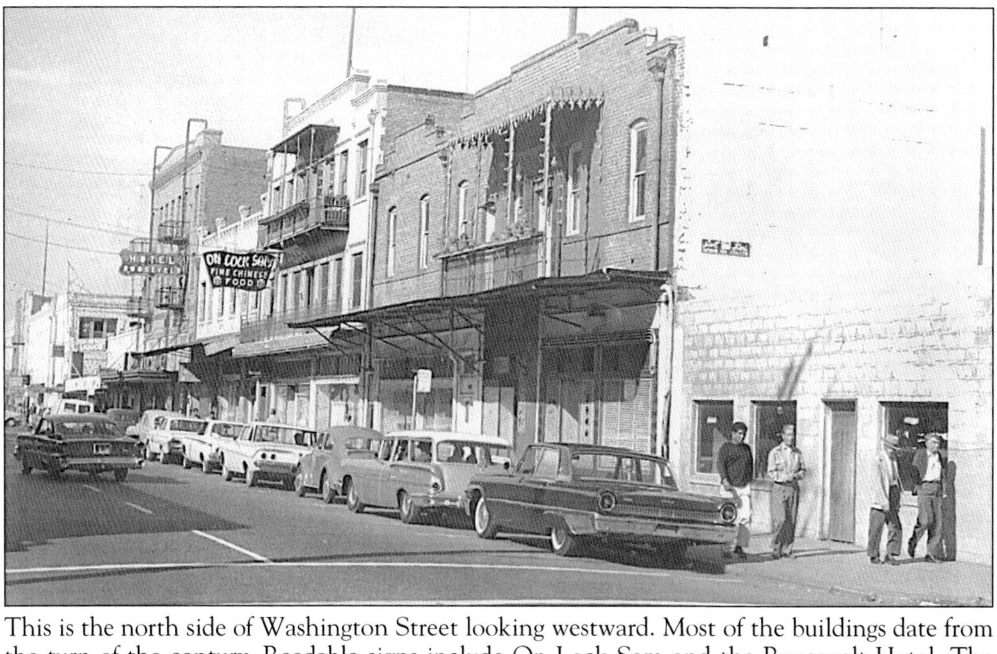

This is the north side of Washington Street looking westward. Most of the buildings date from the turn of the century. Readable signs include On Lock Sam and the Roosevelt Hotel. The ornate balconied building is the Mah Family Association. City redevelopment razed these buildings. *(Courtesy of the Keith Wong Collection)*

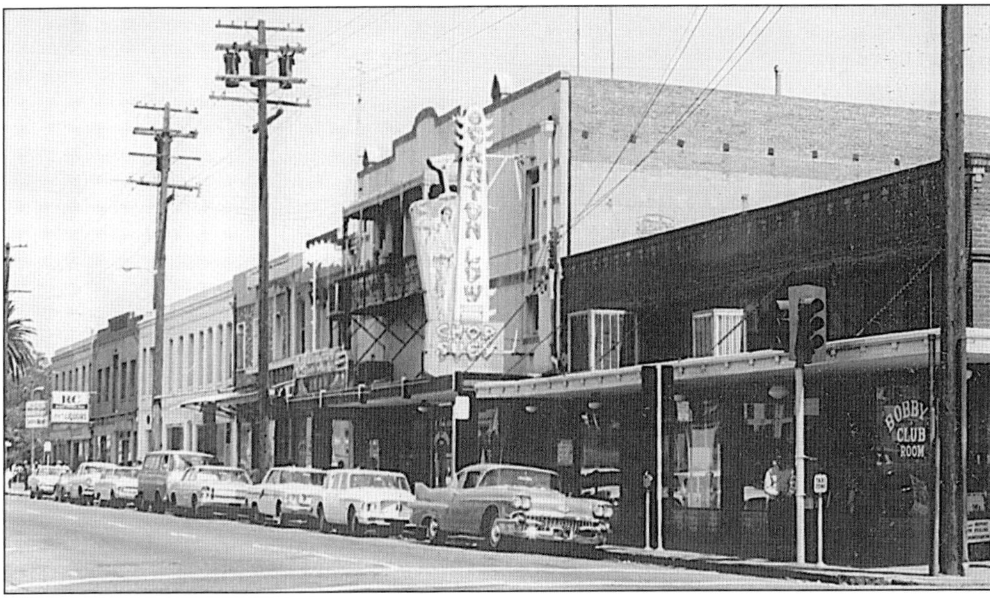

The south side of Washington Street looking east housed a series of small shops including several delicatessens. Stockton Chinatown was noted for its many gambling halls, which were closed during World War II. One reminder of the gambling industry is Bobby's Club Room at the intersection of Washington and El Dorado Streets, site of Tai Fat Choy, a former gambling house. All the buildings on this south side gave way to freeway construction. *(Courtesy of the Keith Wong Collection)*

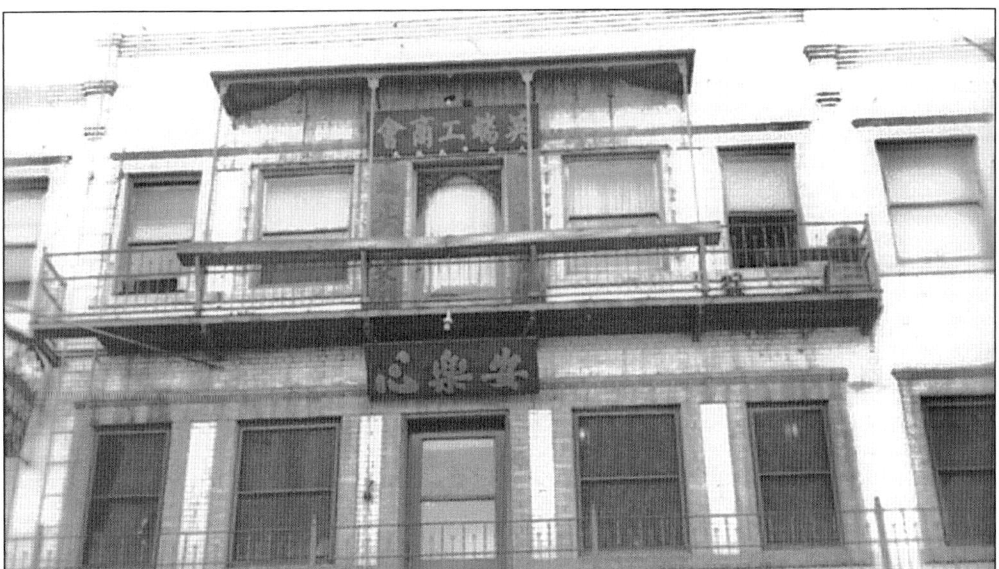

This three-story building stood at 125 East Washington Street. On Lock Sam, (on the second floor with a three character sign board), means "contented heart." It began at that location in 1895. Wong Sai Chun and his two partners, a cook and a noodle maker, bought the restaurant in 1920 and the restaurant still remains in the family. Among the Hollywood notables who have dined there were John Wayne, Willie Mays, Paul Newman, Danny Kaye, Ann-Margaret, Anthony Quinn, and Michael Landon. *(Courtesy of the Norman Lew Collection)*

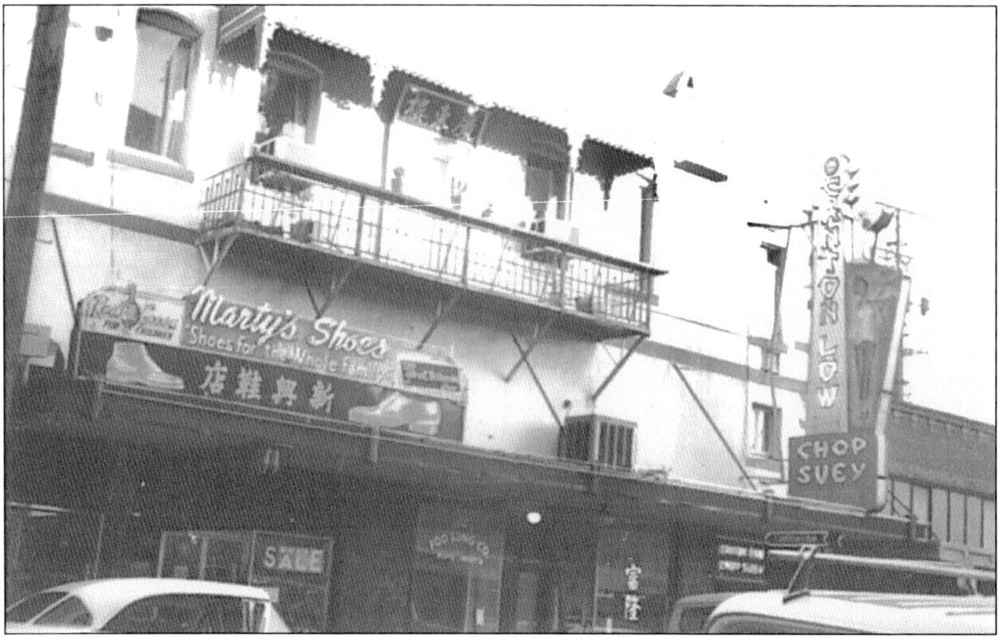

Across the street from On Lock Sam stood Canton Low, another restaurant, on the second floor above Marty's Shoes. Canton Low boasted having the second telephone service in the city of Stockton that the police conveniently used as a substation. Just below the restaurant were two stores. On the right side, the Chinese character and English words clearly visible, is Foo Lung, a Chinese delicatessen owned by the Louie family member, Louie On.

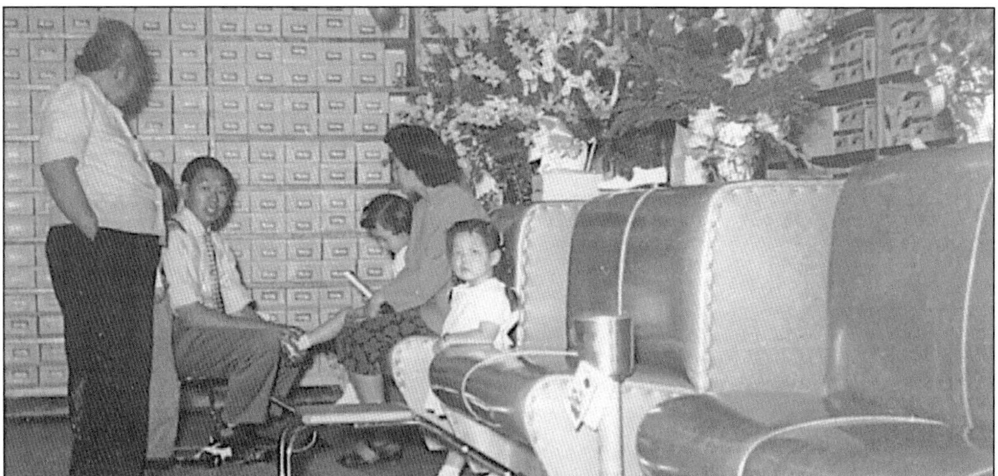

On the ground floor of the Canton Low building was Marty's Shoes started by Marty Yip, his sister Sadie Lee, and her son King Lee in 1950. Pictured here are Sadie and King waiting on a customer. Note the many congratulatory flower arrangements that lined the shop's walls and counters during the grand opening. When Marty died in 1960, his widow Rose, from Terminous Island, took over the business and operated it until redevelopment tore down the building. In 1940, Marty, his sister Sadie, and their father Quong Lee began the Yet Bun Heong Bakery. This bakery moved several times in the Chinatown area and later found a home in the Filipino Center where it remains today. *(Courtesy of Rose Yip)*

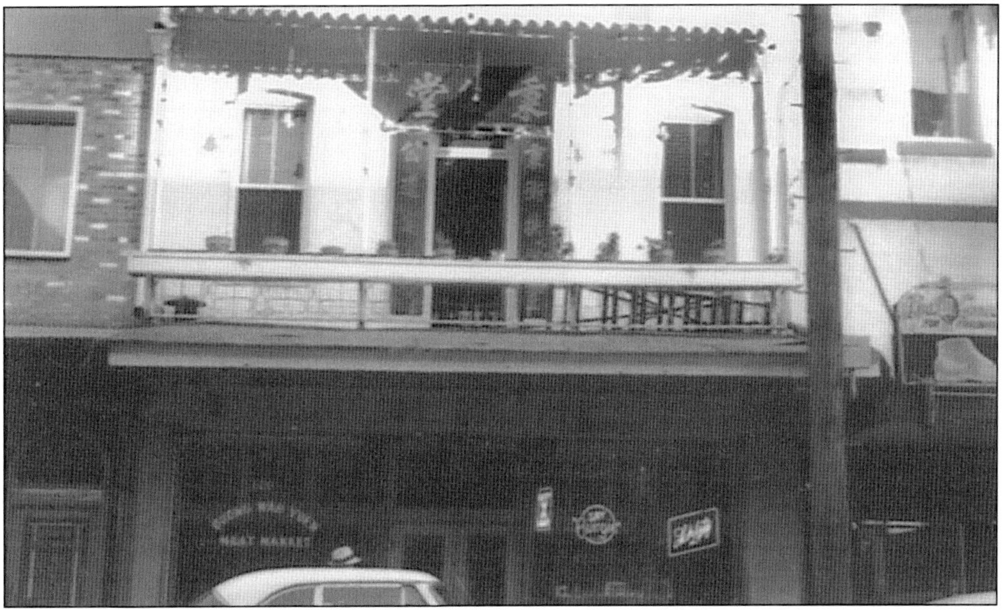

Just east of Canton Low, the Bing Kung Tong Association had their headquarters on the second floor. A fraternal organization mostly composed of younger men, the early history of this organization was replete with activities and tong wars associated with the social entertainment. Still in existence today, the members are older and less active. On the ground floor was Quong Wah Yuen Meat Market, started in 1925 by Wong Sai Chun (of On Lock Sam). Actually a Chinese sausage factory, it was well noted for its traditional pork sausage and duck liver varieties. Through word-of-mouth the factory's "lop cheong" (Chinese for sausage) reputation catapulted into the highly competitive San Francisco and Vancouver, Canada, markets. The delicatessen also prepared roasted pig and barbeque pork on a daily basis. *(Courtesy of the Norman Lew Collection)*

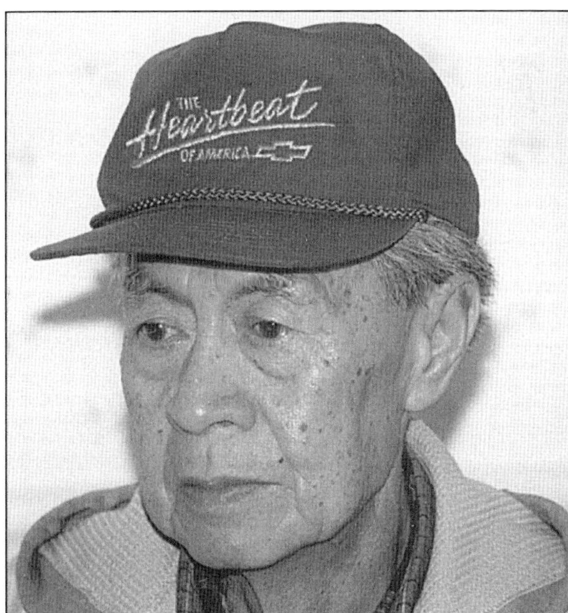

In 1949 William (Bill) Chin took over Quong Wah Yuen from his father-in-law, Wong Sai Chun. A San Franciscan and graduate of Golden Gate College, Bill served in the Army Air Corps in World War II and was stationed for a time in Biloxi, Mississippi. After 40 years in the sausage business and relocation to South San Joaquin Street, Quong Wah Yuen finally shut its doors in 1989. *(Courtesy of Gail Chin Tucker)*

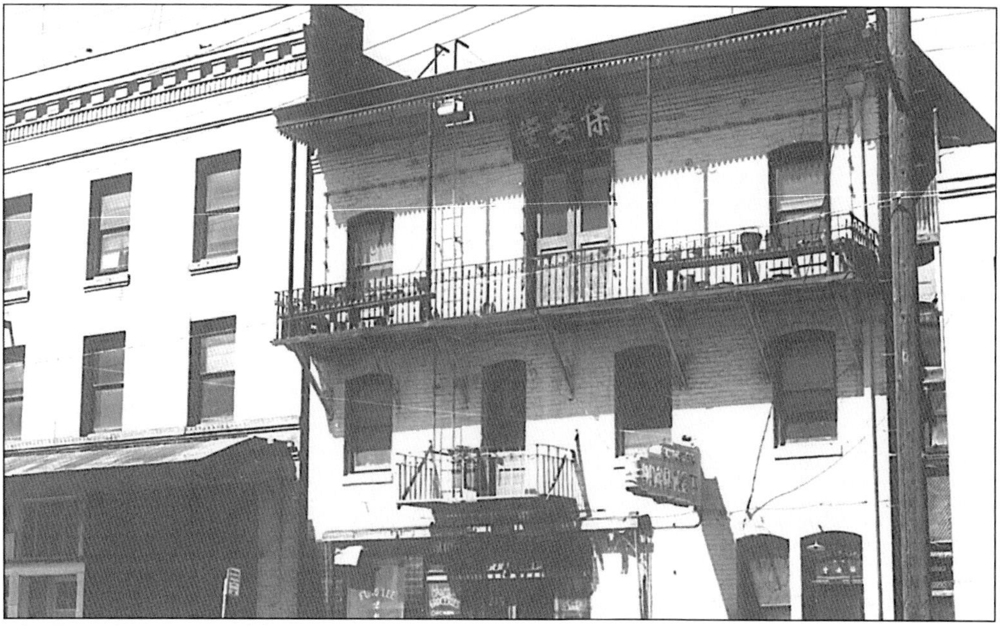

The Bow On Tong Building was on Hunter Street just south of Washington Street. The Bow On Association was created as an enforcement unit of the Kong Chow Association in San Francisco. Membership was limited to having family roots in the Sunwui District in Guangdong Province. Today the focus includes providing scholarships for Chinese high school students and creating social outlets for their aging members. *(Courtesy of the Keith Wong Collection)*

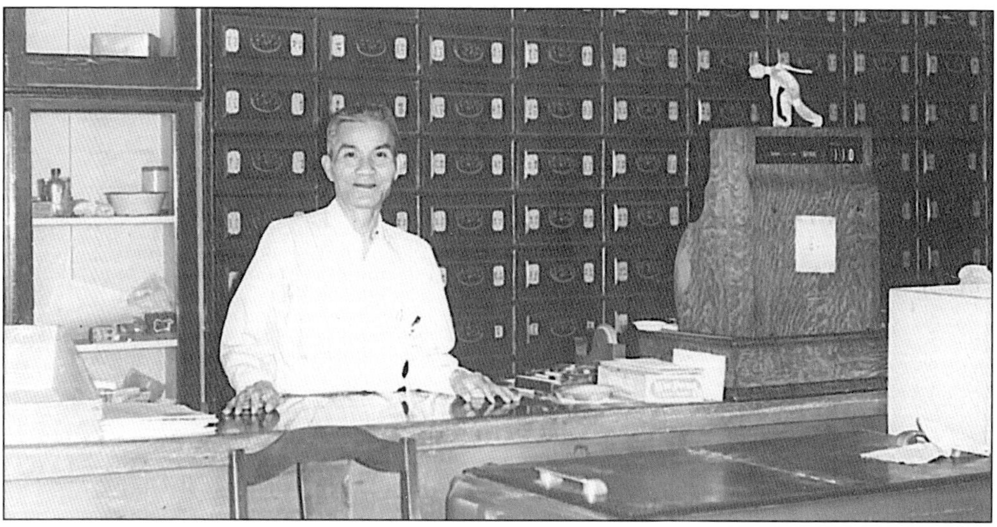

On the ground floor of the Bow On Tong building was the Fung Lee Herb Shop. In this picture, Yee Suey (Chun) Jung stands behind the counter. While Yee Suey sold herbs in the front, he also made tofu in the back for sale. Chinatown had several other herb shops, including Tin Sang Tong and Bow Ning Tong, to name a few. A good herb shop carried from 500 to 2,000 different types of natural herbs. Dr. Paul K. Yee, a local teacher and herbalist, spearheaded the effort to save the store's artifacts before demolition in the late 1960s. The medicine cabinet and paraphernalia are on permanent exhibit at the Haggin Museum on Pershing Avenue. *(Courtesy of the Keith Wong Collection)*

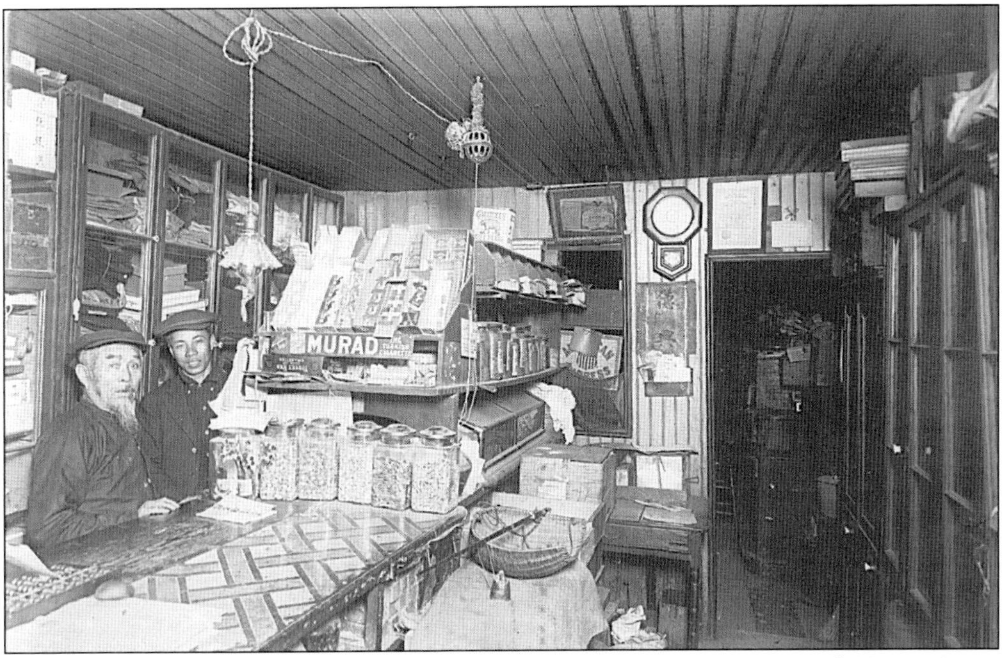

Tuck Hing, a store on Washington Street, moved around the corner to 133 South Hunter Street in 1947 and was renamed Ark Hing. Original owner Lee Foo Nai (pictured above with a beard) arrived in California in the 1880s. Mr. Lee was also known as Lee Lowe. The store sold herbs, groceries, and dry goods. The back room was set aside for men to congregate and play mahjong and other betting games. *(Courtesy of the Freeman Chang Collection)*

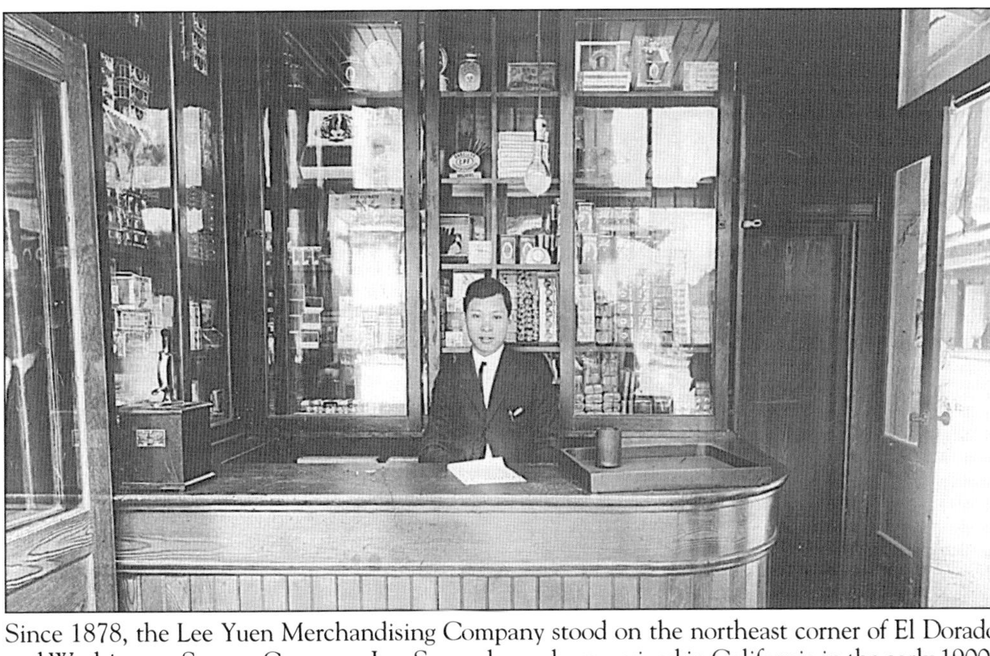

Since 1878, the Lee Yuen Merchandising Company stood on the northeast corner of El Dorado and Washington Streets. Co-owner Lee Soon, shown here, arrived in California in the early 1900s and with due diligence became a prominent leader and benefactor in the community. He served for a time as the county interpreter in cases that involved Chinese.

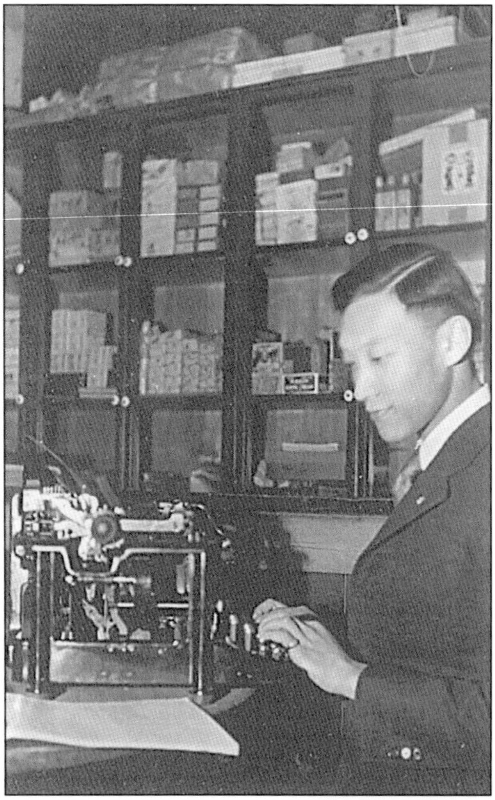

Tuck Y. Lee, a native Stocktonian born in 1907, took over the management of the Ark Hing store when his father Lee Foo Nai died in 1922. Tuck was only 15 years old. He worked at this store for 48 years and returned to China only twice: first to marry in 1935, and second when his children were born. Tuck, with his fellow Lee clansmen, started Lee Co., Inc., a wholesale cosmetic business in which Tuck had shares and served as the company's bookkeeper. The other partners included Lee Soon, Lee Chan Poy, Robert Lee, S.L. Fong, and Eddie and David Lee. Often times clan relatives pooled their resources for startup capital. *(Courtesy of the Freeman Chang Collection)*

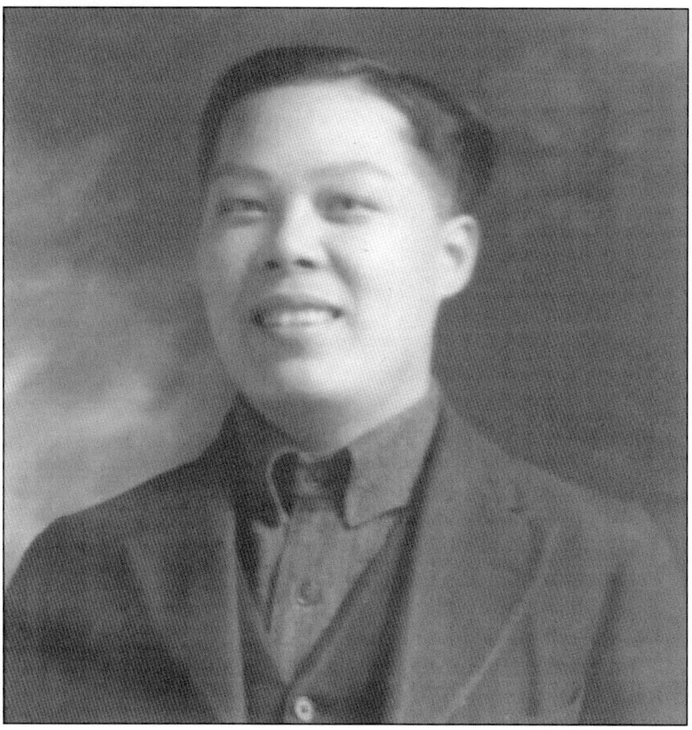

Chan Shang Yee and his wife, Won Shu Chan, like many early Chinese families believed in large families. They had 10 children. Together they invested in a soda fountain, Fook Chong, on the south side of Washington Street near the sausage factory in the 1930s. The business also carried tobacco and other sundries and stayed in operation until the construction of the freeway.

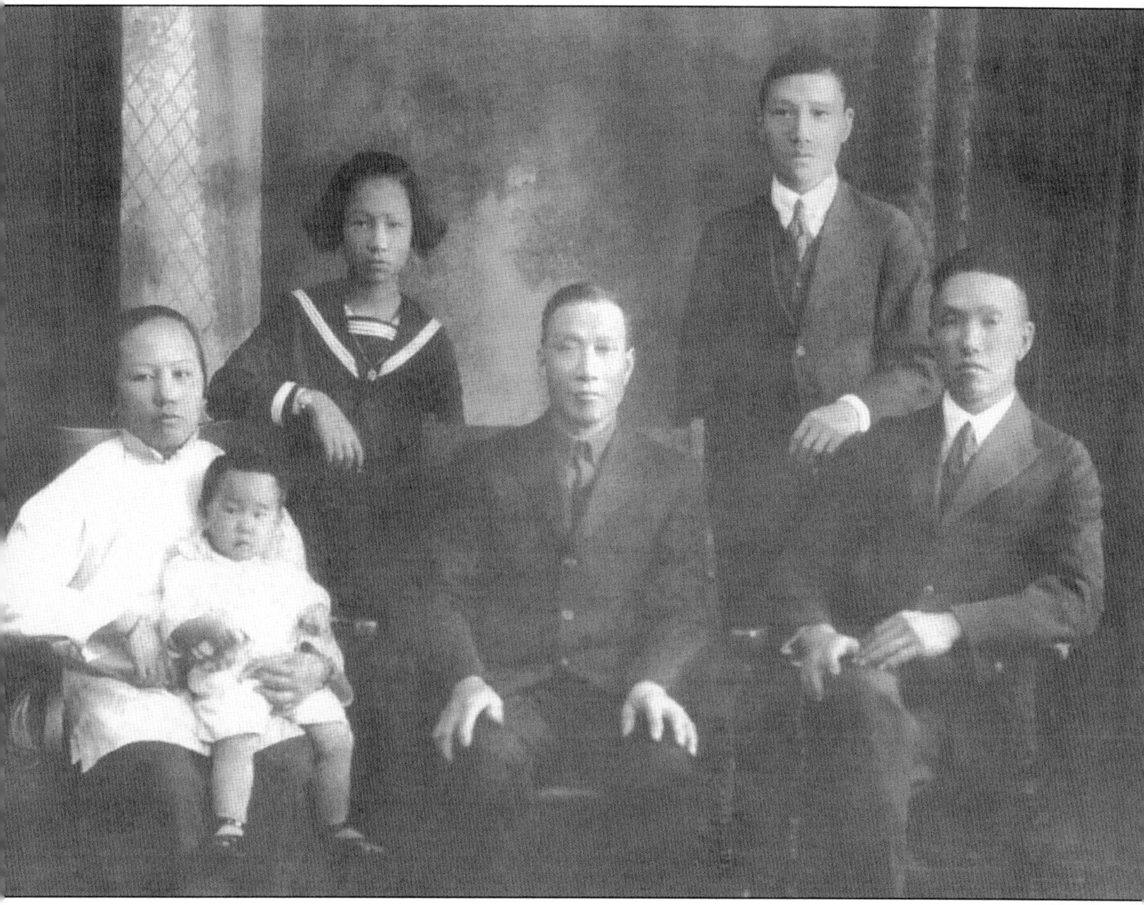

Mr. Siu, center, arrived in California in the late 1890s. When his sons were of age to come to America, Mr. Siu purchased "paper son" documents for them, as Congress had extended the 1882 Exclusion Law limiting Chinese entry to previous residents and citizens of the U.S. Thus, the sons adopted the surname of Low. The eldest son, Jones Low (seated right) started Jones Market on Hunter Street, between Washington and Lafayette. Although born in China, Jones was a veteran of World War I. *(Courtesy of Harry Low)*

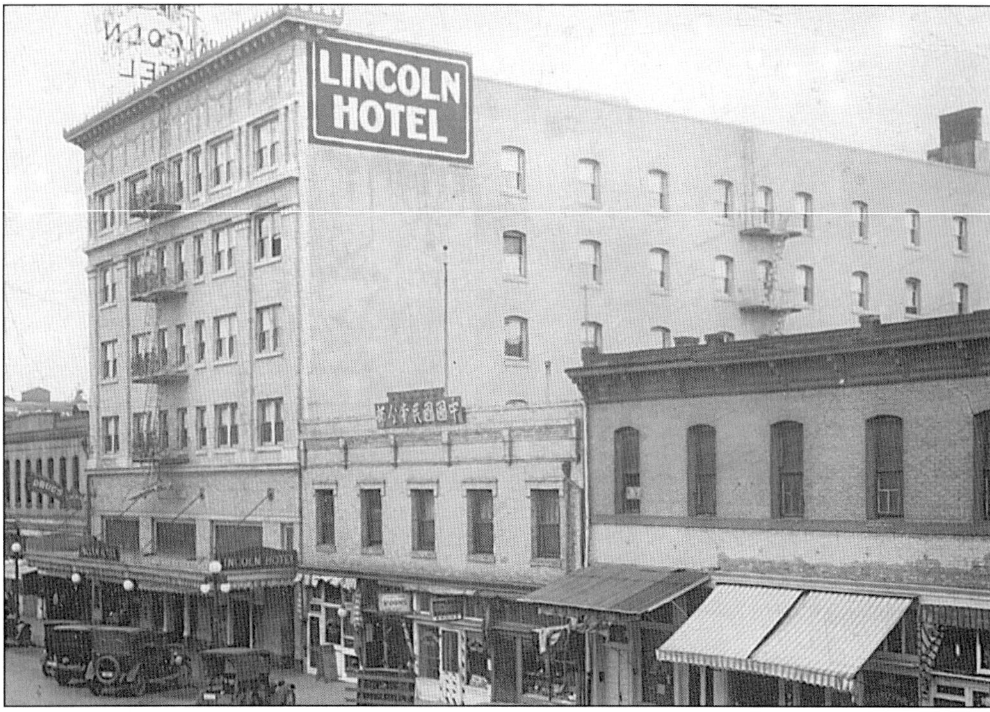

The Lincoln Hotel on South El Dorado Street, built in 1920 by the Wong brothers, was the pride of Chinatown. The five-story hostelry's interior and amenities equaled those of the other first class hotels in Stockton. The hotel was demolished in the late 1960s as part the city's redevelopment project.

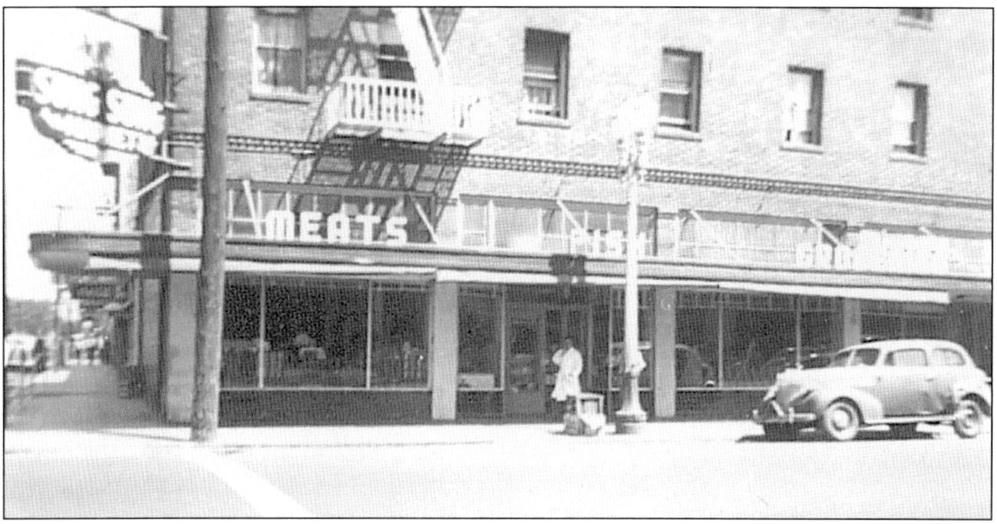

Started in the 1940s, the Sung Sung Meat Market at 302 South Center Street initially operated as a poultry shop with no groceries and no meat. By 1970 and with changes in Chinatown, ownership of the building and the market changed to Vang Market. The property gave way to a McDonald's and a filling station. Old-timers recalled that the earliest of the meat companies was the Mandarin Meats on Center Street whose business began in 1920, relocated once and closed in 1982. *(Courtesy of Dun Fong)*

Frank Yep and his brothers owned the Sung Sung Market. Beginning as a meat market, it evolved into a typical corner store that provided wholesale and retail goods. *(Courtesy of Ida Yep)*

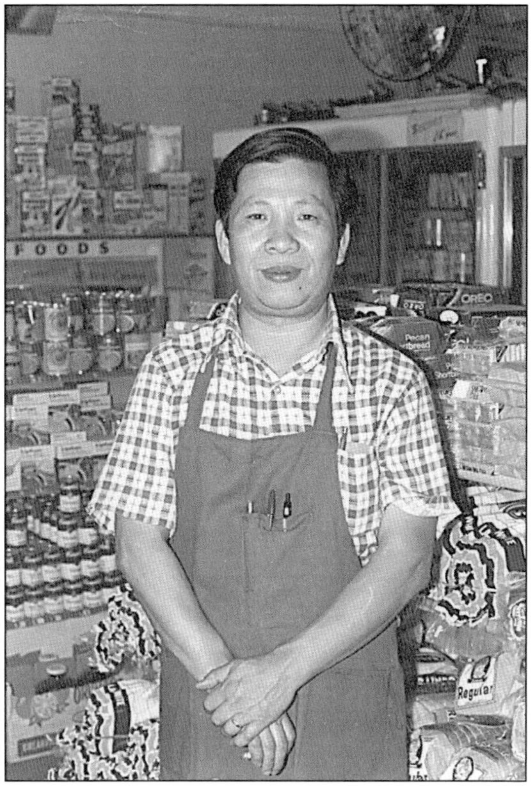

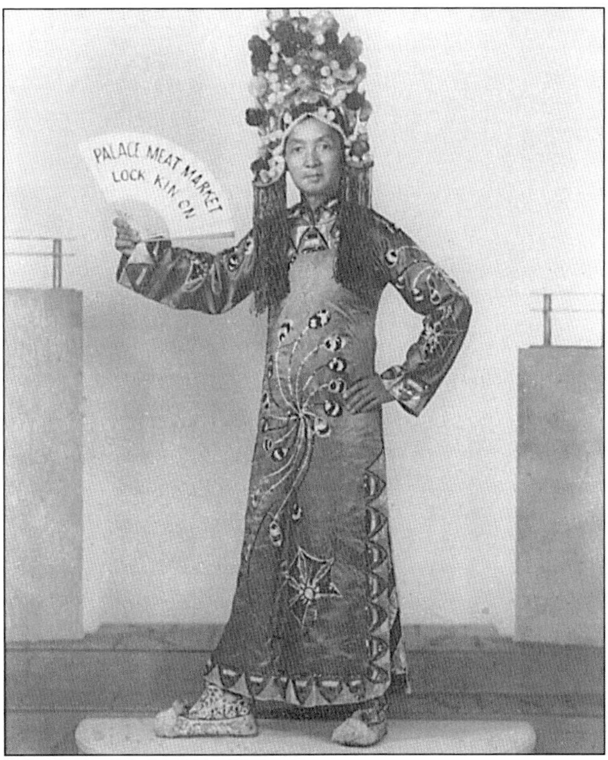

Mr. Lock Kin On came in the 1940s, worked in restaurants, and loved to cook in other people's homes. He ended up operating the Palace Meat Market in the nearby town of Lodi. With his colorful opera-type costumes, he mimicked operatic gestures while strolling as a solo unit in both Lodi and Stockton parades. His form of advertising was unusual to say the least. Many Chinese recalled how he enjoyed "hamming it up" on these occasions. (*Courtesy of Dun Fong*)

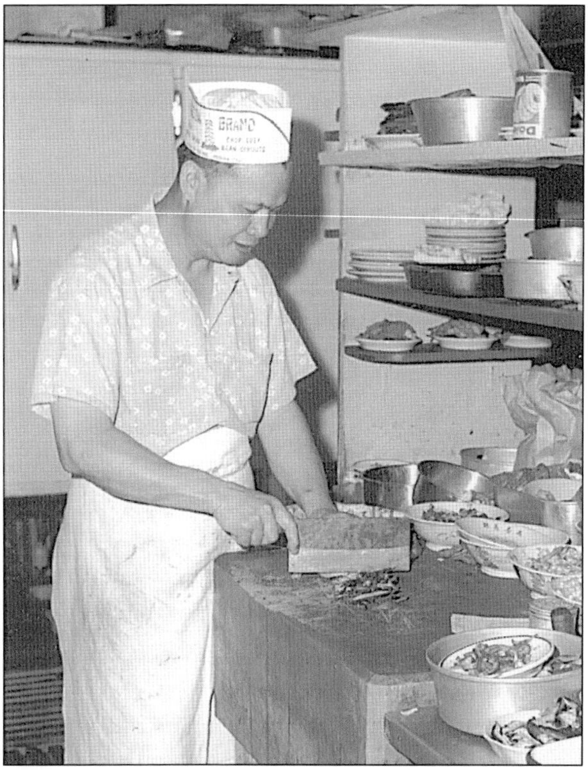

When immigrants first arrived in cities, they often looked for work in restaurants. One went through the various job levels, from dishwasher to busboy and later to second or third-line cook charged with the chopping, dicing, and deep-frying. It took several years to become the *Sifu* (master chef) in an eatery. *(Courtesy of the Norman Lew Collection)*

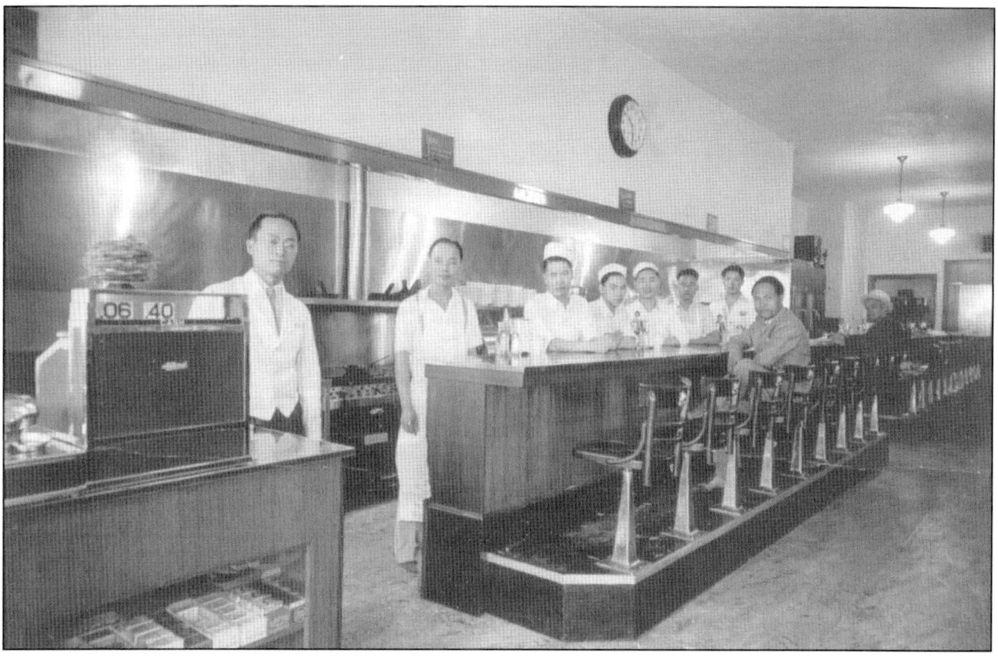

This was the grand opening of King Café on Market Street, a block away from the core Chinatown area. Mr. Eddie Mah is at the cash register and the *Sifu* (master chef) Mah Shew Ngaw heads the staff as noted in the lineup. Chinese restaurants served people from all types of ethnic backgrounds, Filipinos being their most frequent customers. *(Courtesy of Conrad Mar)*

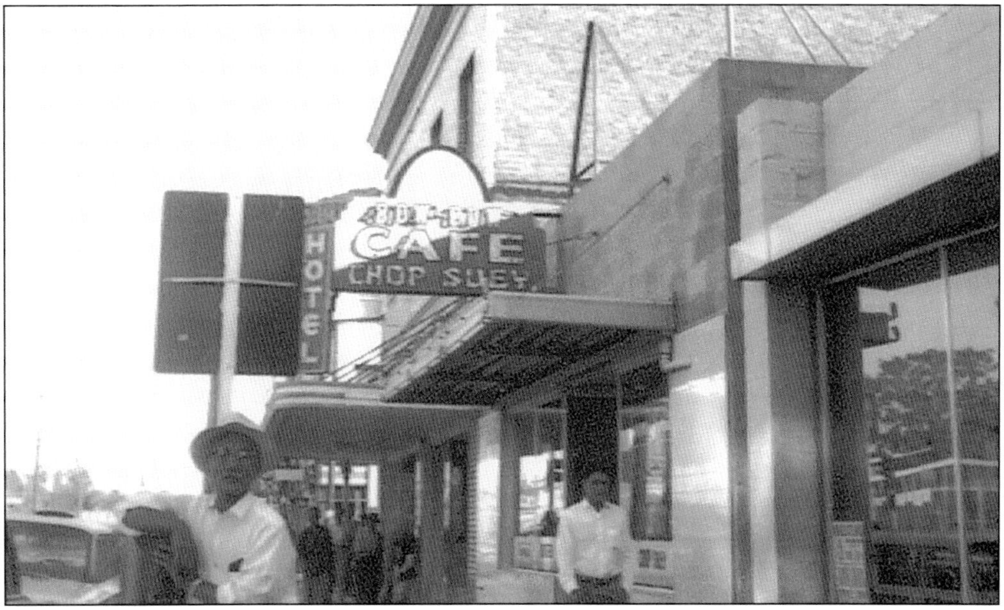

The old Bow Bow on South El Dorado Street, around the corner from Washington Street, was a small establishment and a favorite of the locals. When a customer brought in a freshly caught striped or black bass, the restaurant willingly prepared it for the meal at a nominal charge. Often times there was enough fish to give some to the proprietor. *(Courtesy of the Norman Lew Collection)*

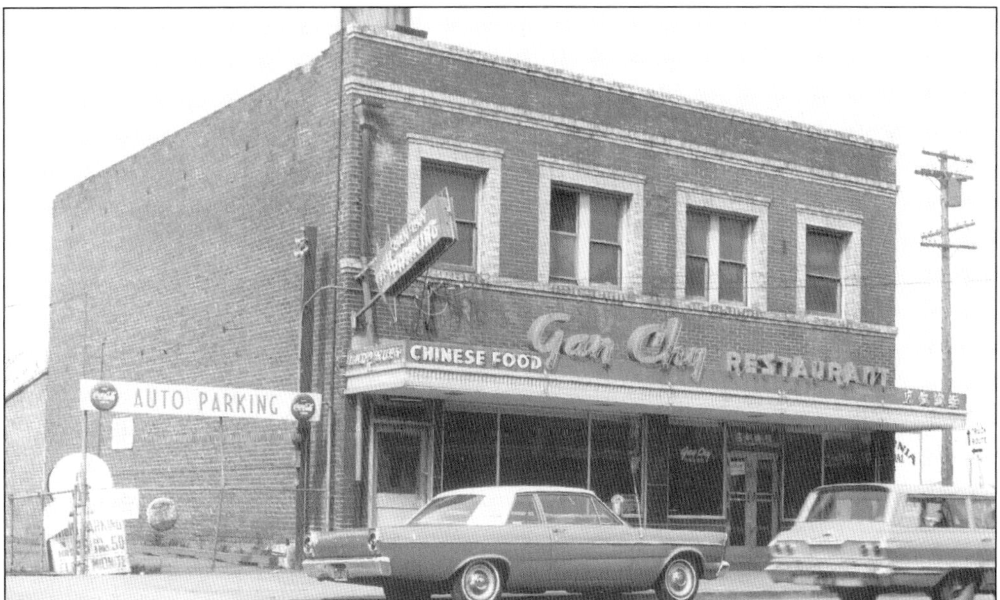

Sai Mow Yip started the Gan Chy Restaurant in 1935 at 215 S. El Dorado between Washington and Lafayette Street. This was another local eatery featuring Cantonese food. At one time the Soo Yuen Tong (clan association of the Louies, Fong, and Kwongs) occupied the top floor, but they moved by 1965 before the building's demolition. Gan Chy itself was forced to relocate five years later. When Mr. Yip retired, his son Henry took over the business.

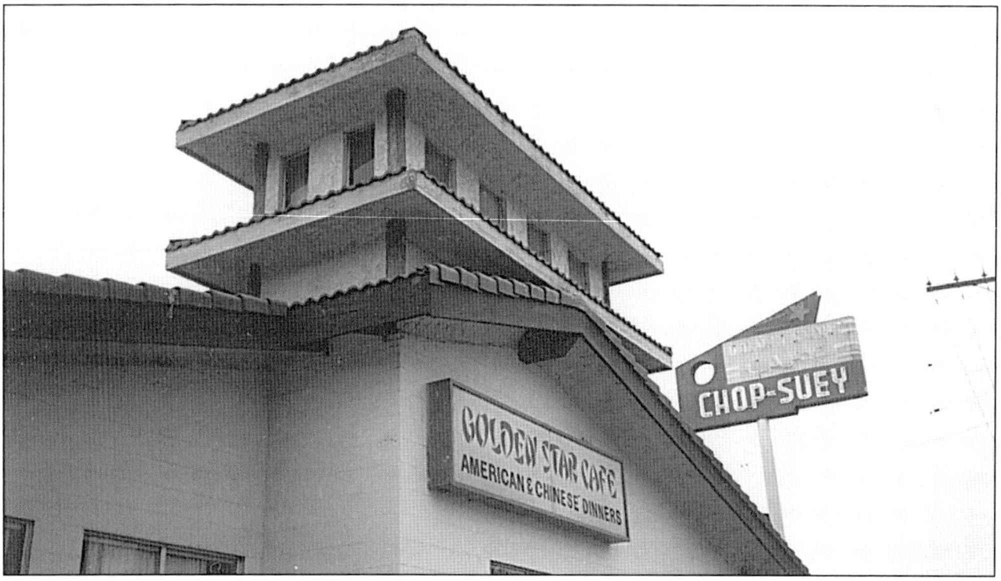

Much farther south of town, the Golden Star Café belonged to Jimmy Yoke Chan's family. His father started the business in 1950; Jimmy ran it for many years until his sons took over the operation. The restaurant, about a mile south of Chinatown, was noted for both western and Chinese food and catered mostly to the Hispanic and African-American families in the neighborhood. With 50 years of history, the restaurant continues a reputation of clean atmosphere and reasonably-priced food.

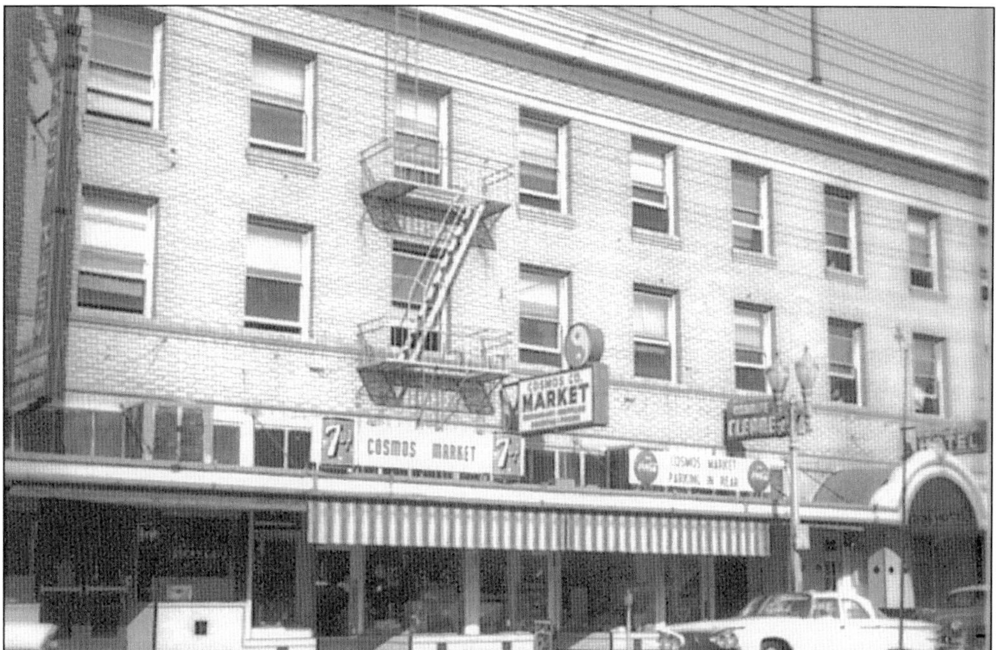

Wing Chan started the Cosmo Market in 1959 and kept the business going until 1971. It was forced to close for freeway acquisition. Wing then opened yet another grocery store in the town of Tracy until his retirement in the early 1990s. *(Courtesy of the Norman Lew Collection)*

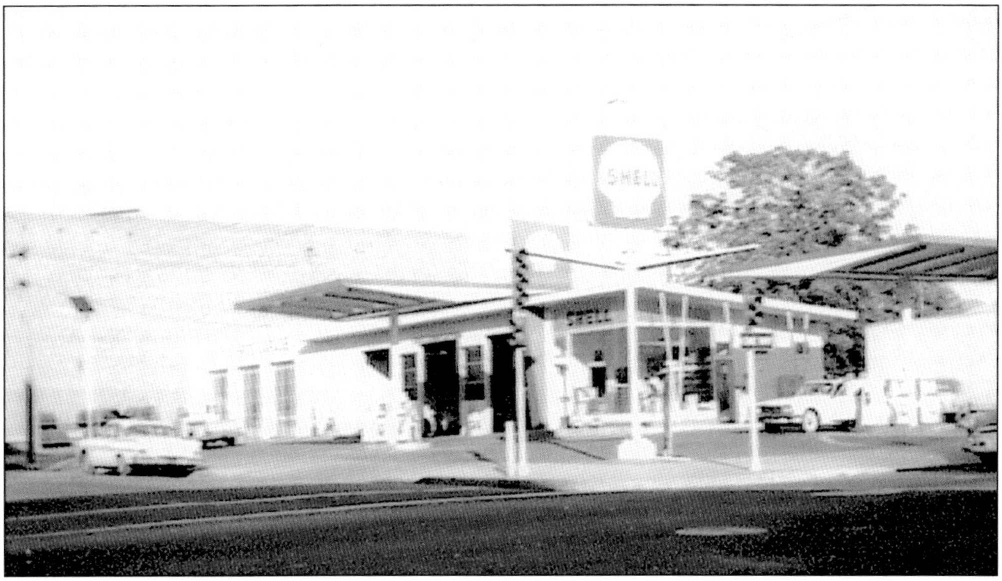

Dilly Ah Tye Jr. had a talent with cars even in his high school days. Because of his natural mechanical skills, his mother Rose suggested the family invest in a service station in 1931. When six of the Ah Tye brothers went to serve in World War II, sisters-in-law Marie and Audrey had no qualms about pitching in to help brother Raymond who ran the station. Initially located on Sonora Street, the station relocated to Lafayette and South El Dorado Street. *(Courtesy of the Norman Lew Collection)*

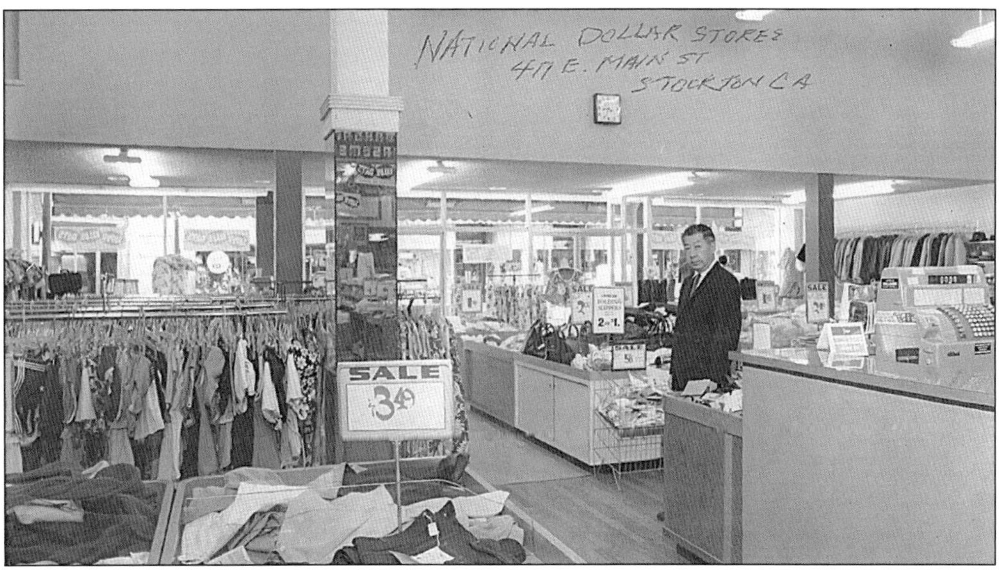

Earl Jann, born in Stockton in 1910 and a third generation Chinese American, began a sales career with National Dollar Store, a Chinese-owned department store started by Bay Area mogul Joe Soong. Mr. Jann's career began in 1930 and after 26 years working in Richmond, Santa Rosa, San Francisco, and San Luis Obispo, he returned as manager of the Stockton store in 1956. Jann was noted for his ability to function in both the western and Chinese world. He was a member of Rotary, the Masonic Lodge, SIRS, and was inducted into the Stockton Athletic Hall of Fame. *(Courtesy of the Jann Family Collection)*

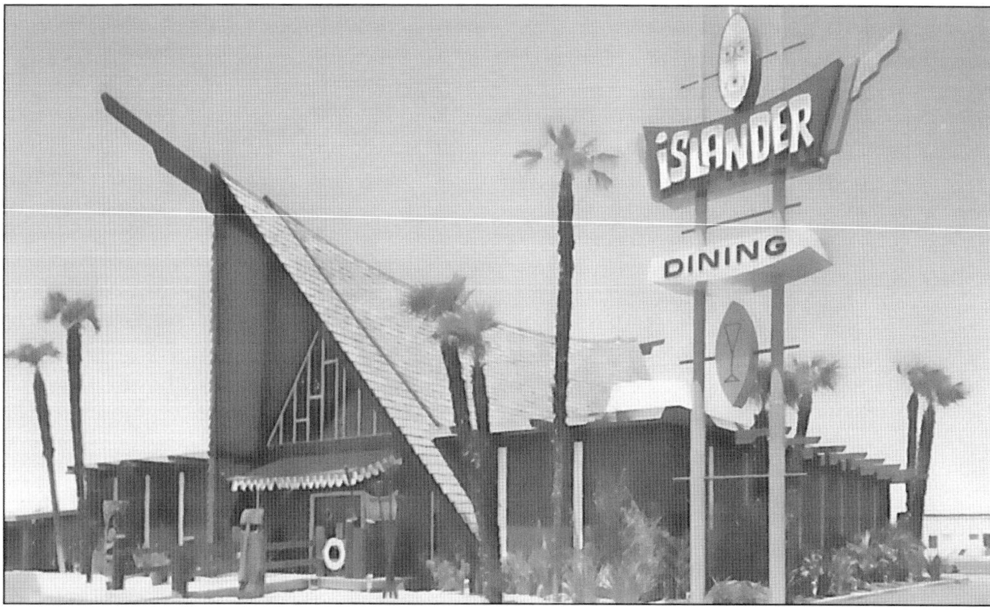

Located in Lincoln Village South (in north Stockton), the Islander catered to the general population. The tropical décor lent to serving a mix of Cantonese and Mandarin cuisine. Many considered the Islander as exotic and upscaled. Started by Tommy Lee in 1966, it stayed in business until 1980. Headliners included Frankie Fannelli. Adjoining the restaurant to the west was Latitude 20, a cocktail lounge with a dance floor. *(Courtesy of Valerie Acoba)*

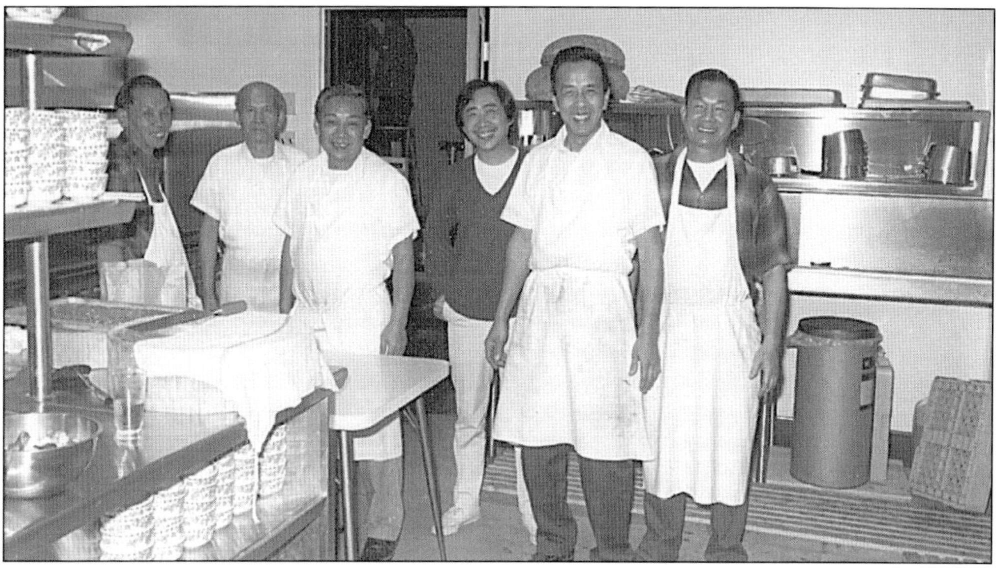

Dave Wong and his partner Raymond Wong were astute when they opened their restaurant on North Pershing Street in 1975. Dave Wong is in the center (in the sweater) next to his partner on his left. This picture was taken on opening day. Dave came to Stockton in the early 1950s and worked at On Lock Sam for a number of years before deciding to go on his own. Catering mostly to the western palate, the restaurant serves basic Cantonese food and has a lively bar. Success in providing good food has now faithful customers looking forward to the grand opening of the new Dave Wong's at a new location in Brookside. *(Courtesy of Dave Wong)*

Another successful restaurant that catered to the western palate was Minnie Gong Lee, a Chinese buffet at 145 East Harding Way. Gong Lee (Leung) went from his native village to New York in 1937 and landed in Stockton in 1947. He worked for a time at both a Chinese restaurant (the Peking) and Lamberts (a local bar and restaurant). With his wife, he bought Minnie's in 1957. He boasts that the buffet lunch cost $1.25 and dinner was $3.85. Gong Lee enjoyed playing the *ye wu* (a two-string Chinese stringed instrument) and writing calligraphy. He served as the Chinese Language School principal for two years and as the president of the Toishan District Ning Yueng Association for five years. *(Courtesy of Kathy Gong Meissner)*

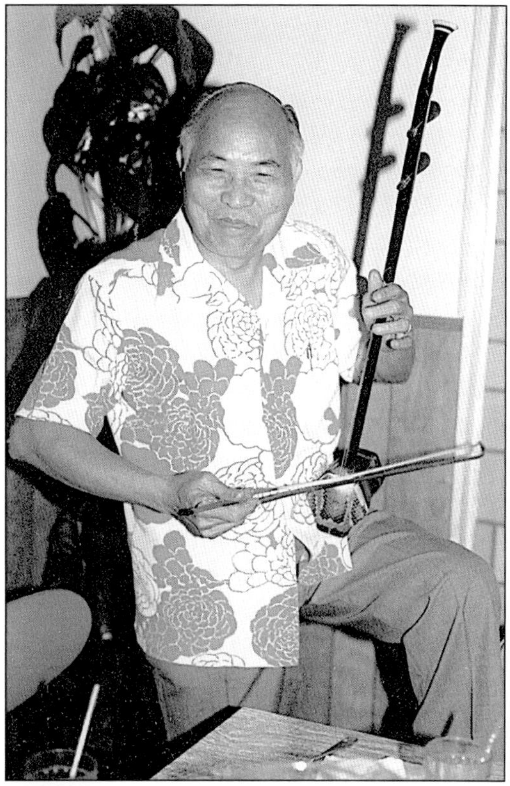

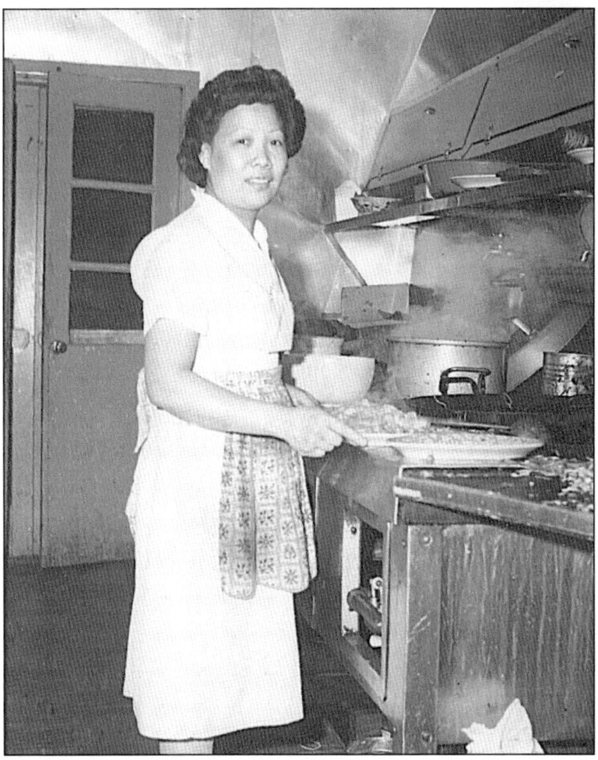

A Chinese married woman, helpmate at home, was expected to work in her husband's business. Mrs. Toy Gong Lee was no exception. She is seen here working in the kitchen of their Minnie Gong Lee Restaurant. Toy came to California in 1953. She married Gong Lee in the mid-1930s before he left China. Even though the Japanese had invaded their village and they were ravaged by war, Toy recalled that they tried to adhere to the old marriage traditions in which Gong Lee gave Toy's family an adequate dowry of numerous cakes, chicken, candies, and whiskey. *(Courtesy of Kathy Gong Meissner)*

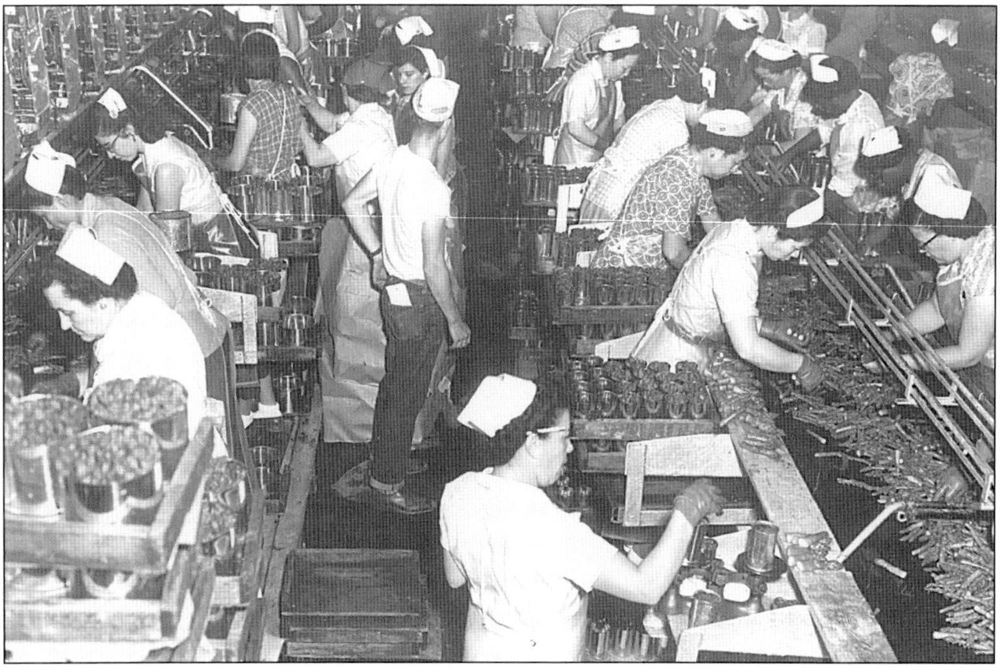

As early as the 1910s, Chinese women formed the greater part of the county's cannery work force. The seasonal work later provided these women health and union benefits, a social outlet with a high degree of psychological independence, and for many their own retirement funds.

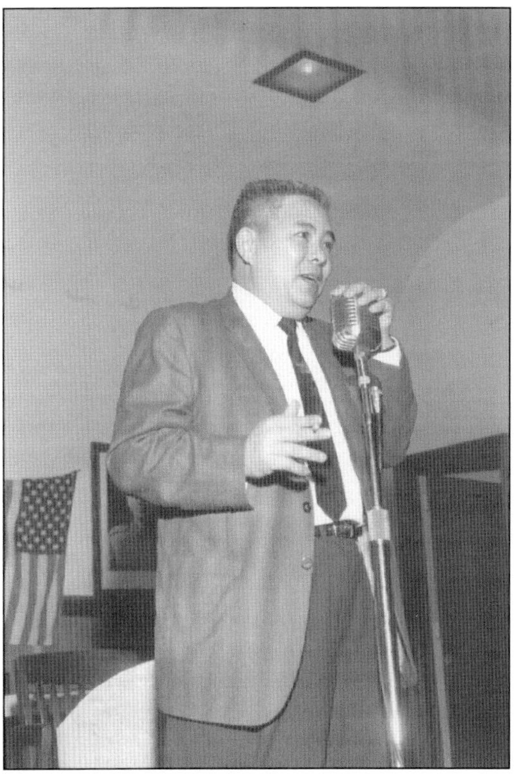

An extremely astute businessman, Sam Wahyou opened the first Daylite Market in 1938 as a meat market. In the following three years he opened three more stores in a neighboring town. Almost simultaneously he started the first Centro-Mart, an emporium that offered food, furniture, and a coffee shop. Daylite Market was a component within the Centro-Mart complex. Catering to the general population, he expanded the business with additional stores through the years, covering several cities as far north as Redding, California. In the 1960s, through a series of mergers the various conglomerations of stores were incorporated into Diamond Properties, Inc., a real estate holding company in San Francisco. When president Sam Wahyou suffered a terminal illness, the operations of the company underwent restructuring in 1973. As an employer, Sam had the ability to look for and place those with management skills in mentoring positions and created his own corporate ladder. *(Courtesy of Jimmy Lam)*

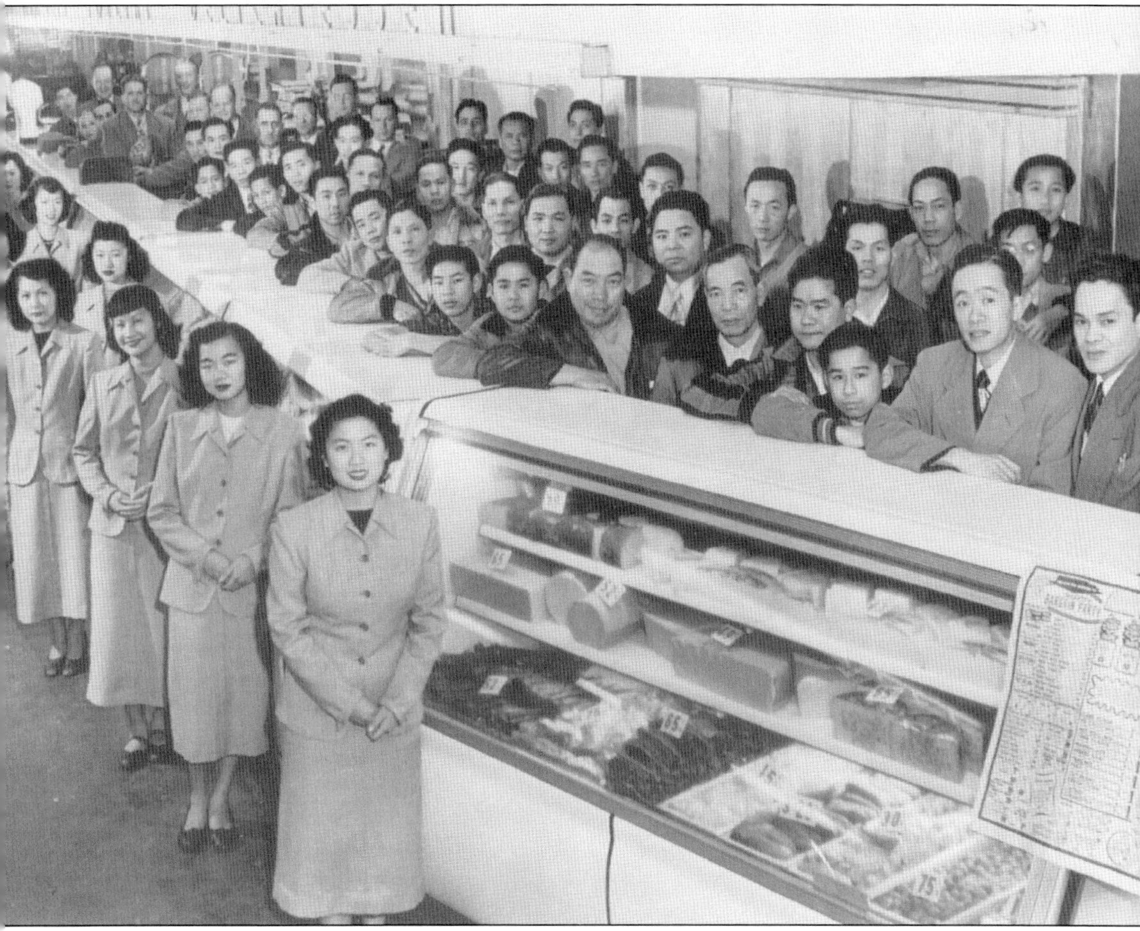

This 1946 photo shows employees gathered around the Daylite Market meat counter in the first Centro Mart on 111 South Center Street. Louie Lee was the first general manager of Centro-Mart. The women employees all wore well-tailored suits as their uniforms. Anna Mae Yip was their supervisor. Tommy Lee, later owner of The Islander, is the second from the right at the meat counter. *(Courtesy of Jimmy Lam)*

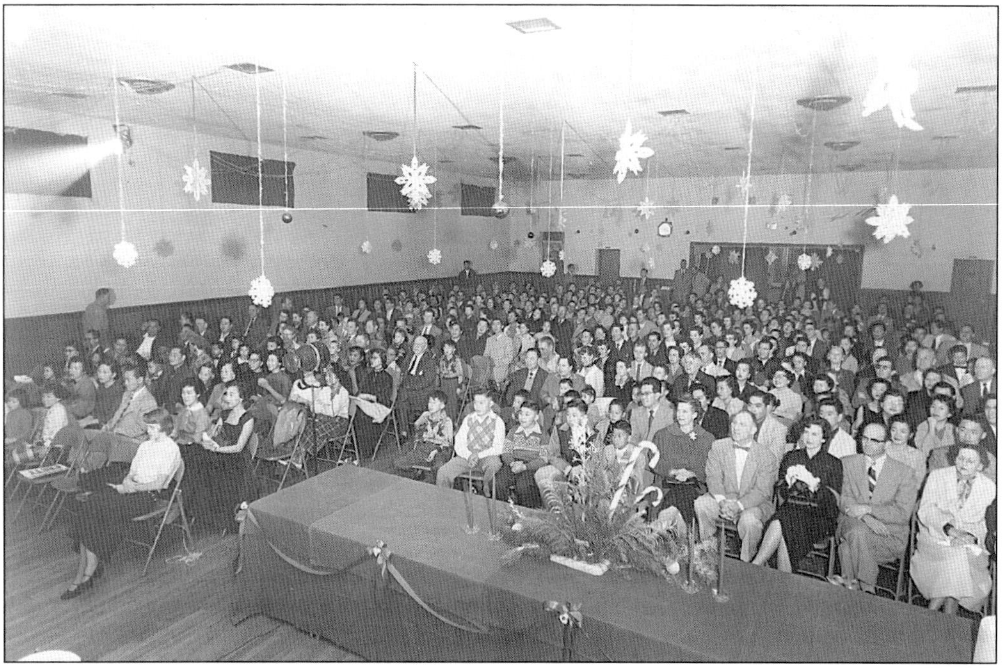

By 1949 there were no less than 31 Centro-Marts in operation. This anniversary commemorated the success of the company. The number of employees present was indicative of the workforce. This occasion was held at the new auditorium inside the Confucius Church (Chung Wah). *(Courtesy of Jimmy Lam)*

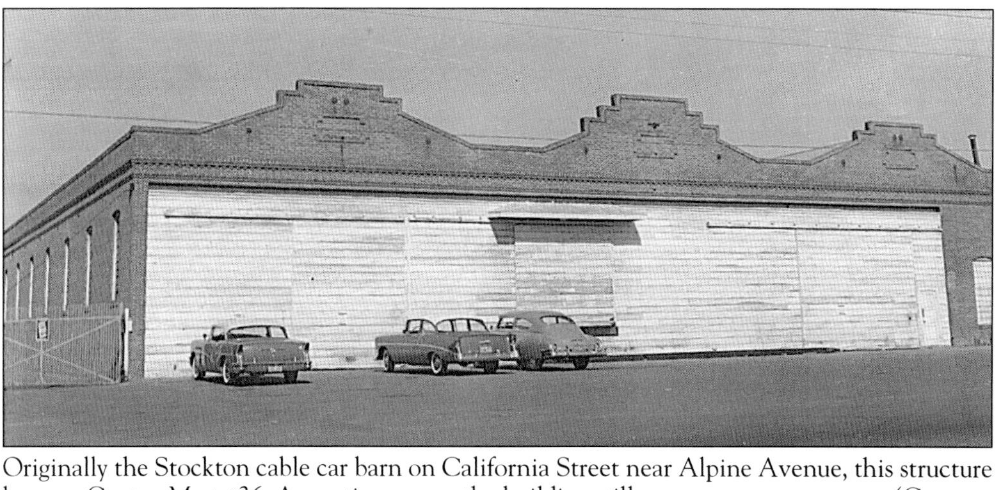

Originally the Stockton cable car barn on California Street near Alpine Avenue, this structure became Centro-Mart #36. A creative re-use, the building still serves as a grocery store. *(Courtesy of Jimmy Lam)*

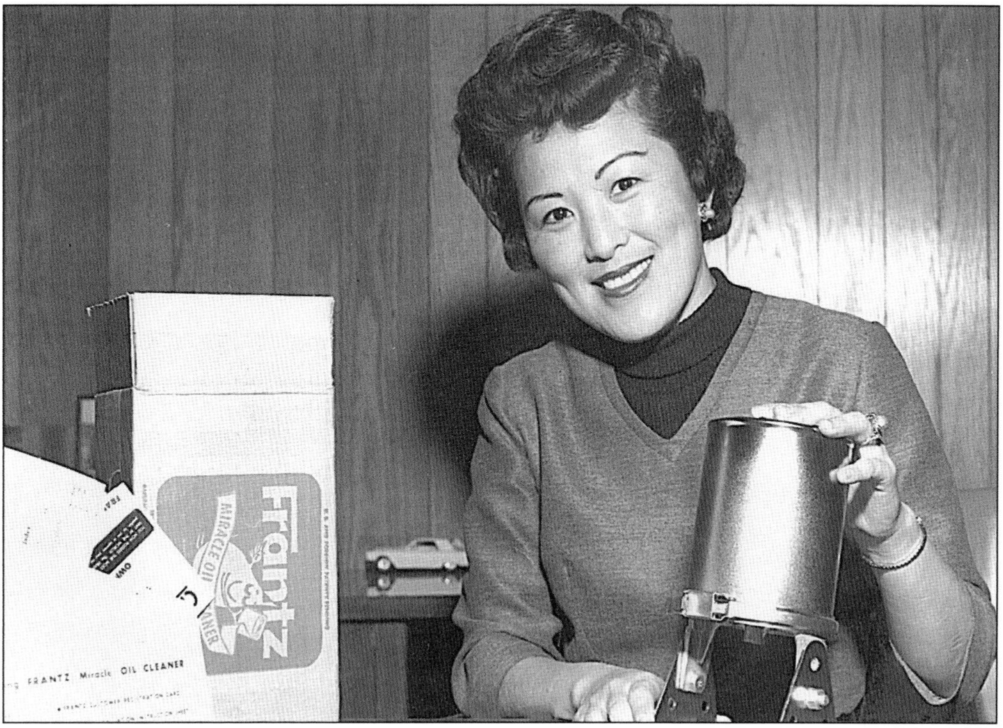

Skipper and Lois Kanagawa Yee became distributor of the Frantz Oil Filter in 1960. The design seen here in 1963 underwent four evolutions. The filters use tissue paper to remove impurities from all oils and fuel. Skipper owned the worldwide patents and started manufacturing the filters in his plant, SKY Corporation, at 1850 South El Dorado Street. Lois began the Lois Yee Cosmetics, Inc. in 1971, a full line of skincare products and recently has gone into food supplements. *(Courtesy of Lois Yee)*

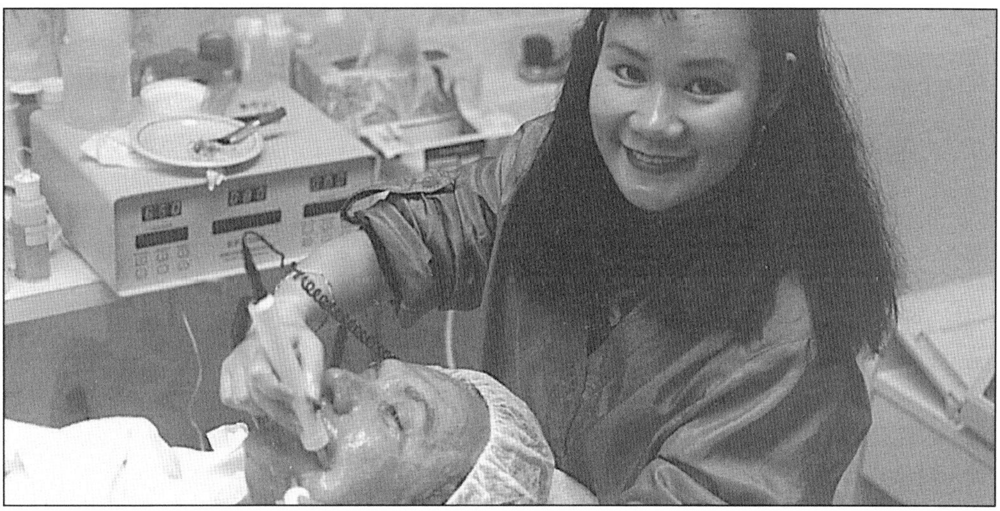

A niece of Skipper Yee, Fawn Yee Liang came to America in 1989. Employed initially at Lois Yee Cosmetics, Fawn continues the strides made by many immigrants. She attended school to improve her English, received her Associates of Arts degree and became an esthetician (facialist). *(Courtesy of Lois Yee)*

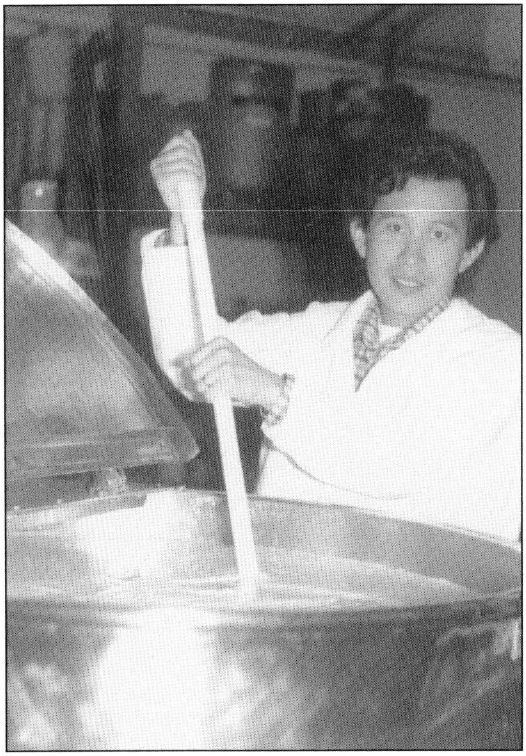

Stocktonian David Yee is a biochemist graduate of the University of California-Santa Cruz, and joined Lois Yee Cosmetics, Inc., the family business, in 1976. The beauty line was the only Asian manufacturing company actually making the product in the U.S. David, active in the Audubon Society, runs an annual birding symposium. *(Courtesy of Lois Yee)*

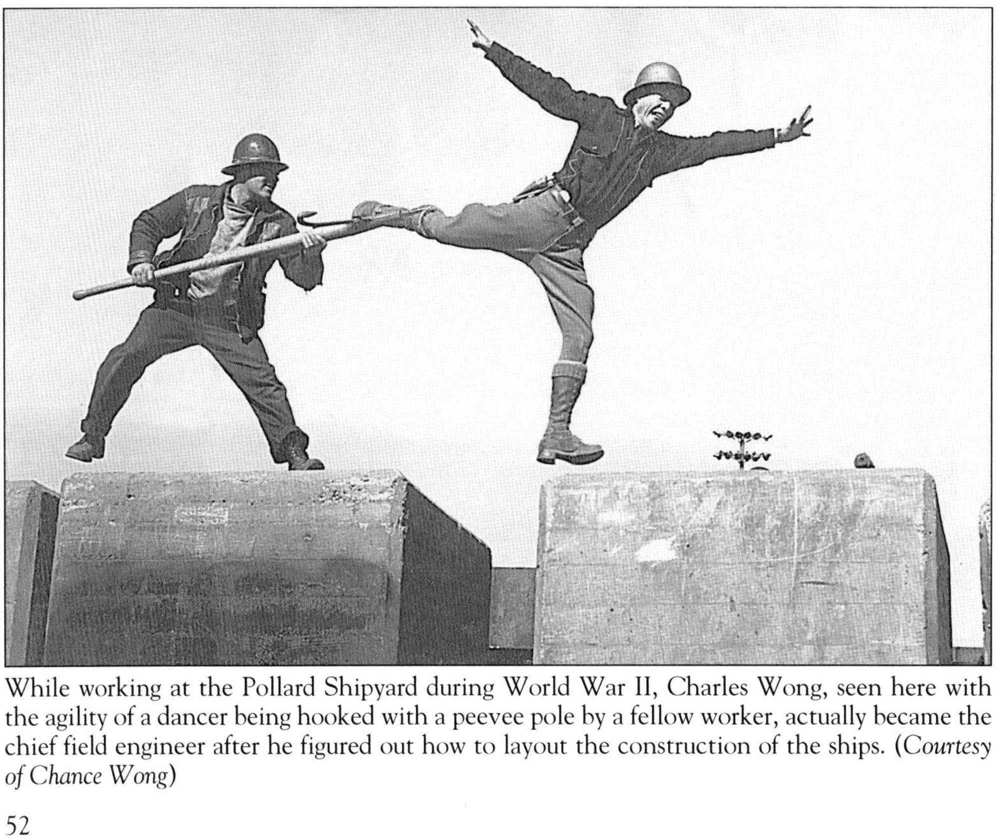

While working at the Pollard Shipyard during World War II, Charles Wong, seen here with the agility of a dancer being hooked with a peevee pole by a fellow worker, actually became the chief field engineer after he figured out how to layout the construction of the ships. (*Courtesy of Chance Wong*)

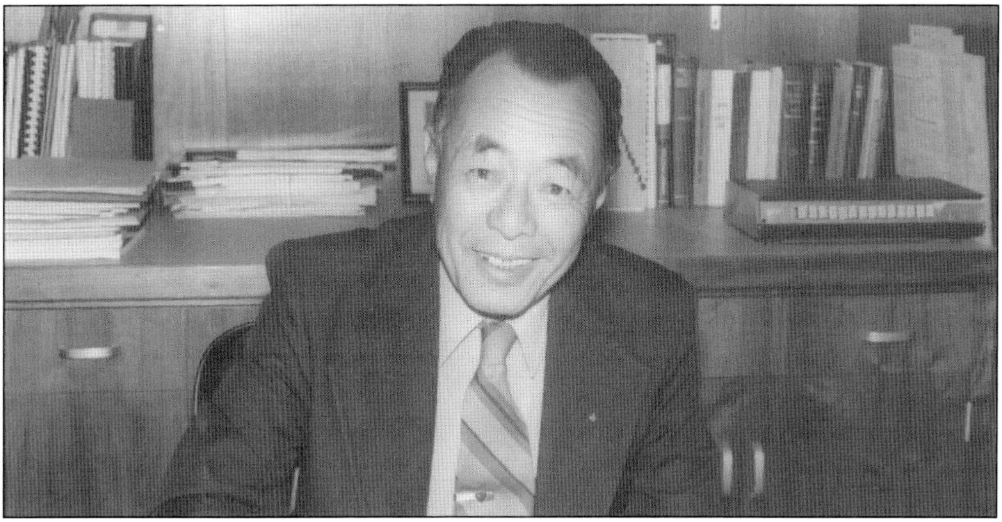

Charles Wong, native of Marysville, came to Stockton with his father who worked as a potato picker. Charles, as a young adult, worked at the King's Café, starting out as a dishwasher and working his way up to being the cook while his wife, Lola, worked at the Shanghai Restaurant on Main Street. After World War II, Charles became a surveyor for the county's Public Works Department and gradually, through self-study and correspondence courses from the University of Wisconsin, passed his civil engineering exams. In 1965 he was appointed the San Joaquin County Public Works Director. *(Courtesy of Chance Wong)*

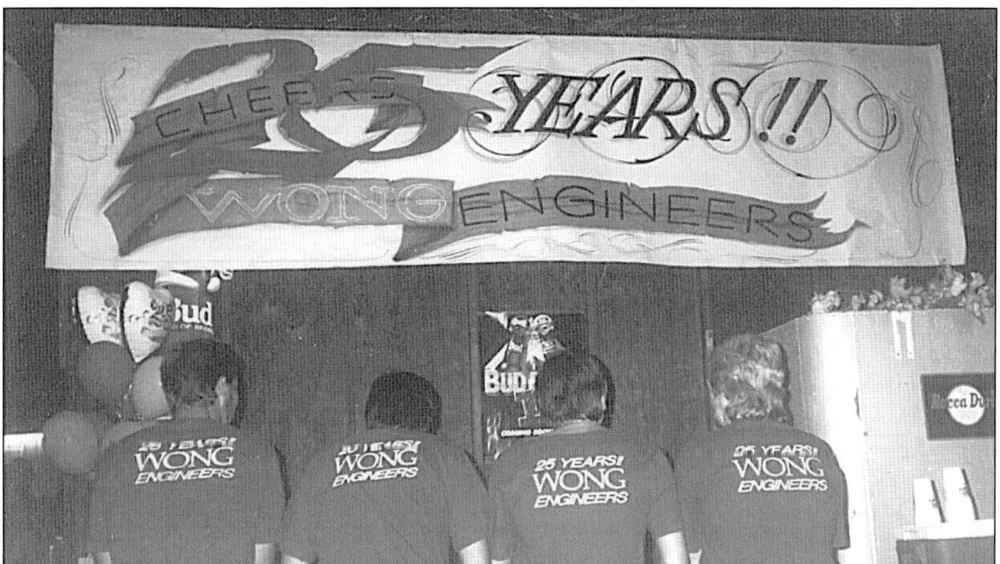

In 1990 the Wong Engineers celebrated their 25th anniversary. Beginning in 1965 by Chance Wong (son of Charles and graduate of University of California-Berkeley), Wong Engineers is a general civil engineering firm providing services throughout Northern California. A large portion of the firm's work is boundary, control and topographic surveys, aerial photography and mapping for public agencies, large engineering, and architectural firms. It is the only Asian engineering firm in the county. With Chance's recent retirement, the firm is now headed by his son Zachary, a civil engineer and licensed land surveyor. *(Courtesy of Chance Wong)*

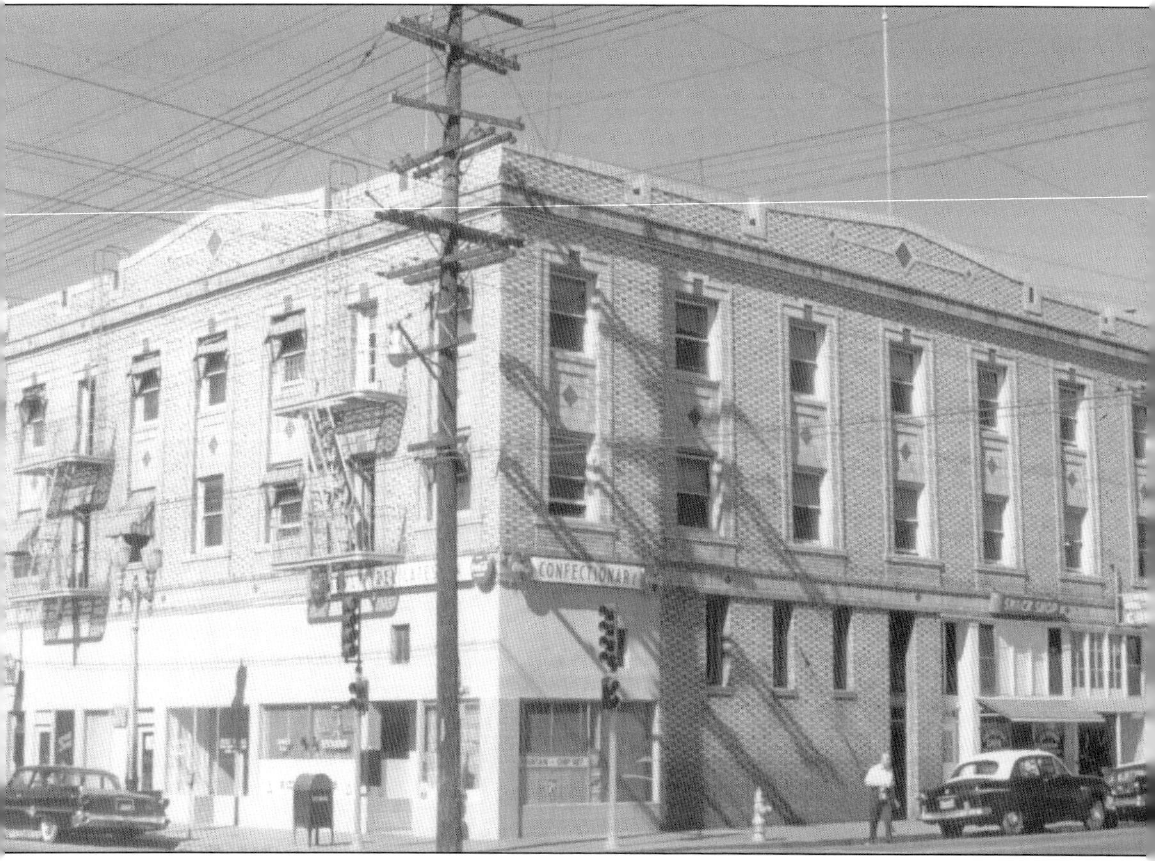

This building was owned by Johnnie and Elsie Lee Chang and sat at the northeast corner of El Dorado and Lafayette Street. A sizeable building took much capital and the Changs scraped together the funds with assistance from relatives. Johnny came to Stockton in 1924 from Indiana. He became a partner in a laundry business and slept in the back room on an ironing board. Pitching in, he washed clothes by hand and used a horse and buggy for delivery. His son, Freeman, recalls that his dad worked 12 hours a day. Later, Johnny ran an herb shop. On the ground floor of the building was Sam Lee, a local coffee shop owned by three partners—Lee Toy, a Mr. Louie, and Johnny Chang. The building stood in the way of the proposed Crosstown Freeway and the owners sold through the condemnation process in October of 1970. Today the eastbound on-ramp sits on the original building site. *(Courtesy of the Freeman Chang Collection)*

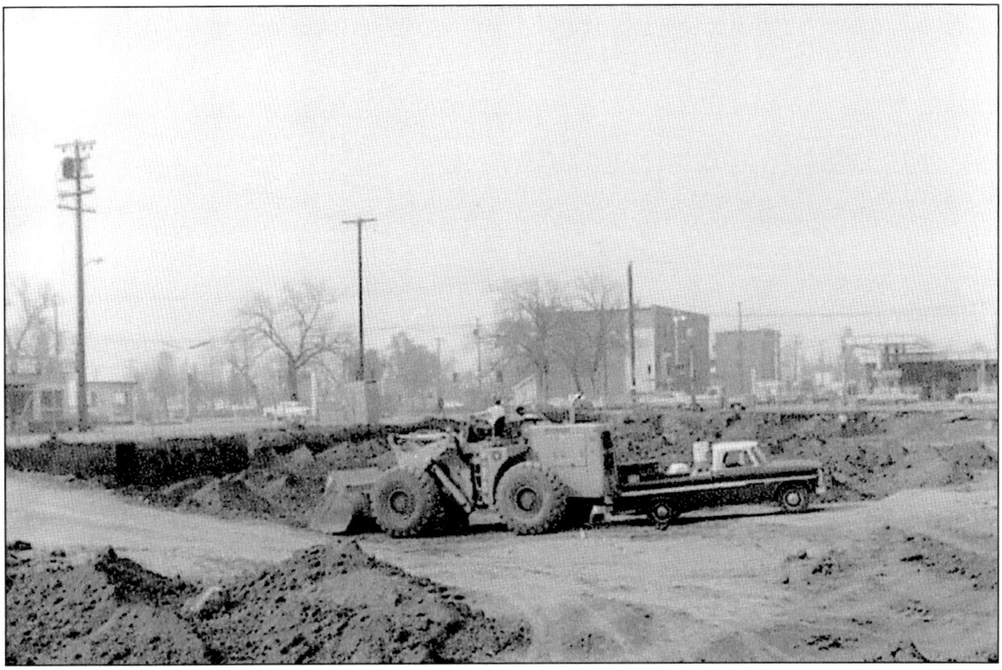

Heavy equipment machinery became a customary sight in the Chinatown area for several years. *(Courtesy of the Norman Lew Collection)*

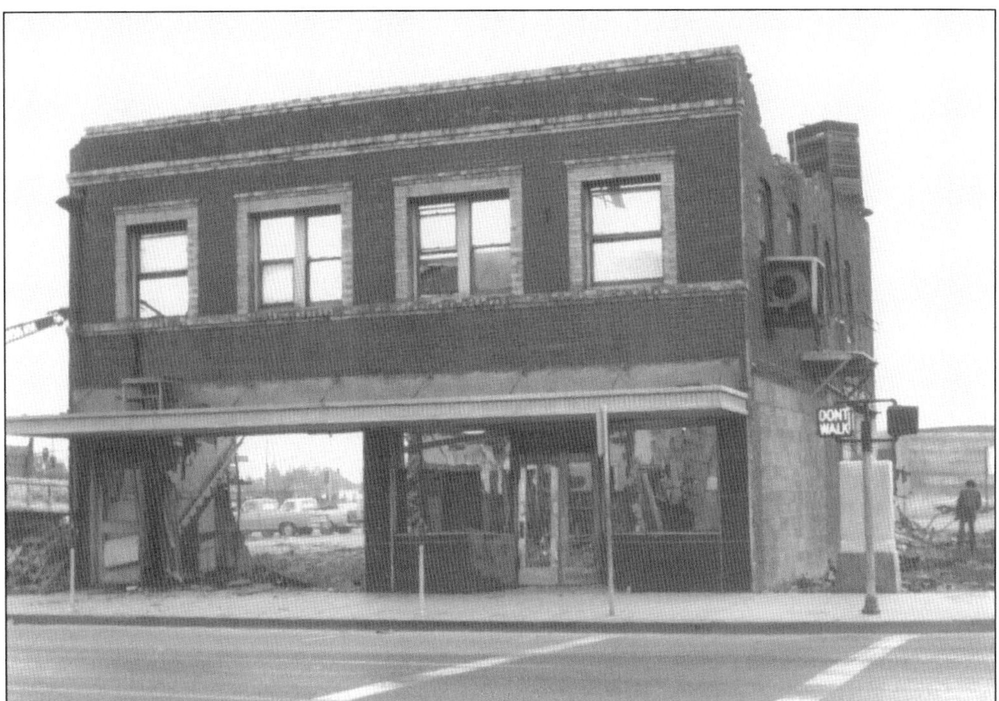

Barely a shell and with the inside gutted out, the final brick and mortar of the old Gan Chy Restaurant on El Dorado Street was ready for the final phase of demolition. The building, built before 1935, came down in November of 1971. *(Courtesy of Henry Yip)*

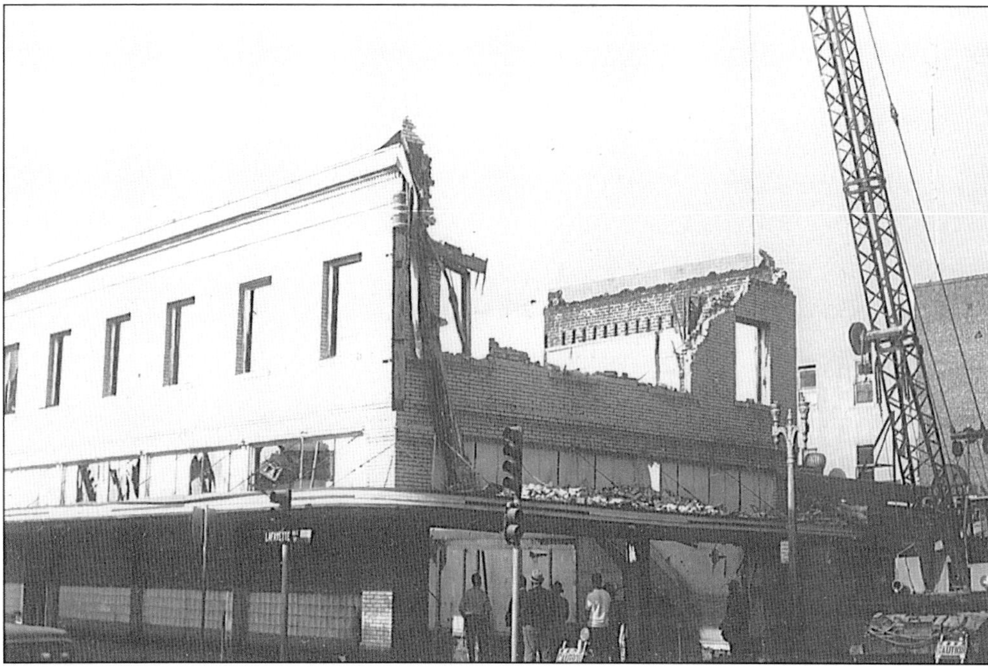

Sidewalk superintendents watched the wrecking ball's activities at yet another large building on Lafayette Street to give way to freeway construction. *(Courtesy of Conrad Mar)*

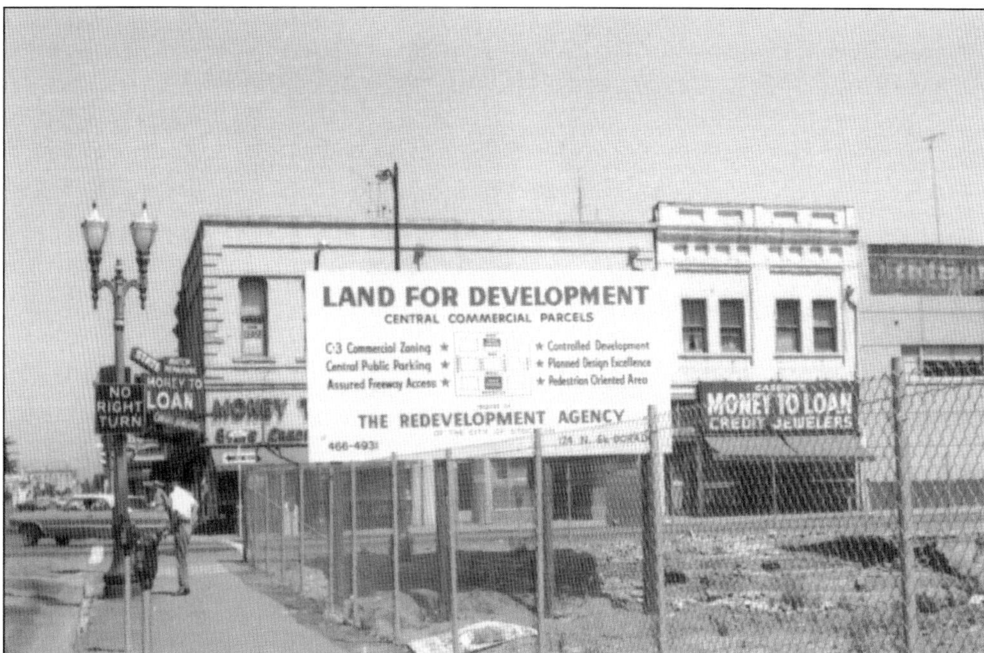

The first redevelopment project for the city of Stockton occurred in the north section of Chinatown. A new experience for both the city and the Chinese, only a few comprehended the process of condemnation and demolition with subsequent offers to return and had the first right to build anew. *(Courtesy of Conrad Mar)*

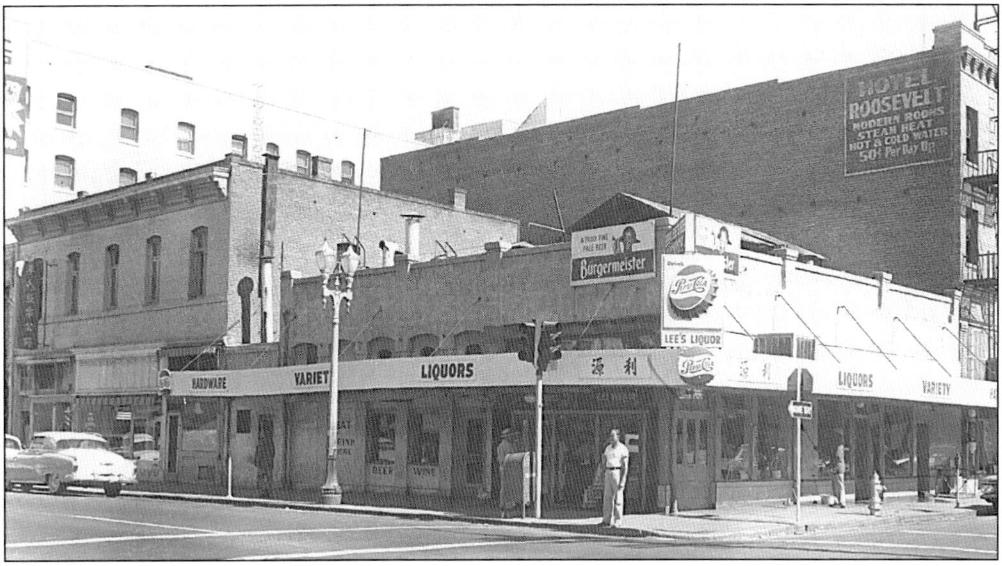

Only one parcel of land was not acquired for city redevelopment—the northeast corner of Washington and El Dorado Street. Some 80 years after the store's beginning, the third-generation Lees (Edward, Lawrence, and David) had the foresight to replace the old structure with a new building in 1958. They expanded northward with a four-unit commercial building and replaced the Roosevelt Hotel adjoining the store to the east with a four-story housing facility. The former Lee Center was renamed the Franco building and used as a senior housing complex operated by the housing authority. *(Courtesy of Mae Lee)*

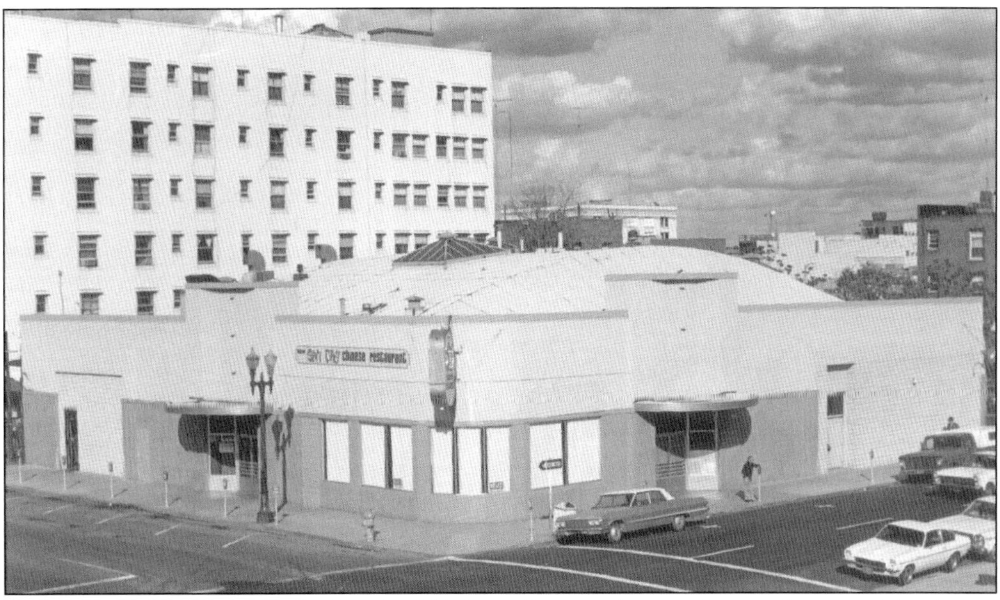

Rather than expending the funds to build, Henry Yip opted to purchase and remodel the former Greyhound Bus Depot at the corner of Washington and Sutter Street. Opening Day for the new location occurred on Chinese New Year in 1972 with lion dancers and well-wishers. The tall structure in the back was the Clark Hotel that was torn down in the 1990s to make way for a city parking structure. *(Courtesy of Henry Yip)*

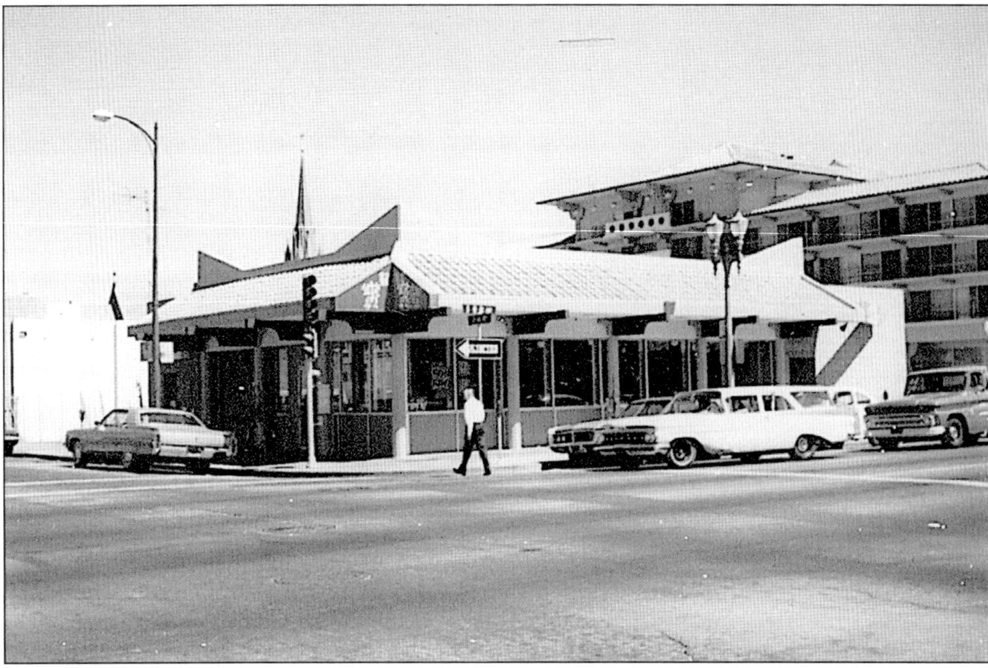

The original Bow Bow relocated to the southeast corner of El Dorado and Market Streets in 1970. Back in the 19th century, Peter Musto operated a spaghetti factory and Italian delicatessen at the same location. Unlike the old small restaurant, the new facility included a large banquet room in the back that seats about 225 people. *(Courtesy of Darryl Yee)*

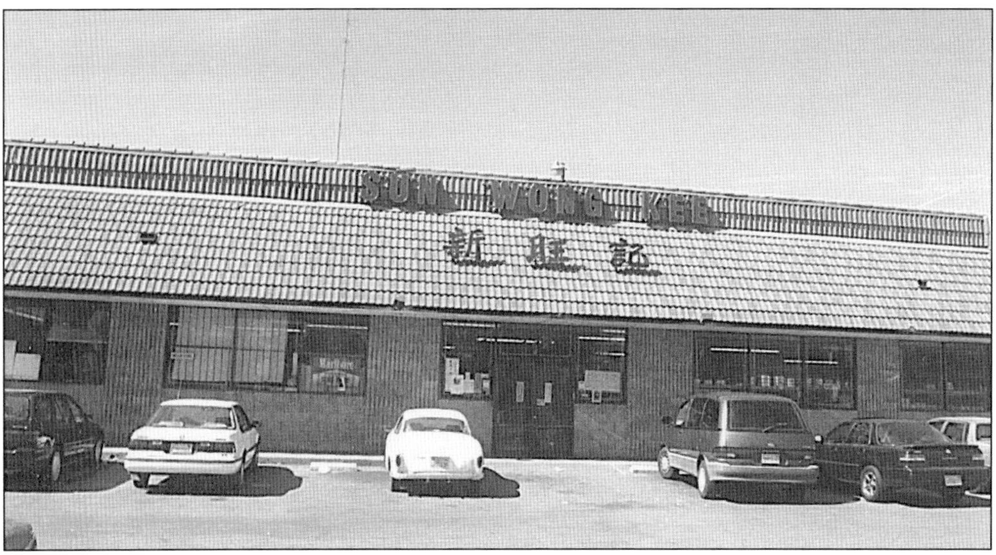

The Sun Wong Kee, at Sonora and Hunter Streets, is a grocery store established in the 1970s to fill the needs of the Chinese who lived south of the Crosstown Freeway. Another grocery store a block away is Kwong Tuck Wo, which was formerly on Washington and then Hunter Street before relocating to San Joaquin Street at Hazelton Avenue.

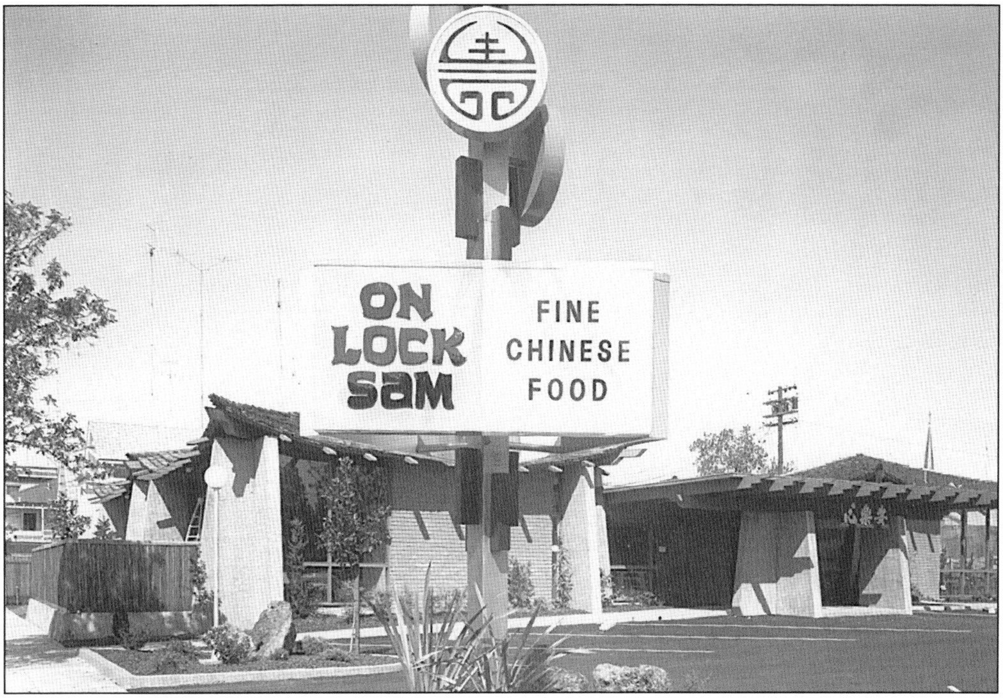

Hanging the old On Lock Sam signboard above the entryway, the Wongs built this modern structure with the thought of keeping some of the old touches including retaining some intimate dining booths. Quite recently the restaurant received the Century Recognition Award from the San Joaquin County Historical Society. This family business has spanned three generations: Wong Sai Chun, Jimmy Wong, and now Robert Wong with his late brother, Jenkin. *(Courtesy of Robert Wong)*

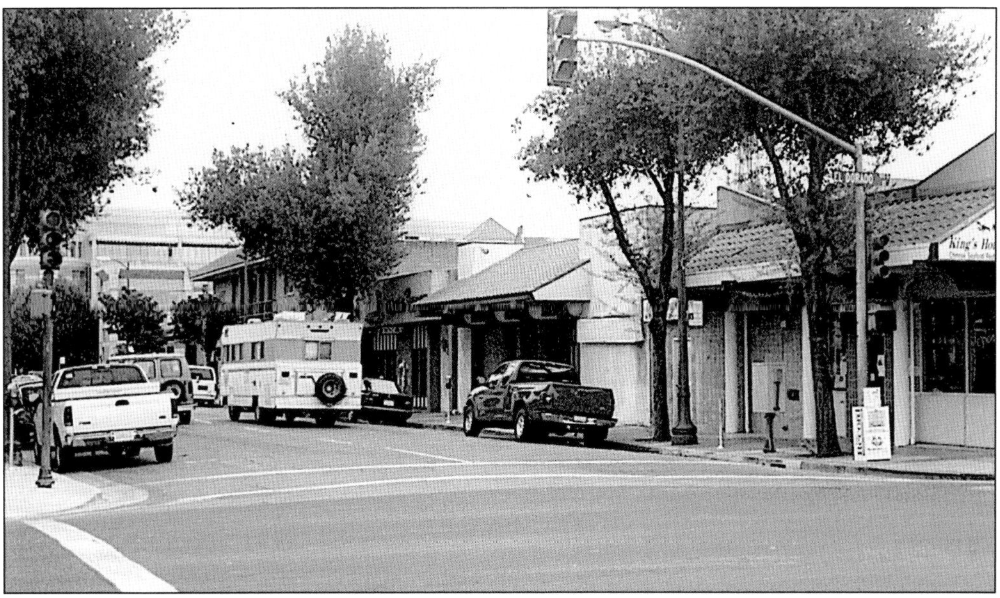

A very recent photo of Market Street without the ambiance, foot traffic, and excitement of the past.

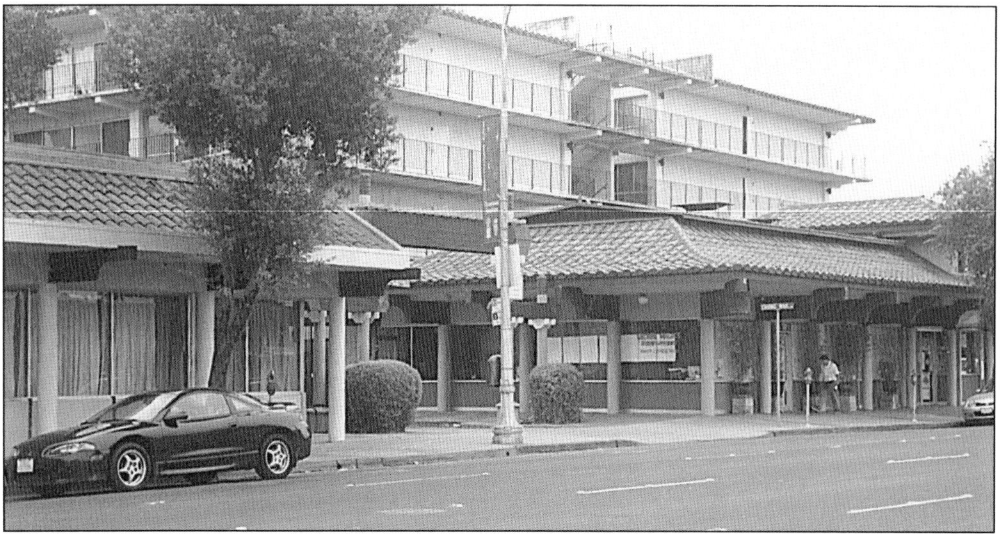

One can see the large, four-story Franco Building (former Lee Center) in the background. The Lincoln Hotel had once occupied the area where one now sees a walk/driveway to the mosaic inlaid path of Chung Wah and Mun Kwok Lanes. Within this path had once been the infamous Stockton bordellos.

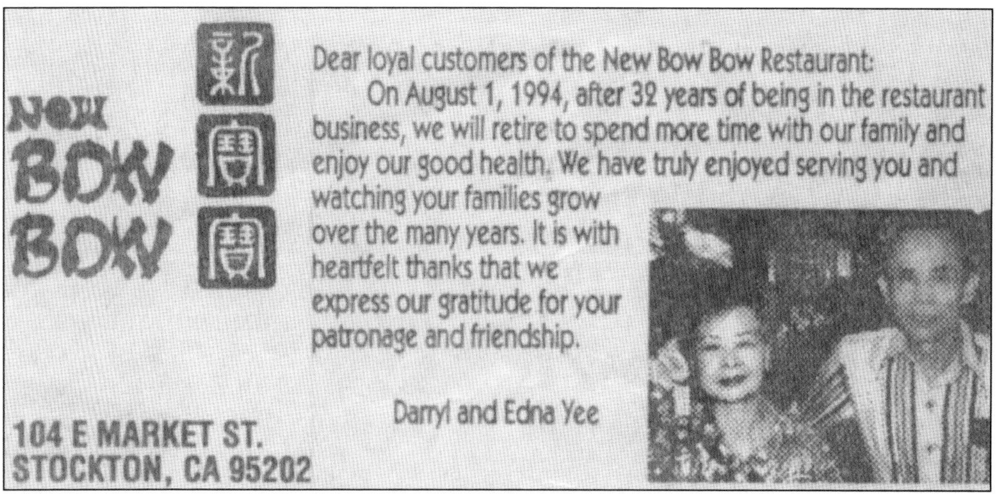

This newspaper ad placed in the Stockton Record foretold not only the retirement of Darryl and Edna Yee, but was indicative of the generation of merchants, restaurateurs, and others in the business community who provided the economic energy to the Chinese community for nearly seven decades. Infrequently, however, did the next generation follow in their parents' footsteps. *(Courtesy of Darryl Yee)*

Four

Family, Friends, and Events

In the mid-1930s a scholarship question arose: "Am I American or am I Chinese?" This question plagued many of the high school and young adult-aged, second-generation Chinese, particularly when Japan invaded China. Many began to wrestle with their bi-culturalism since the ties to the old Motherland were not as strong as that of their parents. Yet, there were blatant legal as well as subtle barriers to full rights and privileges, even for the second-generation, American-born. California's enactment of the Miscegenation Law in 1872 prohibited marriages of white persons with minority races that included the Asians. This law was not rescinded until 1948. A de-facto housing practice existed in Stockton until the mid-20th century whereupon Asians could not buy new homes in the north part of town. Children were also prohibited from swimming in the municipal pools when white children were in the pool and Chinese men found themselves locked out of civic organizations. These were the challenges.

Yet, the Stockton Chinese made great strides. The young had received dual guidance as they matured—from their parents and activities associated with the Chinese Christian Center. In essence, they focused on their own Americanization process and their own community. Barriers seemingly disappeared in time.

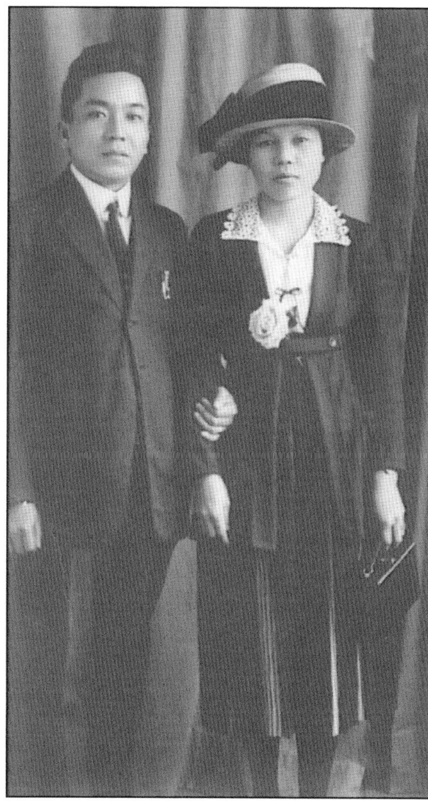

Long-remembered as a benefactor to the Chinese community, Wong Sai Chun and his wife, Fong Hau Ng, came to America in 1918. Young and astute, two years after his arrival he acquired the On Lock Sam restaurant with two partners. Five years later he began a sausage factory. His support of the community's activities included leadership in Chung Wah, the Chinese Language School, and participation in endless family and district associations. The Wongs were parents who saw to the well-being of their two children and that of the entire community.

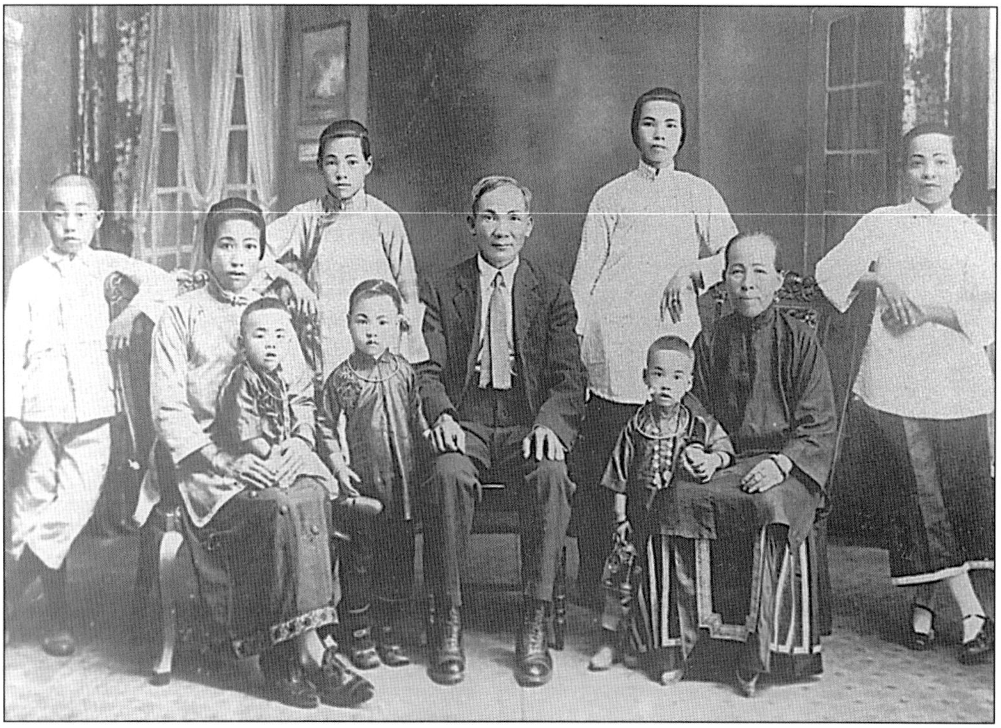

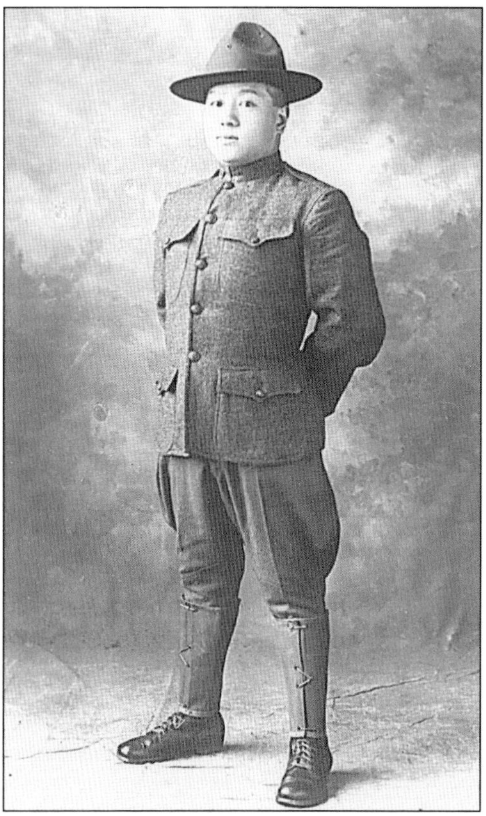

It was not unusual for Chinese men to have more than one wife. Goon Hing Yep is pictured here with his two wives and the children from both. Coming to Stockton with his first wife and children, Goon Hing Yep took up potato farming in the delta and became quite affluent. (*Courtesy of Mary Huey*)

Many sons of the early Chinese pioneers, as first-generation Chinese Americans, served the U.S. in World War I. Gong Cheung Ka, owner of the A-1 Meat Market, as well as Jones Low of Jones' Market, were both fairly new arrivals and served their newly-adopted country.

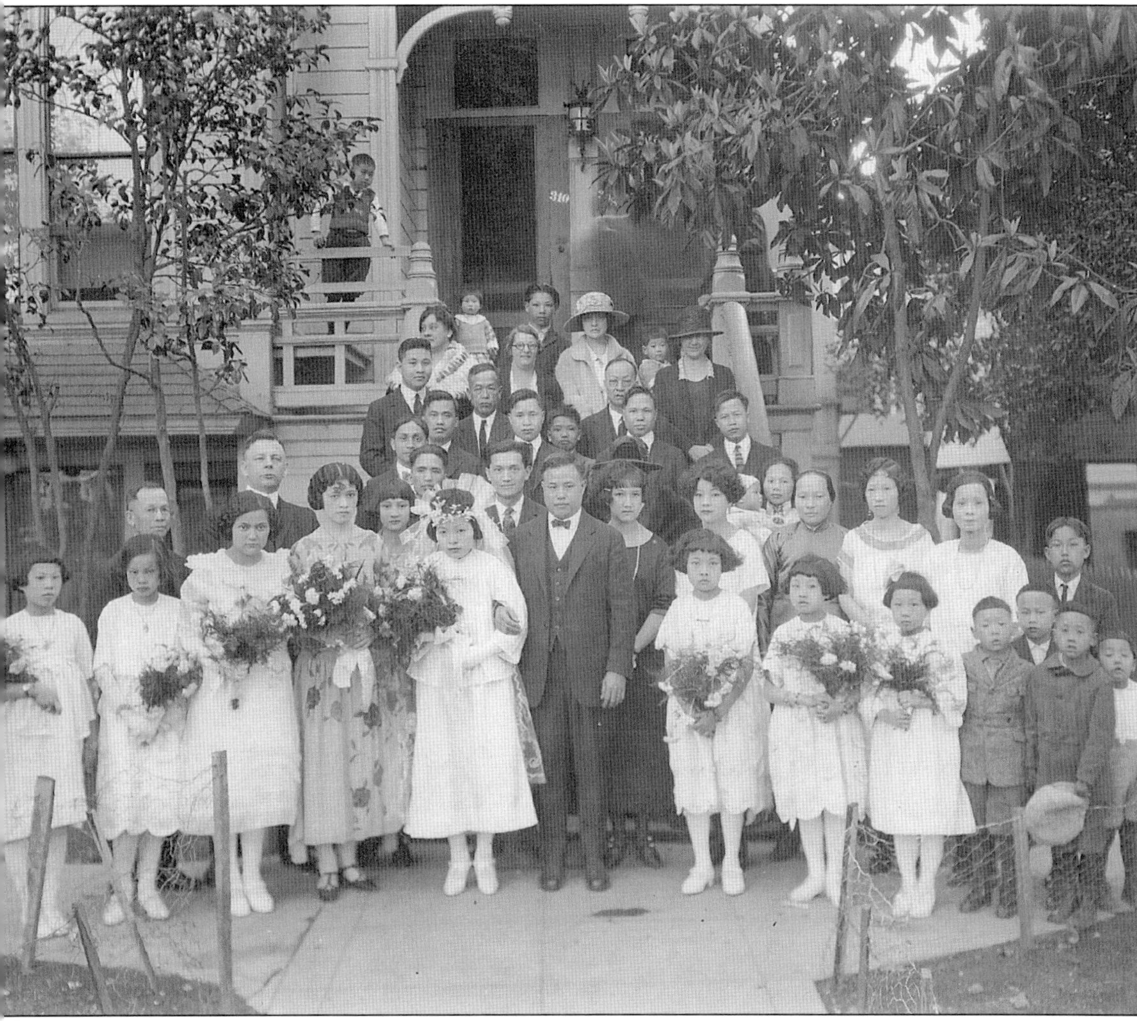

The marriage of Men Coon Fong of Sacramento and Ka Yep (whose English name was Alice) in 1922 was celebrated with many close and distant relatives. The daughter of Goon Hing, Yep was born in China in 1903. She joined her husband who had worked at a variety of trades in Sacramento. Together, they had six boys and six girls. *(Courtesy of Mary Huey)*

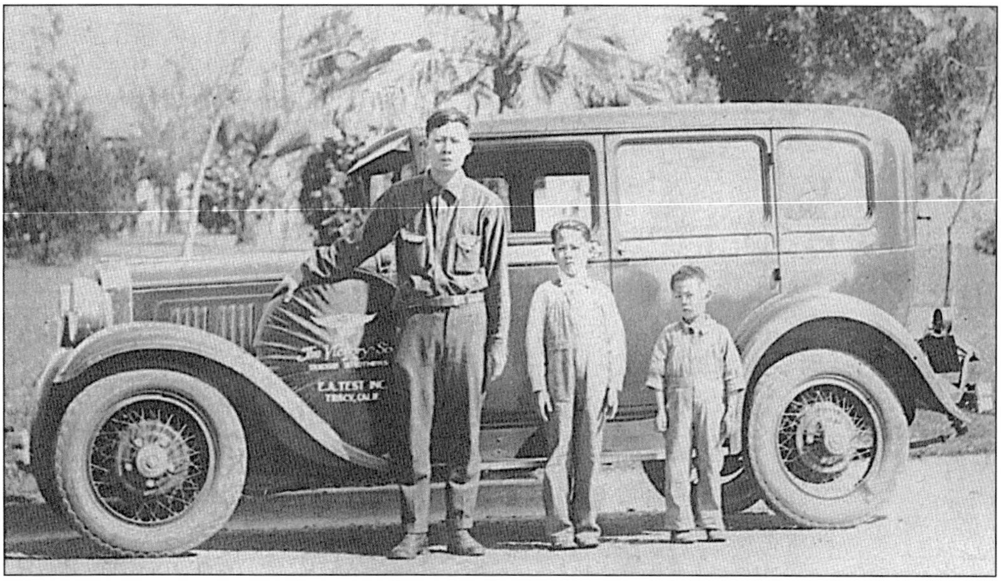

One could not tell which Mar Hing Lung was more proud of, his 1929 Dodge or his two fine sons, Ken and Wing. Both boys were born in Stockton. Although Mar Hing Lung died early, his sons recalled their mother working long hours in the canneries to assure that the boys would receive an education that would have made their father proud. Ken became a dentist and Wing a medical doctor. *(Courtesy of Ken Mar)*

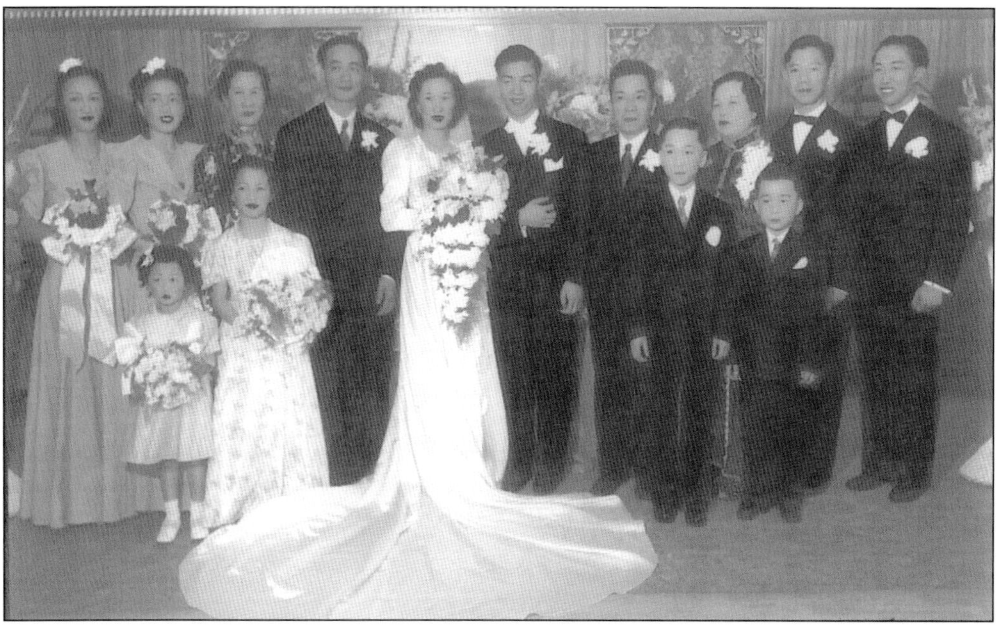

The wedding of Jim S. Wong, son of Wong Sai Chun and Lillian Hom, suggests all the trappings of a very large wedding. Flanked by their parents on both sides, the wedding party also included Wilbur Choy (on the far right) who became well known in the community for his activities in the church. Oftentimes, couples preferred a western ceremony followed by a Chinese banquet. This photo was taken at On Lock Sam. Jim took over the reins of On Lock Sam when his father passed away in 1953. *(Courtesy of Robert Wong)*

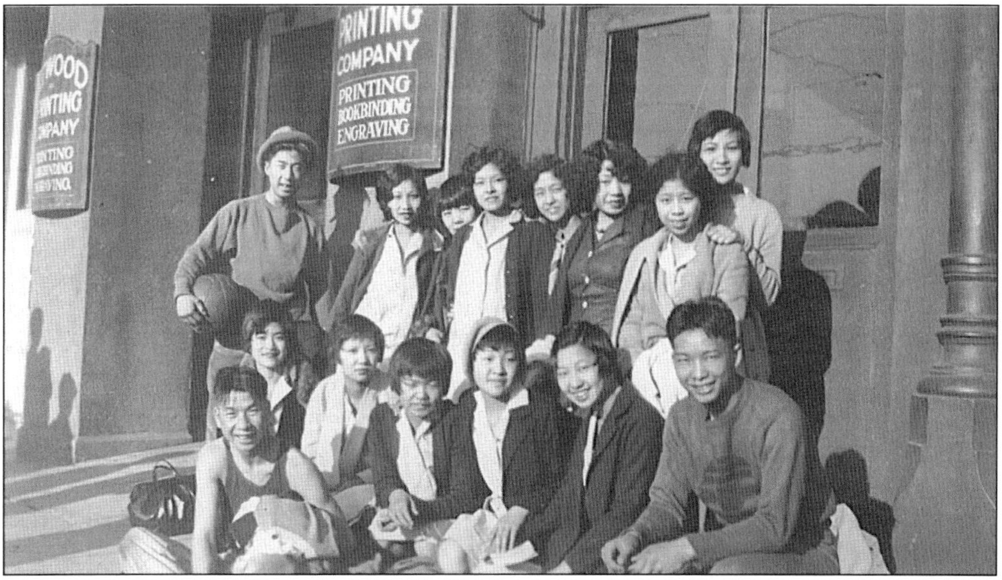

In 1928 the formation of a girls' basketball team was not unusual for a group that was mostly born and raised in Stockton. Unlike their mothers who were not allowed to fraternize in public, these young ladies were active and competed with other teams. Many remained steadfast friends for a lifetime and some are now in their late 80s. Identifiable are: Florence Jann Won, May Lee Low, Hazel Chang, Sadie Fong Chan, and Nellie Lee. *(Courtesy of the Jann Family Collection)*

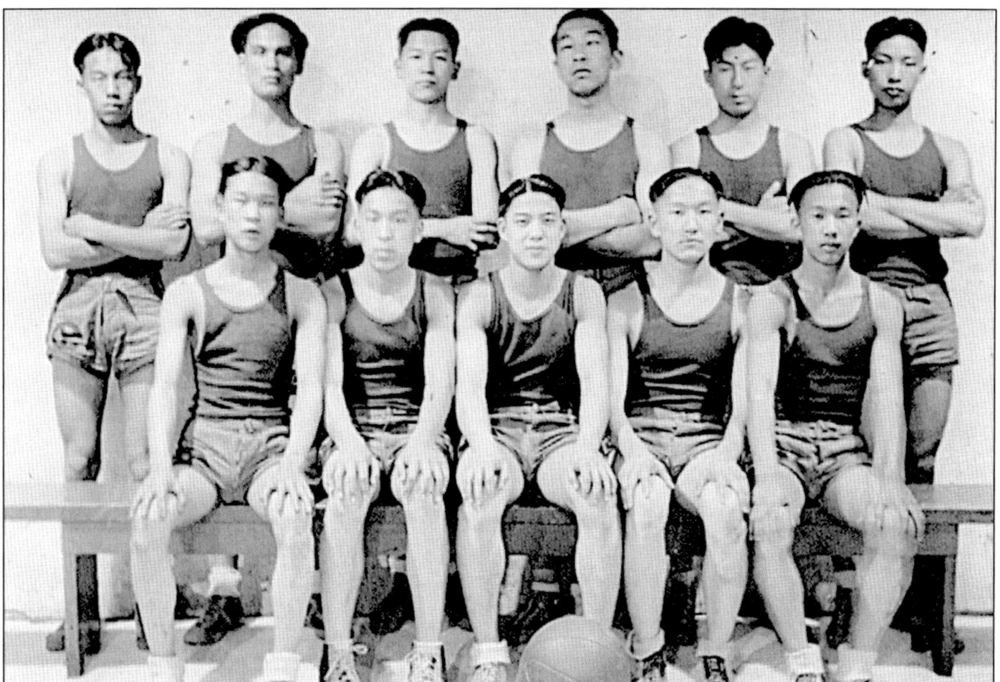

Boys formed their own Chi Y Basketball team in 1929. Known as the Wolf Club and connected to the local YMCA, the teenagers also became involved in football and baseball. Chinese gambling houses often donated the uniforms. *(Courtesy of the Jann Family Collection)*

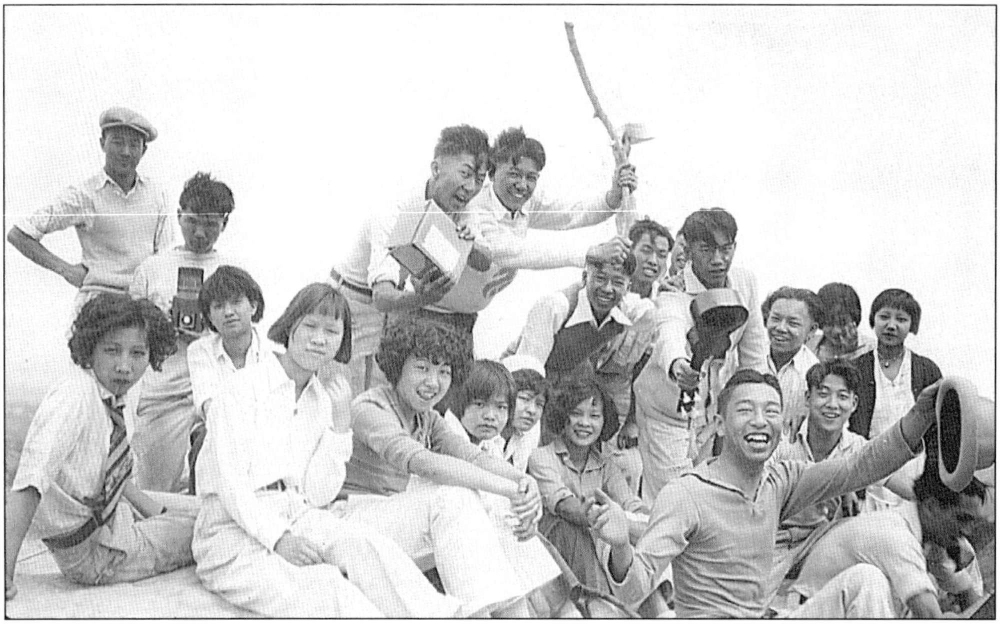

In this 1929 photo of a perfect boy-meet-girl situation, many remembered the picnics at Jenny Lind in the eastern foothills outside of Stockton. Chung Wah and even the Y clubs sponsored these annual events. The Stockton youth enjoyed exploring tourist areas such as Yosemite, Monterey, Carmel, and the South Bay. Their geographic visits expanded knowledge of other Chinese-American communities and increased their pool of potential mates, quite unlike their parents, who depended on arranged marriages in China. *(Courtesy of the Jann Family Collection)*

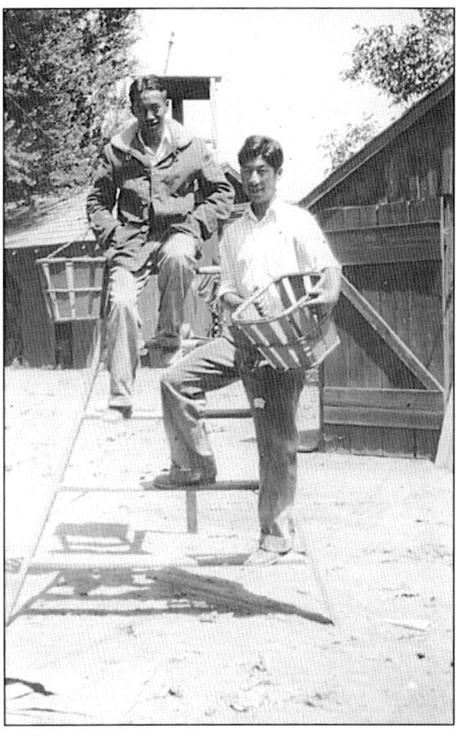

Never afraid of hard work or the ability to earn money during the summer months picking peaches and pears, Earl Jann (right) and Lock Chinn worked at the C.C. Wing Ranch in Walnut Grove. Other ranch areas in the delta where youth found employment were in the communities of Courtland, Franklin, and Locke. Ranchers provided meals and even lodging but the hours were long and the work tough. Girls also worked at the ranches sorting the fruit. *(Courtesy of the Jann Family Collection)*

All children enjoy Christmas. Achieving the ultimate in every boy's dream, Freeman Chang received his very own train set and tracks that ran continuously around the beautifully decorated tree. Elsie Lee Chang made sure her son, Freeman, was decked out in new holiday garb. *(Courtesy of the Freeman Chang Collection)*

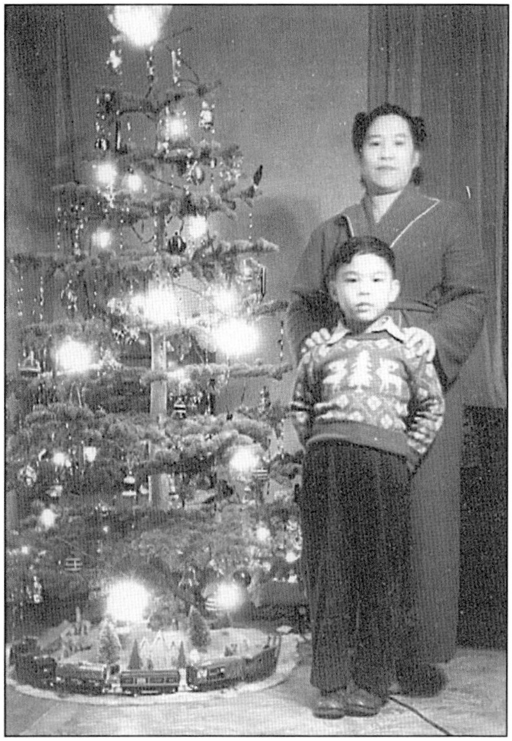

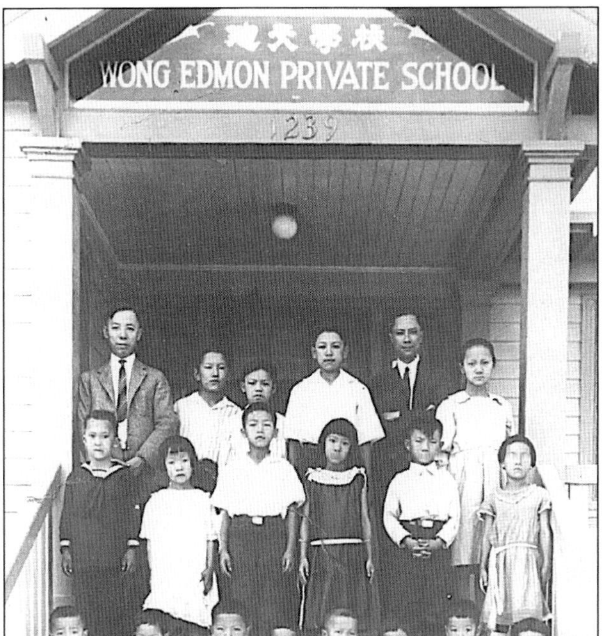

Children of several wealthy Wong families gather for the dedication of their family-funded, private enrollment language school on October 16, 1923. The Wong Edmon Private School was located on the corner of Monroe and Clay Streets.

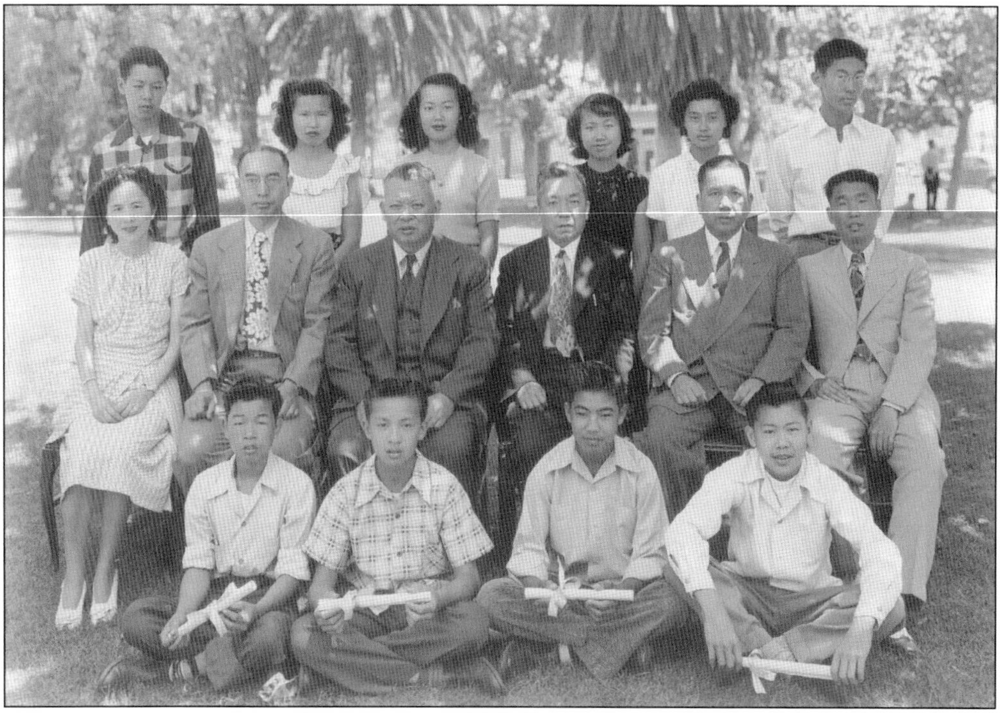

This was a graduating class of the Chinese Language School, taken at Washington Park across from the Confucius Church. In the middle row, starting on the left, are two teachers, Lee Soon, Wong Sai Chun, S.L. Fong, an herbalist, and an unidentified man. Several of Chan Shang Yee's children are in the photograph: Albert, Charlie, and Birtie. Classes are not based on age but reading levels. Therefore siblings are, at times, in the same grade. *(Courtesy of Violet Chan)*

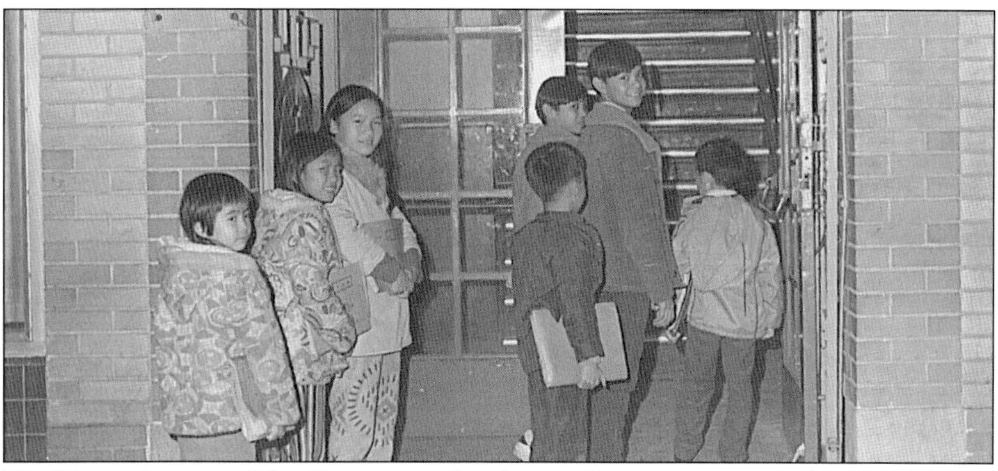

The Chinese Language School has remained in the same location, occupying the second floor of Chung Wah, since 1924. The number of days and hours of attendance have relaxed appreciably since the early decades when families lived closer to Chinatown and students were required to attend Chinese school right after regular school and Saturday mornings. Due to transportation difficulties and other interests, today's students only attend three hours on Saturday mornings. *(Photo by Bryan Chan)*

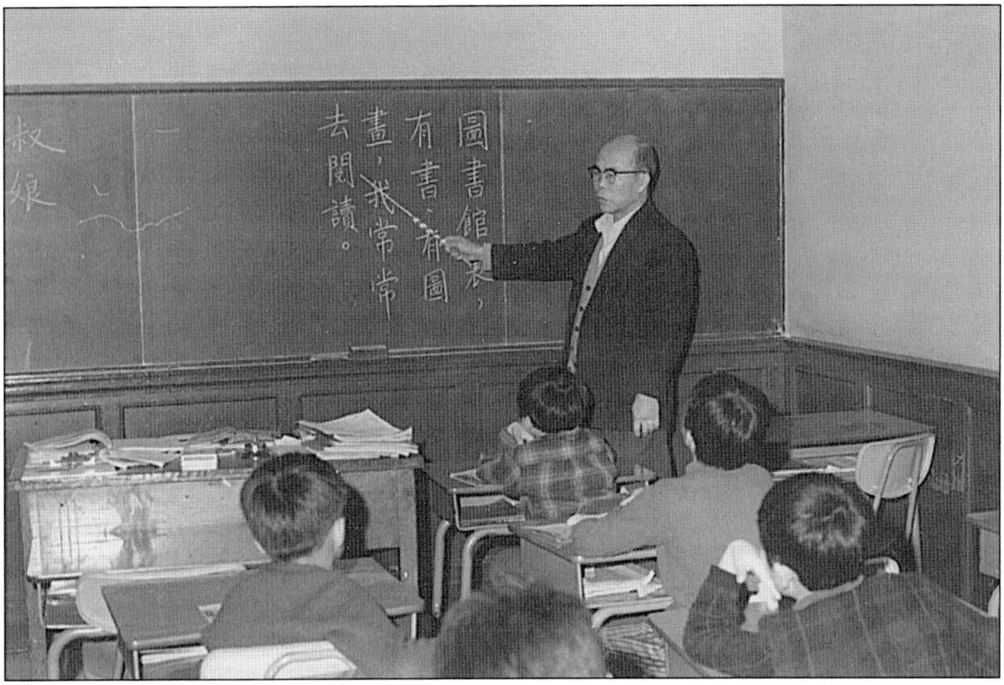

Mr. Hong boon Ma is shown teaching the students using a repetitive method whereby the students read each character in unison and often with a rhythmic beat, c. 1973. *(Photo by Bryan Chan)*

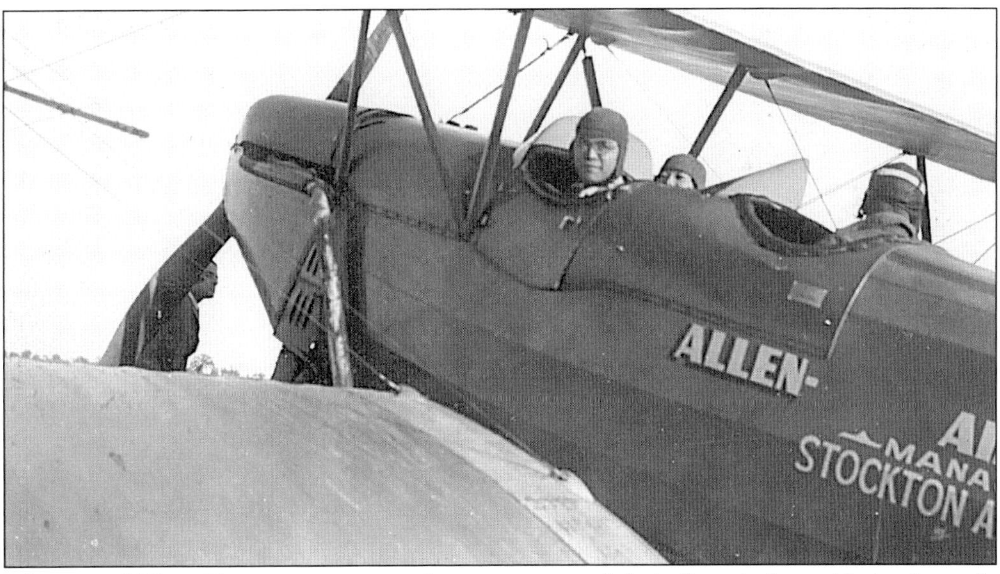

Johnny and Elsie Chang are enjoying the experience of their first airplane ride in the early 1920s at the Stockton Airport south of town. Upbeat, the young couple's sense of adventure lent to learning and experiencing new activities of the time. When they had sufficient funds they purchased the Chang Building at the corner of El Dorado and Lafayette. They, like the other young couples, also saved enough to make periodic trips back to China. *(Courtesy of the Freeman Chang Collection)*

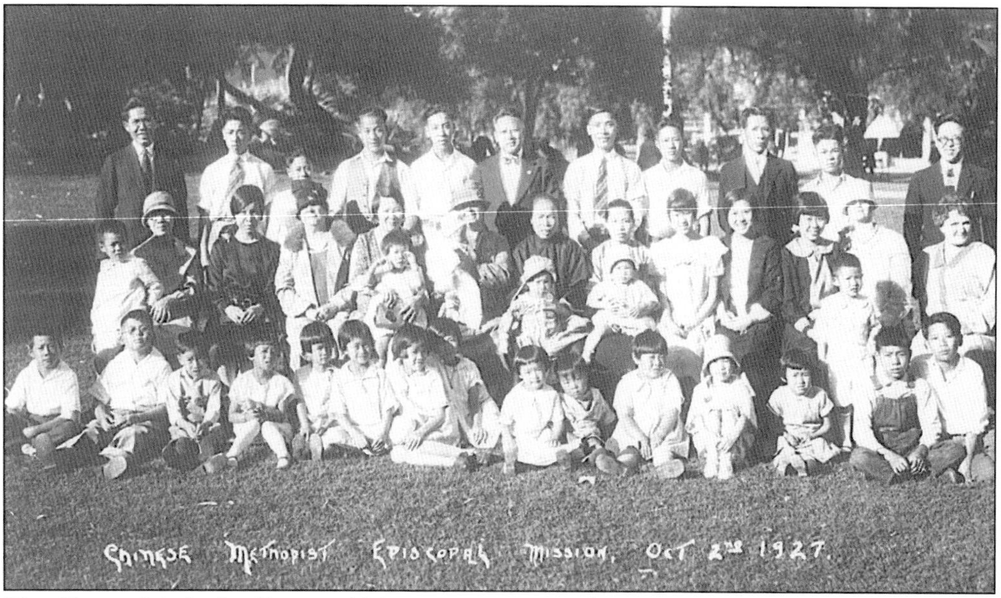

The Chinese Methodist Episcopal Mission was organized in 1905 and used a converted store on South Hunter Street to hold their services. This is the first official Christian unit. Previously, the Chinese from time to time saw sidewalk preachers who periodically visited Chinatown. Home mission concept was introduced in the late 1890s. *(Courtesy of Margo Chin Mah)*

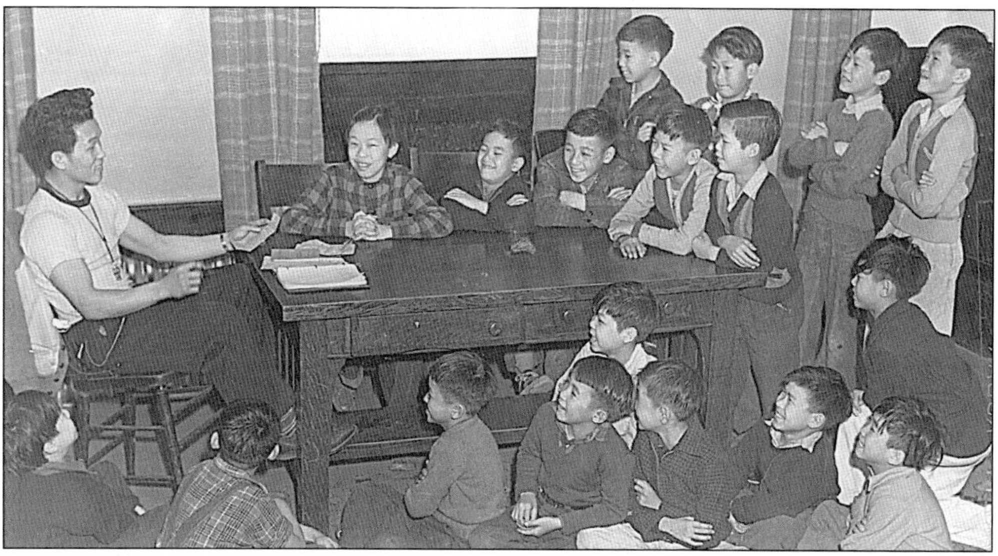

The Friendly Indians continued at the YMCA and operated in conjunction with the older teens' activities at the Chinese Christian Center. Skipper Yee, pictured here, was the youth leader of the group. Skipper came to America at the age of 9 and into Stockton at 16 with a promise of a job at the YMCA. From 1936 to 1954 Skipper continued his work with Chinese youth stopping only when he joined the Air Force in World War II. In later years Skipper married his college sweetheart Lois Kanagawa. Skipper was inducted into the Stockton Hall of Fame in Industry. The Chinese Cultural Society honored him as Outstanding Citizen of the Year in 1999. *(Courtesy of the Keith Wong Collection)*

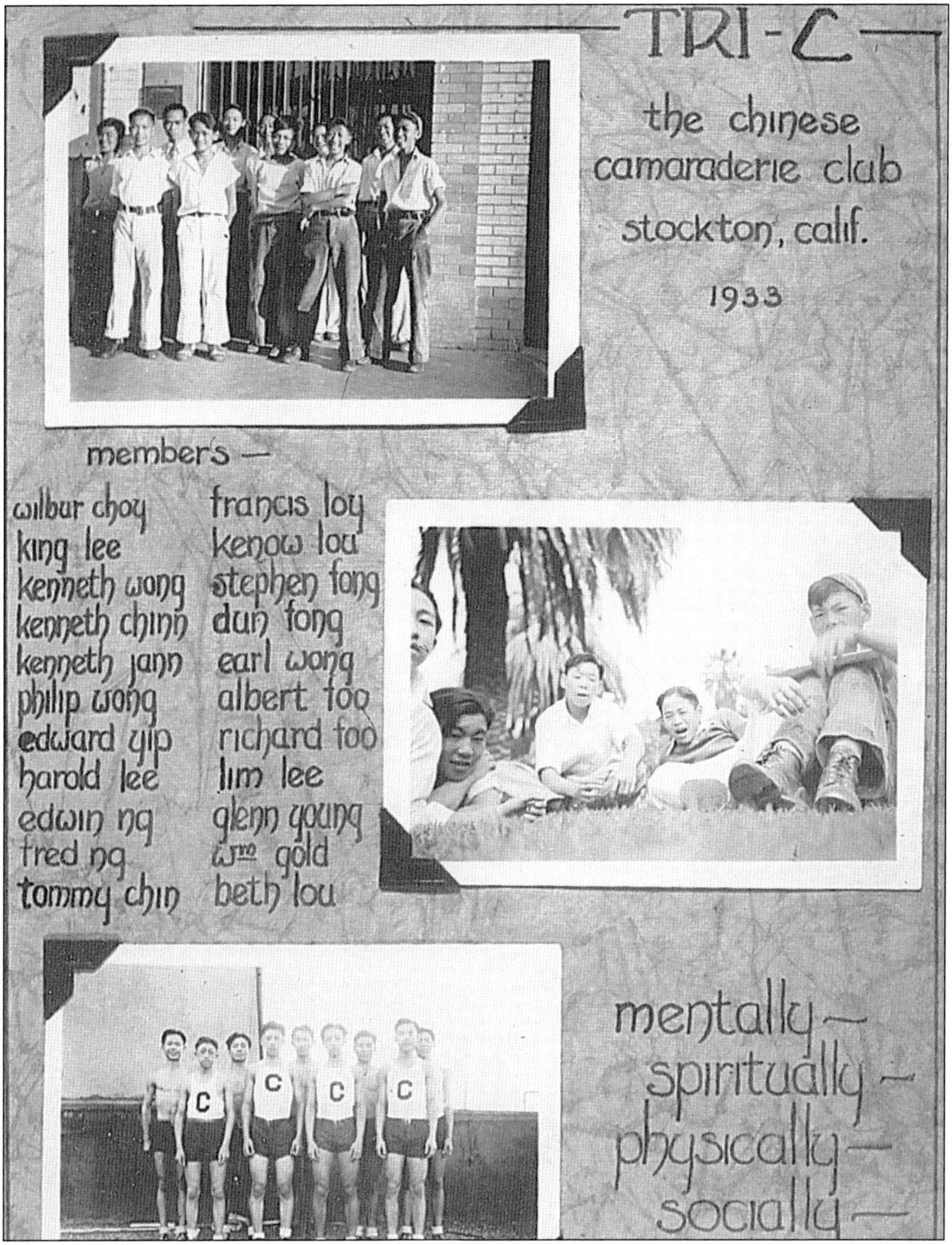

Many Protestant churches in the city and student pastors from College of the Pacific provided the guidance for the Chinese youth. Lim P. Lee, a student at College of the Pacific, organized a Boy Scout group in 1928, but switched their affiliation to the YMCA where the group was known as the "Friendly Indians." Much to the delight of the young men they had use of the basketball court and the swimming pool. The older teens formed the Tri-C and met at the mission that had moved into the Chung Wah building on Lafayette Street. From the Tri-C (being the oldest) other youth clubs followed based on the age set: Dragon, Chi Knights, Confucius, Mencius, Laocius, and Kwangtze among others. *(Courtesy of Kenow Lou)*

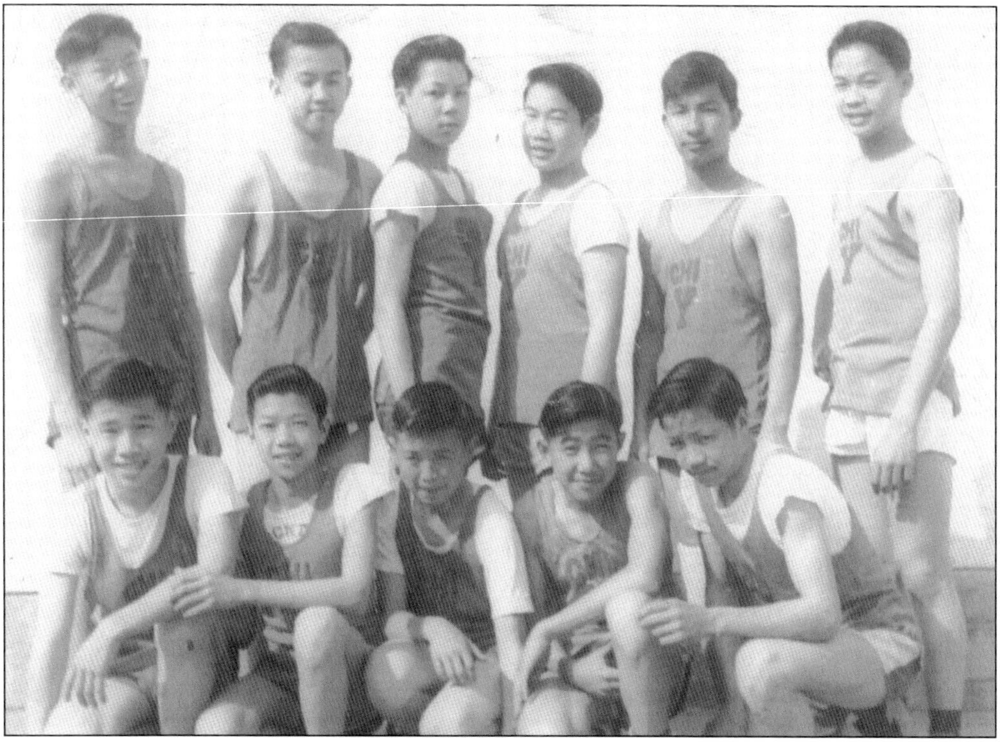

The early teenagers formed the Chi-Y basketball team at the Chinese Christian Center. Friendships built then continue even today. Pictured from left to right are (top row) Ted Lee, John Jue Goy, Charlie Chan, Wesley Hing, Albert "Sonny" Wong, and Jerry Hing; (bottom row) Ray Chan, Bob Lee, David Toy, Henry Wong, and John Low. *(Courtesy of Violet Chan)*

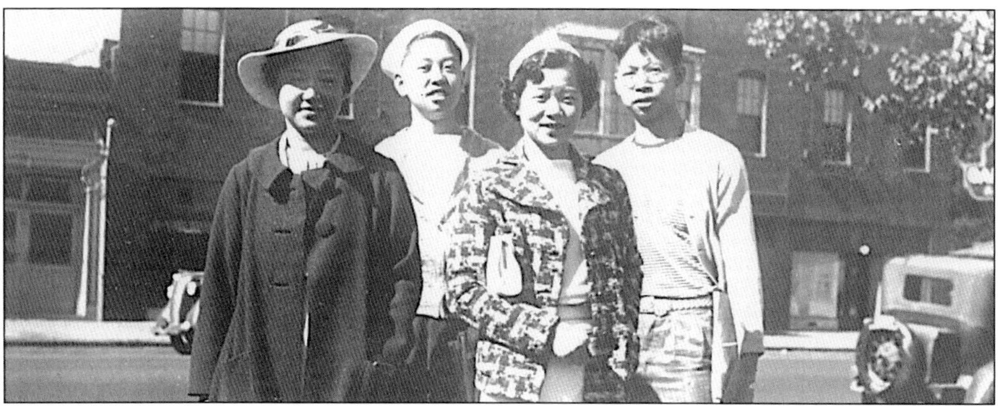

This picture, taken in 1937, shows four members of the Chinese Christian Center. An Arizonian by birth, Dora Ames Lee Wong (in the black coat), received her medical degree at University of California Medical School in San Francisco. Dora is the first woman doctor in the Chinese community and interned at the Stockton State Hospital. She founded the San Joaquin Visiting Nurses organization and was the first woman to serve on the Metropolitan Parks and Recreation Commission. She was also on numerous citizens' committees in urban renewal and community improvements. She has been recognized for many of her medical and professional accomplishments as well as her good works at the local, regional, and statewide levels. *(Courtesy of Dun Fong)*

Pictured here are three fellows—Francis Loy, Kenou Lou, and Dun Fong—in 1935 at a happy reunion in China. All three had been sent back to China for high school, as was the practice of some families. Once there, Stocktonians often looked for each other to compare life's experience. Kenou (center) stayed in Guangdong throughout the Japanese invasion from 1934 to 1940. He returned quickly in 1940 and began his college career, first in junior college and then at University of California-Berkeley before he entered the U.S. Army. Dun Fong (far right) stayed in China for three years and returned by 1936. His family needed his help at the Mandarin Meat Market. Francis Loy returned and entered college. He later became an engineer for the Bechtel Company in San Francisco. *(Courtesy of Dun Fong)*

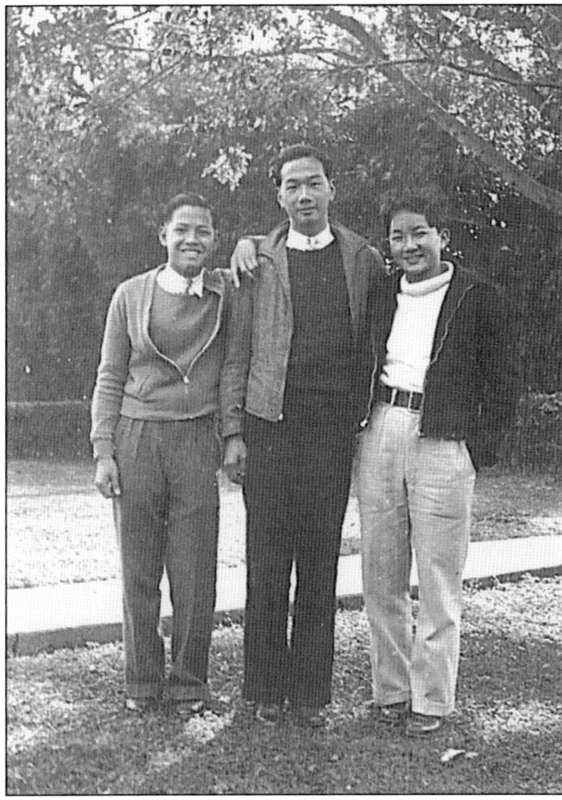

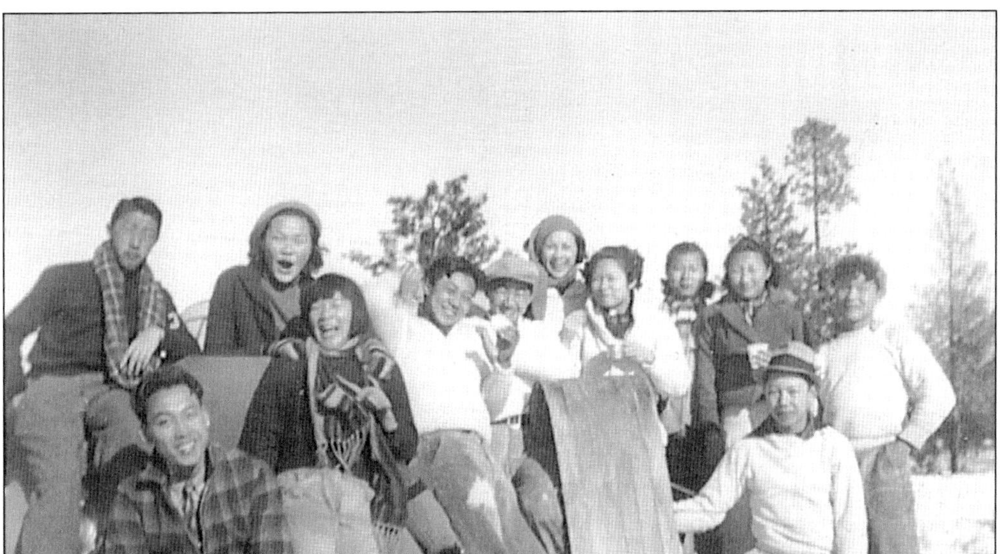

This was a church-sponsored snow trip in 1937 for the young adults. *(Courtesy of Dun Fong)*

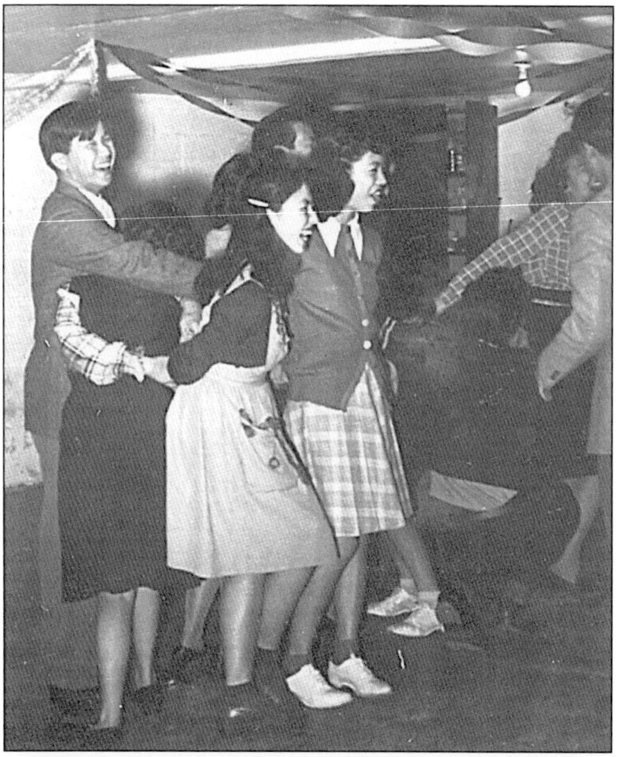

Definitely with a western flair, the teenagers took delight in learning folk and square dancing. Adults converted the basement of Chung Wah into a recreation hall for the young people. This was a period when the Chinese leaders worked closely with the Chinese Christian Center. c. 1944 *(Courtesy of the Keith Wong Collection)*

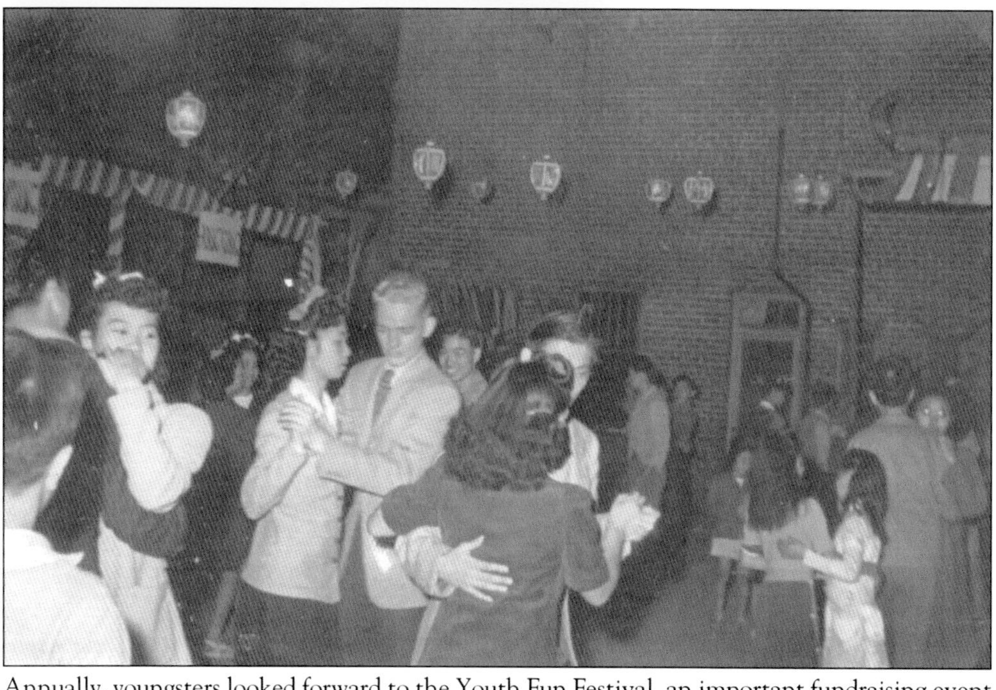

Annually, youngsters looked forward to the Youth Fun Festival, an important fundraising event that included booths, games, and culminated the evening with dancing. These outdoor evening activities took place behind the Chung Wah building prior to the auditorium additional. c. 1945 *(Courtesy of the Keith Wong Collection)*

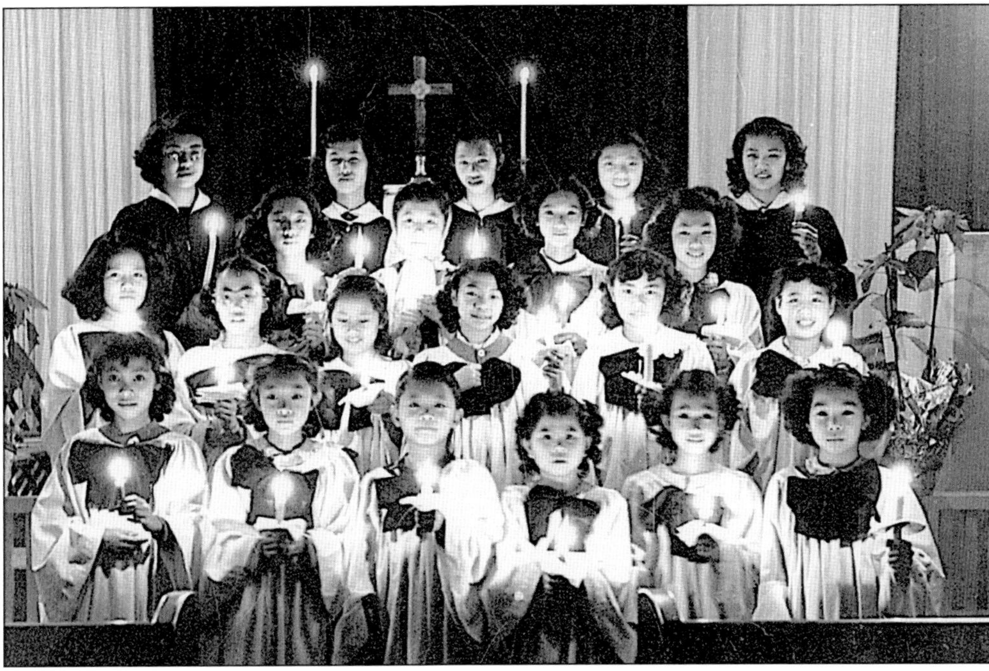

The junior choir of the Chinese Christian Center was a delight. They drew the interest of girls between the ages of 10 to 14. Here they performed for the Yuletide in 1947. *(Courtesy of the Keith Wong Collection)*

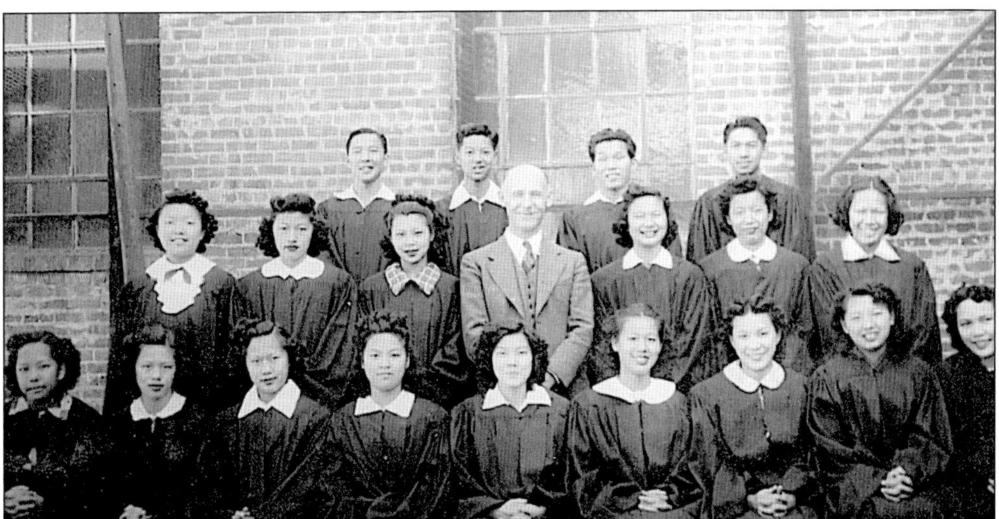

The senior choir of the Chinese Christian Center flanks Dr. George H. Colliver, minister of the Christian Center. The Center had become the heart of the Chinese youth movement in the community. *(Courtesy of the Keith Wong Collection)*

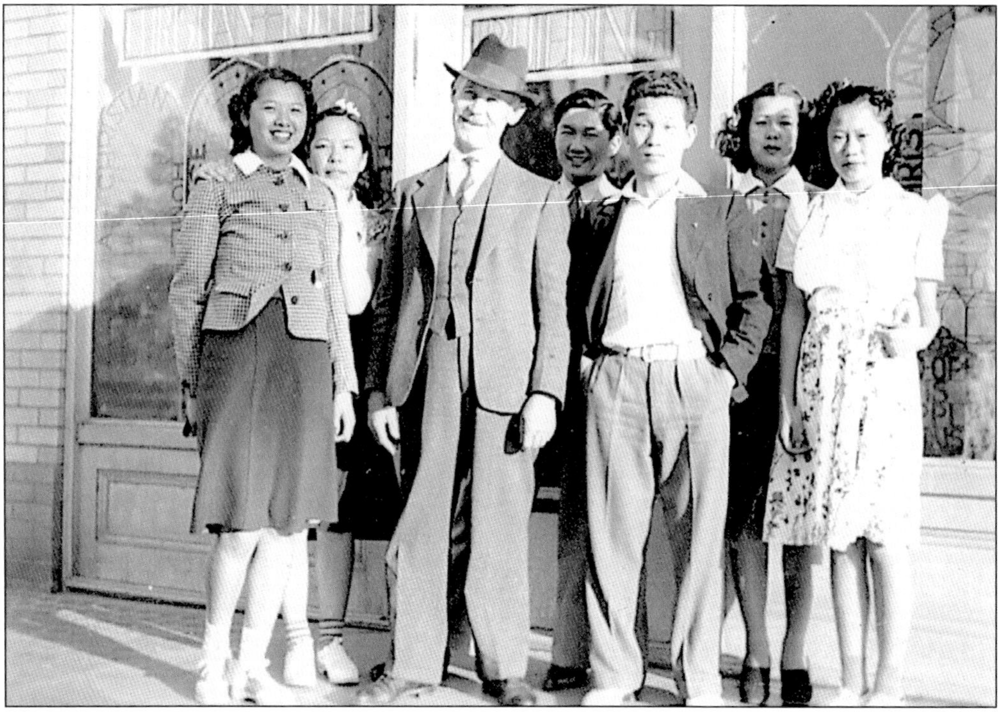

Dr. George H. Colliver, a guiding light to the teens of the 1930s and '40s, was a professor of Bible and Religious Education at the College of the Pacific and was the pastor of the Chinese Methodist Episcopal Mission from 1936 to 1949. It was through his influence that many young adults completed their baccalaureates at what is now the University of the Pacific. Skipper Yee and Beulah Ong Quo flank Dr. Colliver in this 1930s picture along with other youth leaders. *(Courtesy of the Keith Wong Collection)*

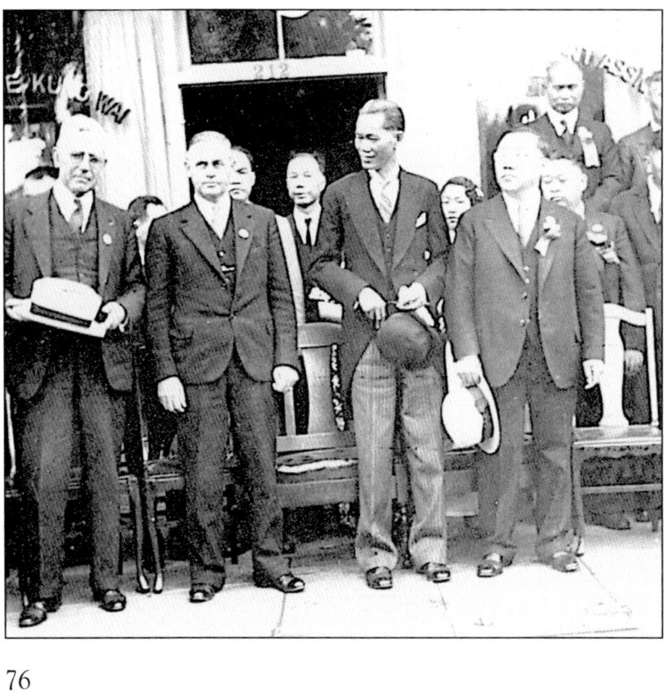

Gen. Tsai Tin Kai, commander of China's 19th Route Army, is flanked by Stockton city manager Walter B. Hogan and Mayor Con J. Franke on the left and a dignitary from the Republic of China on the right. The general arrived on November 17, 1934, while on a goodwill tour to raise funds for China's war victims. Activities associated with the general's visit remain a highlighted memory among the Chinese.

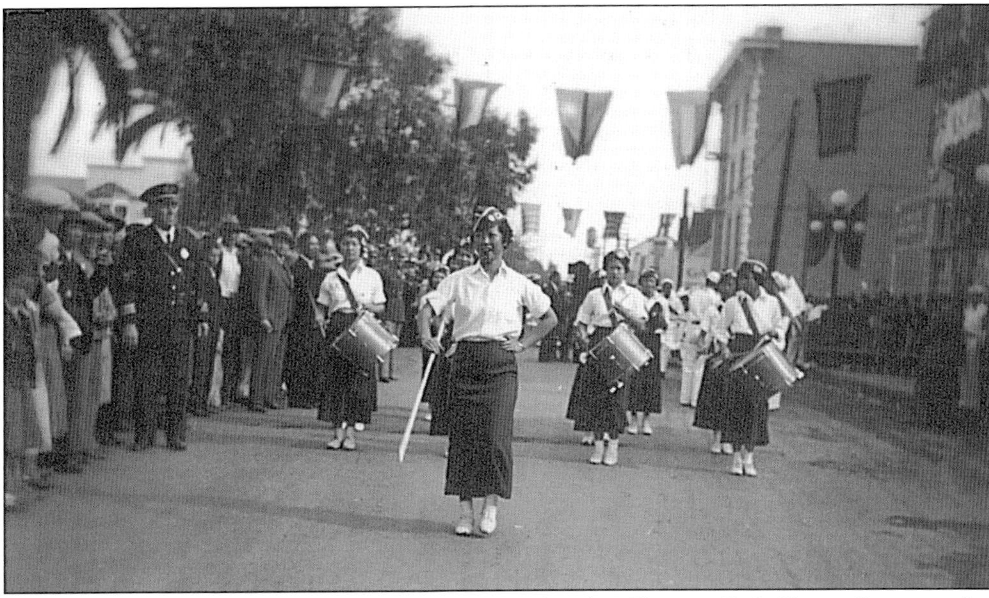

Welcoming Gen. Tsai Tin Kai to Stockton in 1934, the Chinese Girls Drum Corp marches down Lafayette Street in front of Chung Wah and Washington Park. Mary Wong Fong is the majorette. *(Courtesy of the Keith Wong Collection)*

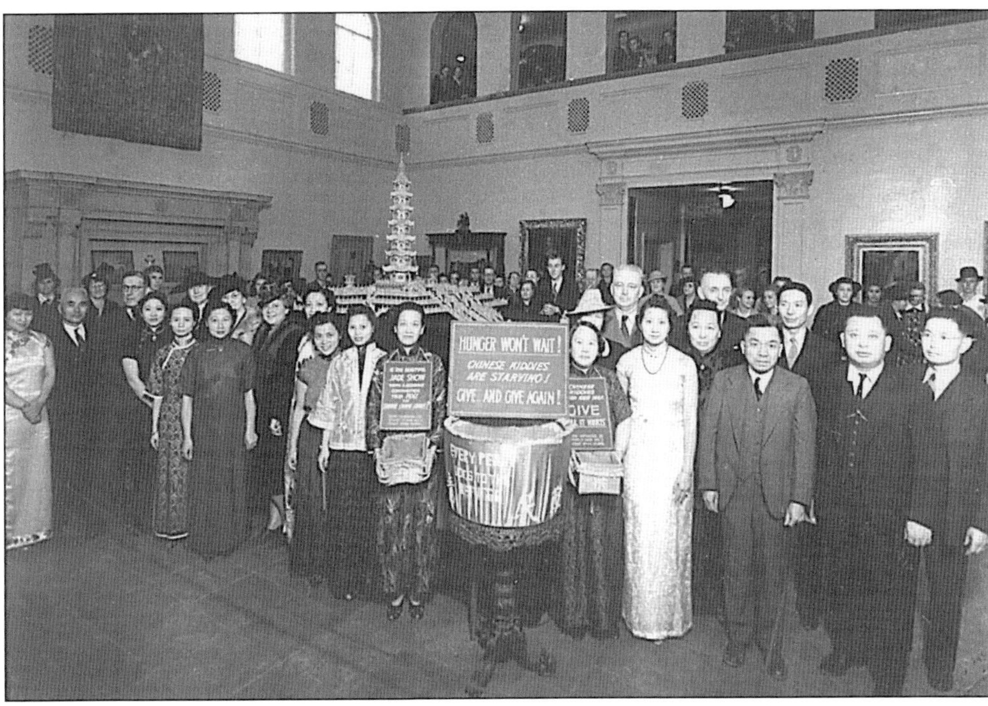

One of the many fundraising events for China's war victims was held at the Haggin Museum in 1939. This exhibit was transferred to the Oakland Museum when the county assessor deemed the jade collection worthy of assessment even though it had been a public display artifact. Stockton not only lost a valuable asset but with the Loma Prieta Earthquake in 1990, the Bay Area Museum suffered damage, as did the exhibit.

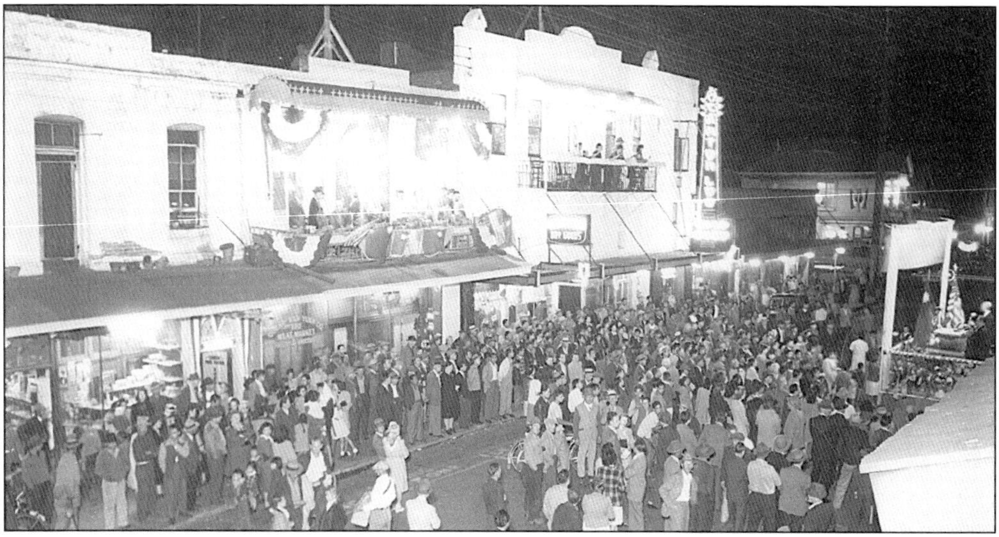

This aerial view of the 1940 Rice Bowl event taken on Washington Street demonstrates the extensive support of the community in the China War efforts. Stockton community alone contributed $411,132.42 towards the overall American-Chinese contribution of over $5,000,000. There were other special drives, including war bonds and community activities. The Rice Bowl Campaigns annually marked Japan's attack on Peking (July 7). Everyone was expected to donate one day's wages to the cause. This photograph taken on the On Lock Sam balcony shows all the businesses on the south side of the street lit up. Bing Kung Tong headquarters is the one with bright lights and bunting. *(Courtesy of Violet Chan)*

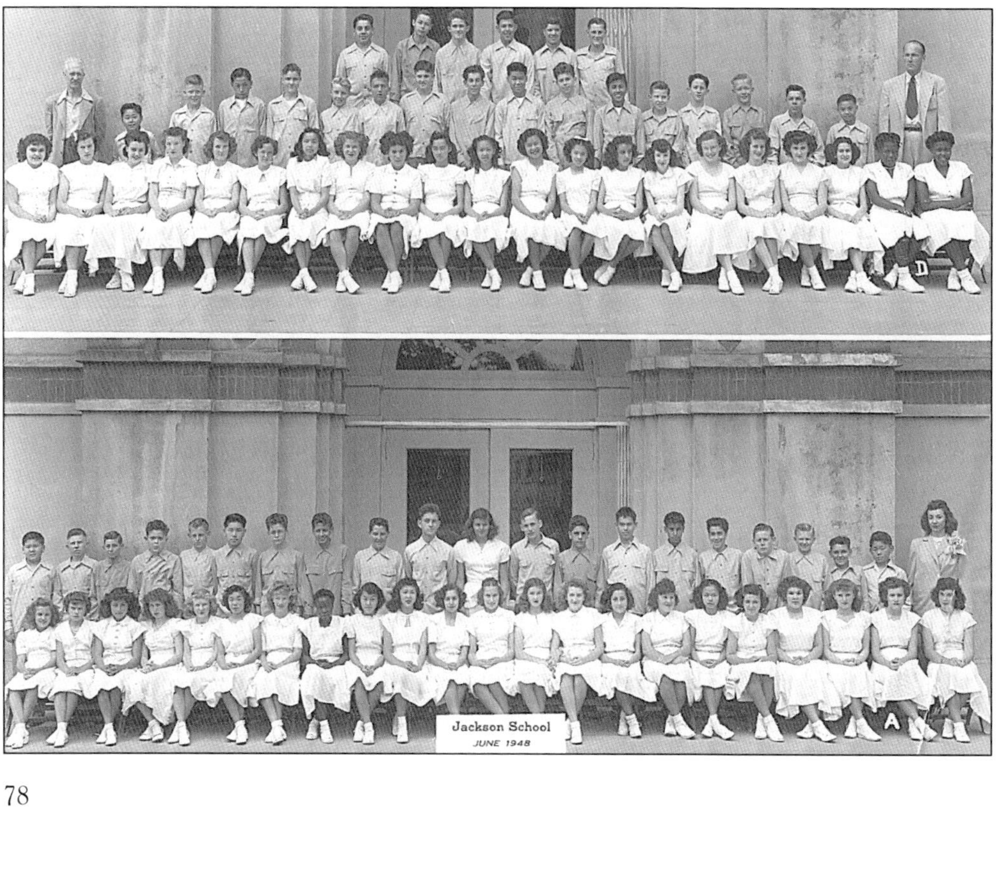

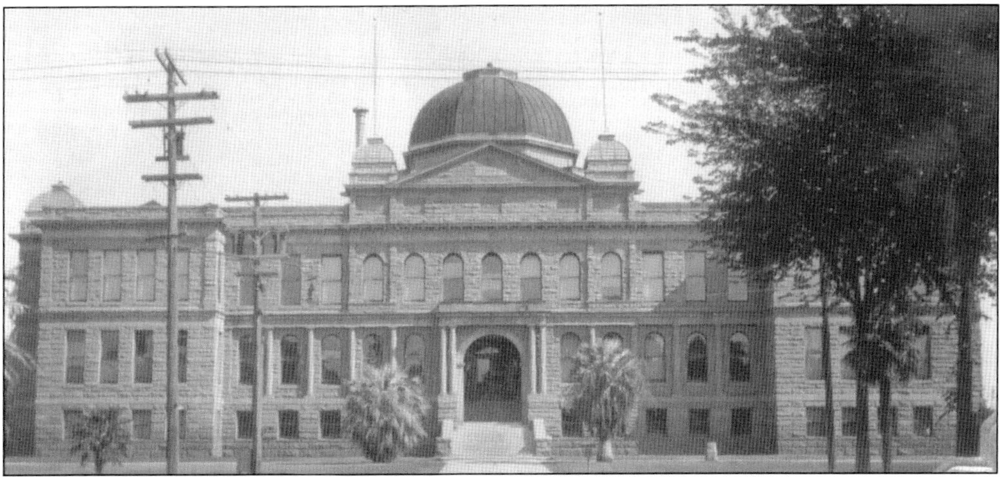

Whether the students went to Jackson, Franklin, Lafayette, or other elementary schools, they all attended Stockton High on Harding Way, built in 1904. A seven-building complex, it served the students until 1968. New legislation deemed old buildings as unsafe during earthquakes. A slow abandonment process took place and by March 1978 the demolition process began. At the abandonment ceremony in 1968, Reverend Wilbur Choy, a graduate, gave the invocation. Stockton High was the only high school until Edison High School was built in 1942. *(Courtesy of the Freeman Chang Collection)*

(right) Strolling through the campus, Ken Mar took early courses at the College of the Pacific then attended University of California-Berkeley for the pre-dental program and later graduated from U.C.-San Francisco Medical Center. Ken, oldest son of Mar Hing Lung, received great encouragement from his widowed mother. He made dentistry his career in Stockton. *(Courtesy of Ken Mar)*

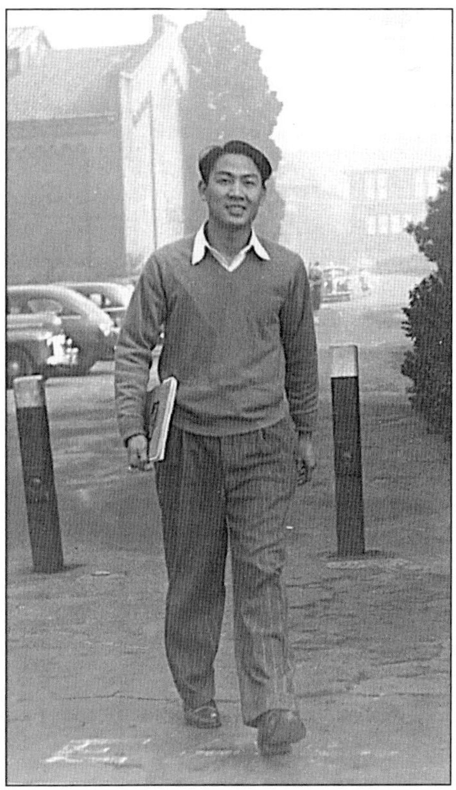

(opposite, below) This graduating photo of the spring and fall 1948 classes of Jackson Elementary School shows a number of Chinese among the students. In the upper picture one can identify Hong Huey, George Lam, Leo Fong, Lovebele Wong, and Grace Ng Mar. In the June class, Sonia Ah Tye, Shirley Fong, Nora Lee, Clara Wong, and Joe Yee are identified. From Jackson the students then went to Stockton High School. *(Courtesy of Hong and Mary Huey)*

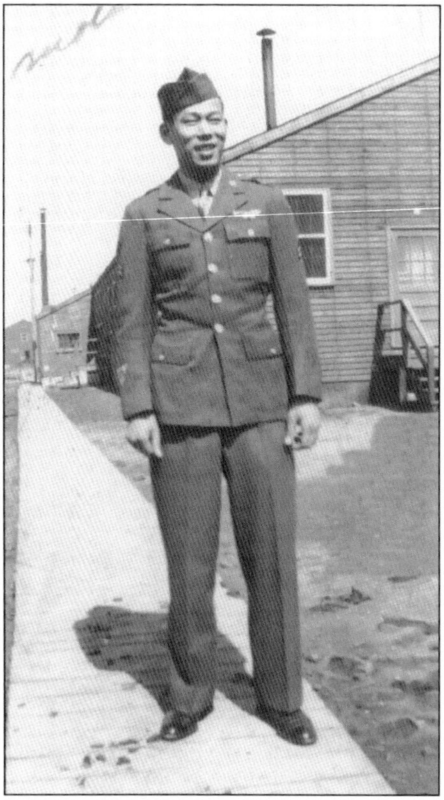

Edward Ah Tye, number three son of Mrs. Rose Ah Tye, served as a top turret gunner on a B-17 in World War II European Theater. The Ah Tyes had five sons and one son-in-law serving their country while their mother actively participated at the surgical headquarters of the local Red Cross.

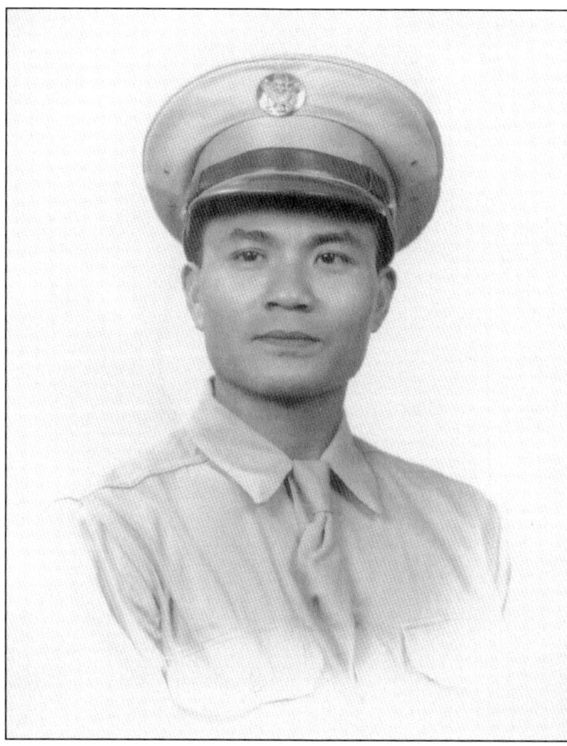

Yee Shey (Gin) Jung was assigned as a combat-infantry member of the 8th Army, 36th Texas Division. As a sharp shooter, he saw action in the Italian Campaign and in Germany. Few were aware of his war efforts. The community only knew that he was the gentle herbalist who helped out at his father's original herb store Bo Wah Tong at 130 E. Washington Street. After the war the herb store moved around the corner to 215 S. Hunter Street and was renamed Fung Lee. *(Courtesy of the Freeman Chang Collection)*

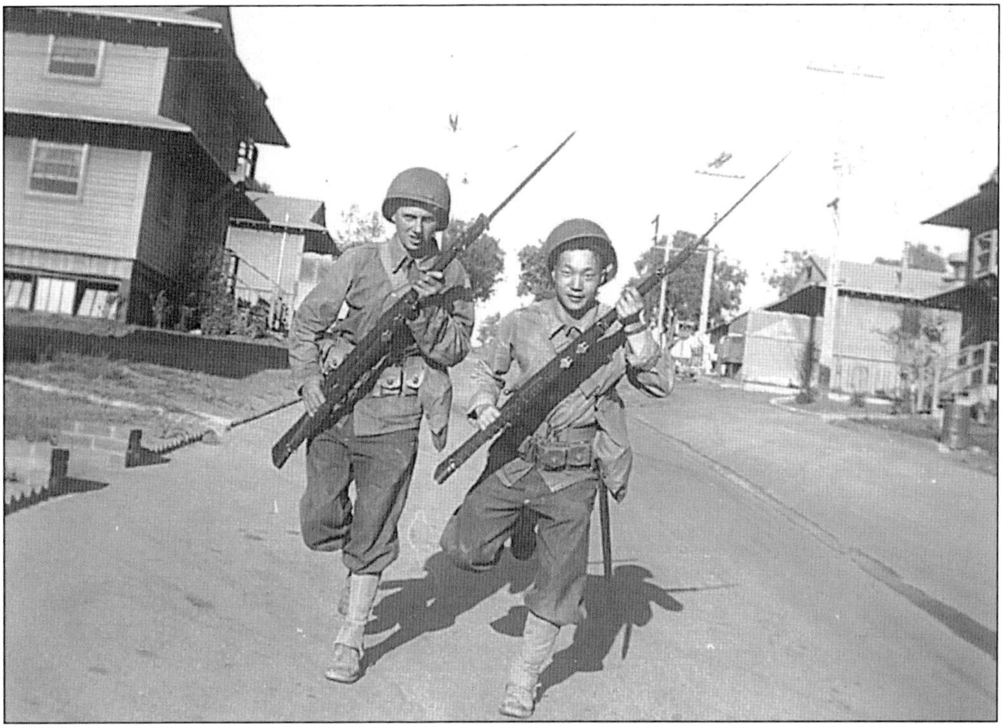

It became obvious to Bing Chang and another unidentified enlistee that running a drill course was not easy when it included carrying a model 1903-A-3 Springfield rifle with the long bayonet. The rifle weighed at least 10 pounds and stood 5 feet long from the bottom of the butt to the tip of the blade. Later bayonets were reduced to 11 inches. Bing himself was only 5-feet 8-inches tall. *(Courtesy of the Freeman Chang Collection)*

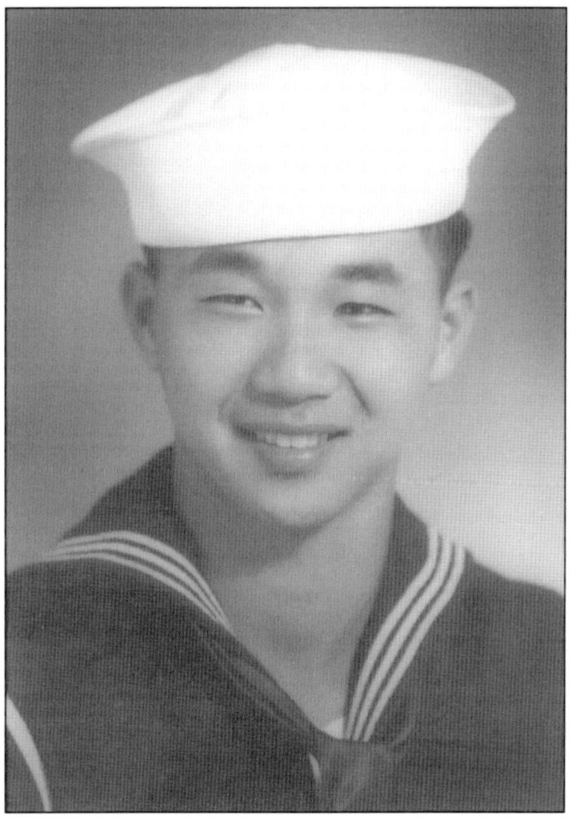

Keith Wong, fresh out of high school, was assigned to the Navy and served on the land base at Subic Bay, Philippine Islands. Classified as Seaman, 1st class, he served as a radar operator. Following the service, he returned to attend Stockton College under the G.I. Bill and later College of the Pacific. *(Courtesy of the Keith Wong Collection)*

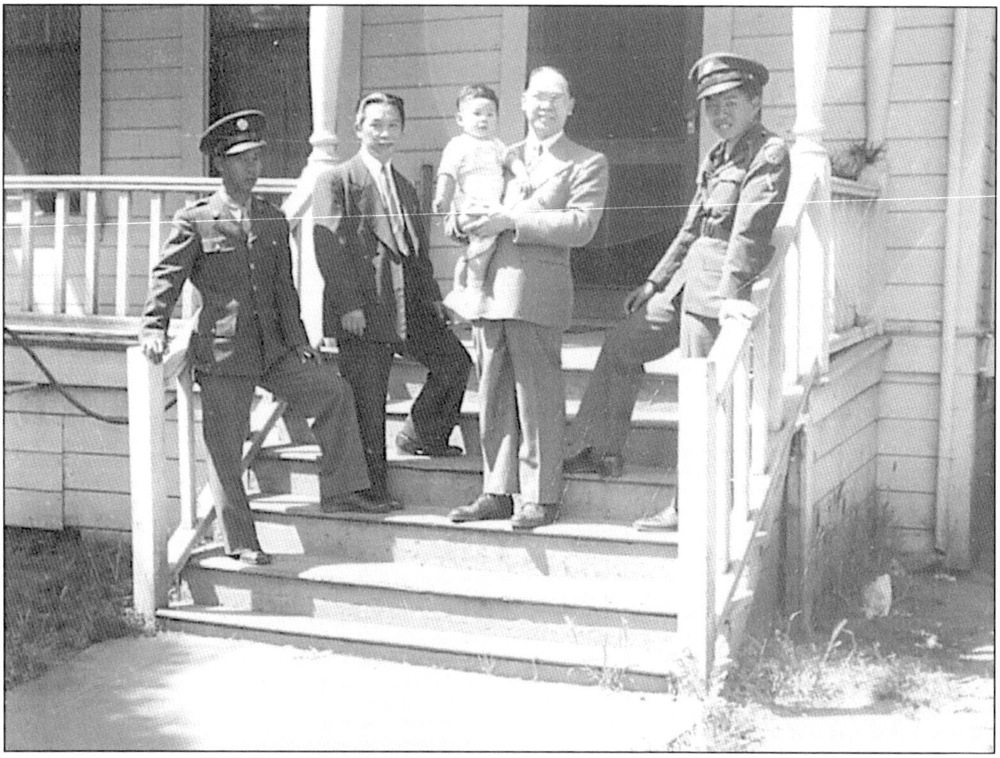

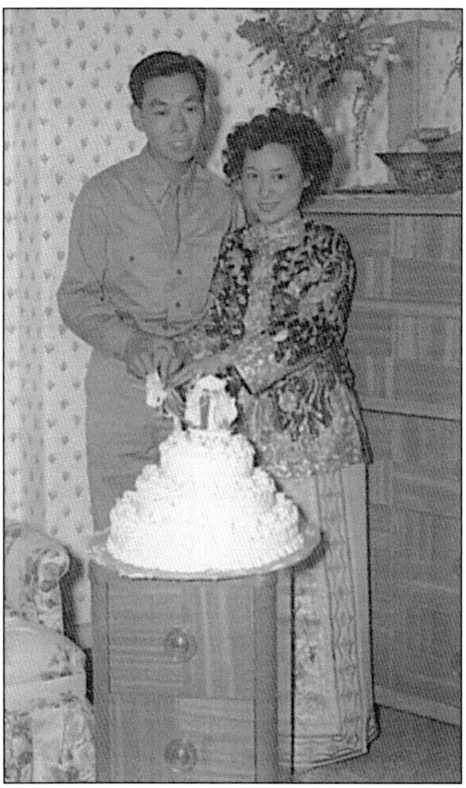

When at all possible, liberty included coming home to family and friends. Several GIs are seen here visiting with Johnnie Chang at their Sonora Street home. A greater number will testify today that the greatest benefit was the ability to continue their education at a much lower cost than they could have originally thought. *(Courtesy of the Freeman Chang Collection)*

Private 1st Class King Lee and Rosie Chew are cutting their wedding cake. They were married at St. Mary's Church in San Francisco with Wilbur Choy as the best man. The former Rosie Chew of Oakland met King in the shipyards in Oakland where he was a welder. The couple's wedding took place just before he was shipped out to Guam where he was promoted to a T4, Technical Sergeant. Previously, he served at the Army Ordinance Station in Aberdeen, Maryland, in the automotive division. King came home to Stockton and worked in the family's bakery, Yet Bun Heong. Rosie passed away in 1987. They had three children. *(Courtesy of the Freeman Chang Collection)*

The Chinese were proud that many served in the war. Even children wanted to play soldier; in this case it was playing sailors. This is Freeman Chang at age four in 1945. *(Courtesy of the Freeman Chang Collection)*

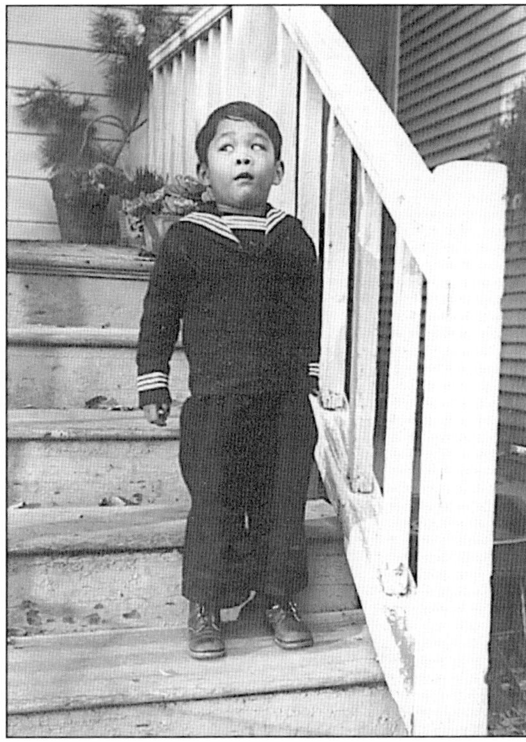

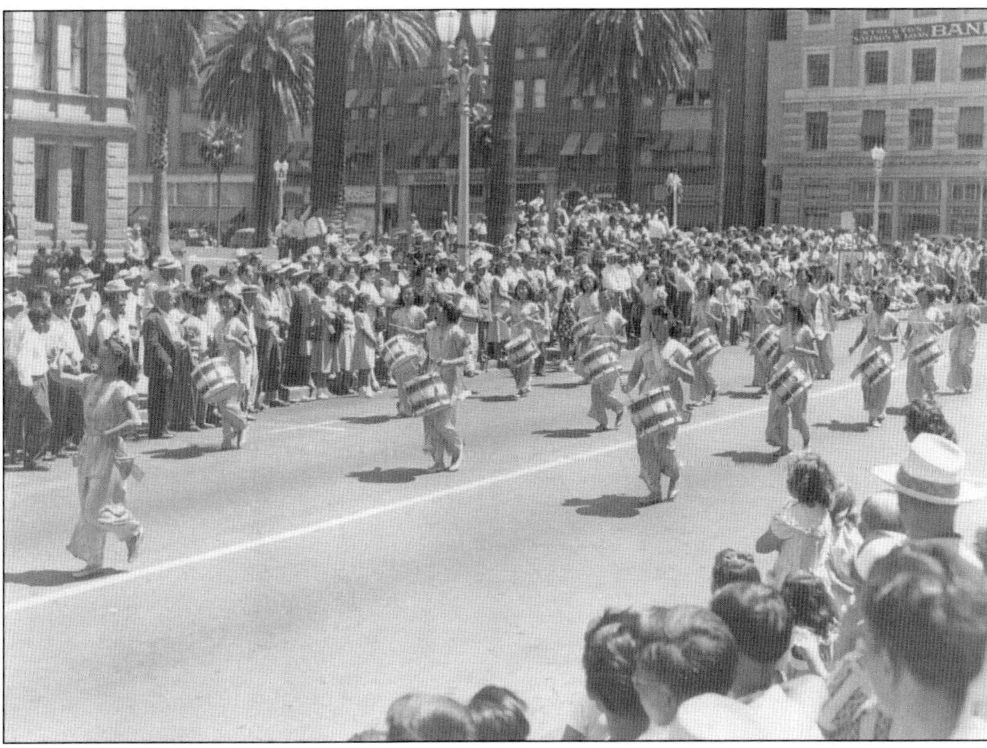

During World War II, parades during the Fourth of July were important. The Chinese Drum Corp marched down Main Street in front of the Fox Theatre. *(Courtesy of Violet Chan)*

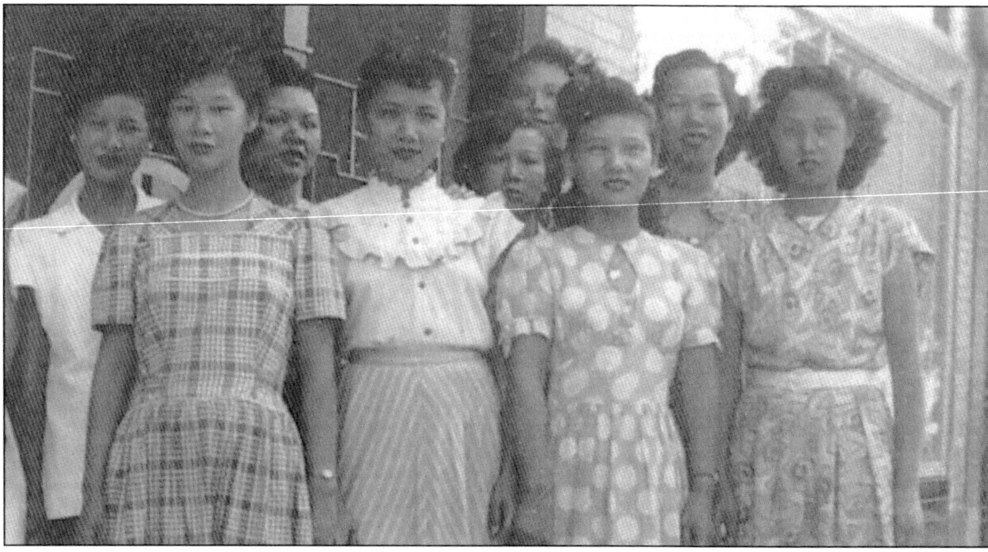

With the end of war, soldiers returned to China for the brides they left behind. These are the wives who came in 1948 and were in the English language course given at Chung Wah. In the front row (starting to the left) are Jane Fung Fong, Monica Leung Low, and Nancy Jung Fong. *(Courtesy of Harry and Monica Low)*

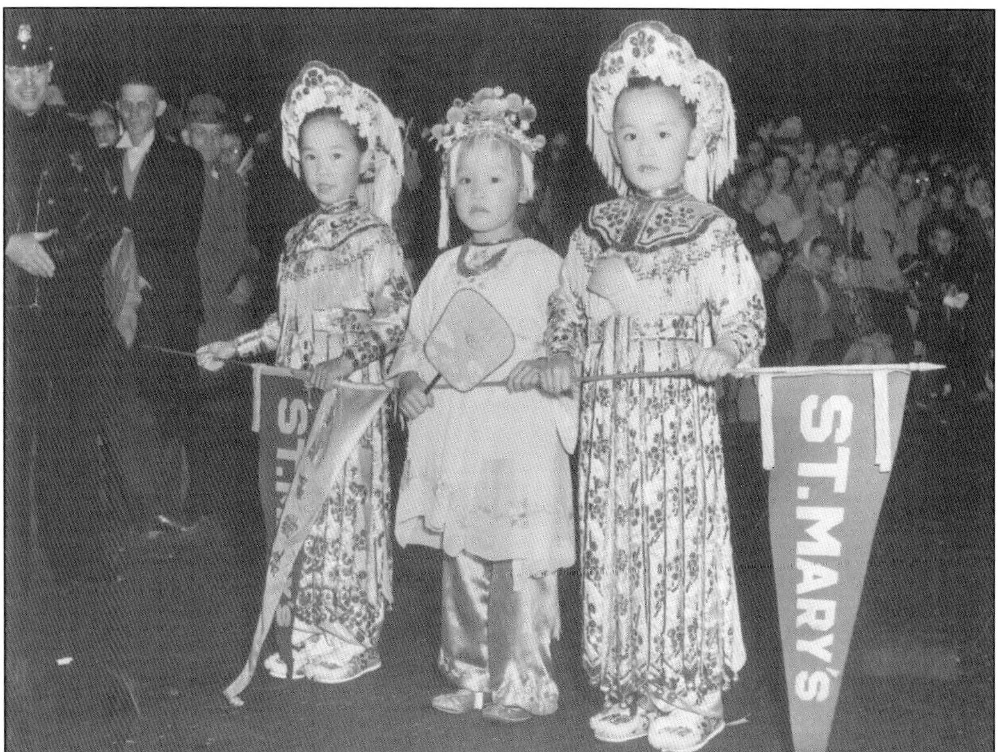

The end of the war and Veterans Day was an important occasion. Chinese participation added to the community pride. The St. Mary's School's students from San Francisco were always crowd pleasers, c. 1948. *(Courtesy of Violet Chan)*

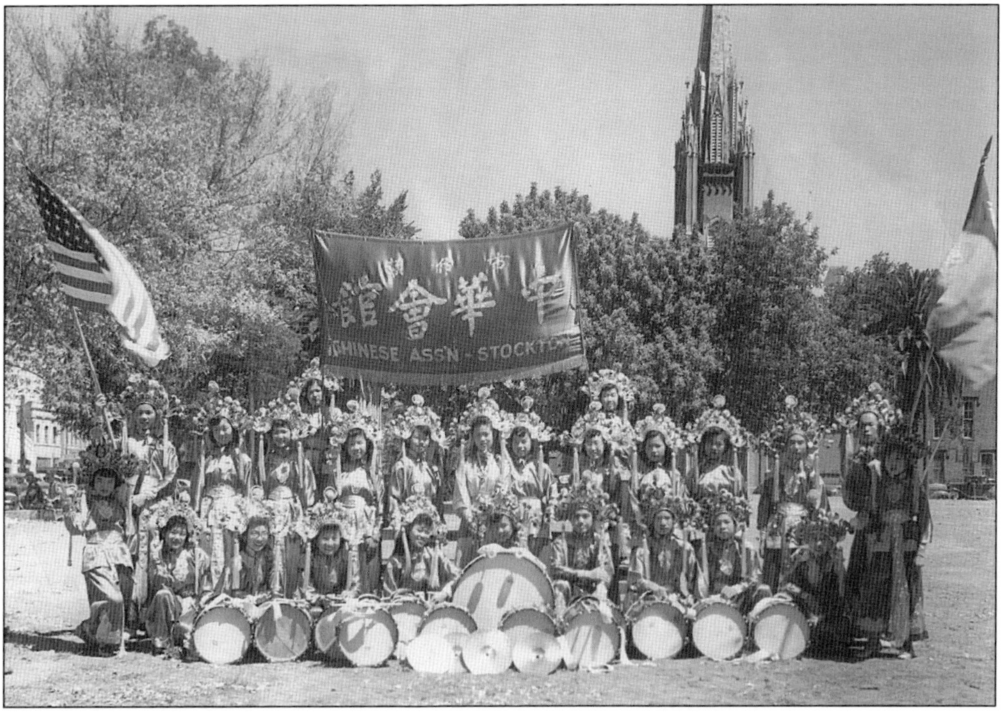

Here is another July Fourth parade in 1951 with the Chinese Drum Corp participating. This photo was taken at the Washington Park. The steeple in the back is that of St. Mary's Catholic Church. The Chinese always flew the U.S. flag at all important occasions and it took precedence over the Chinese flag. *(Courtesy of Wing Chan)*

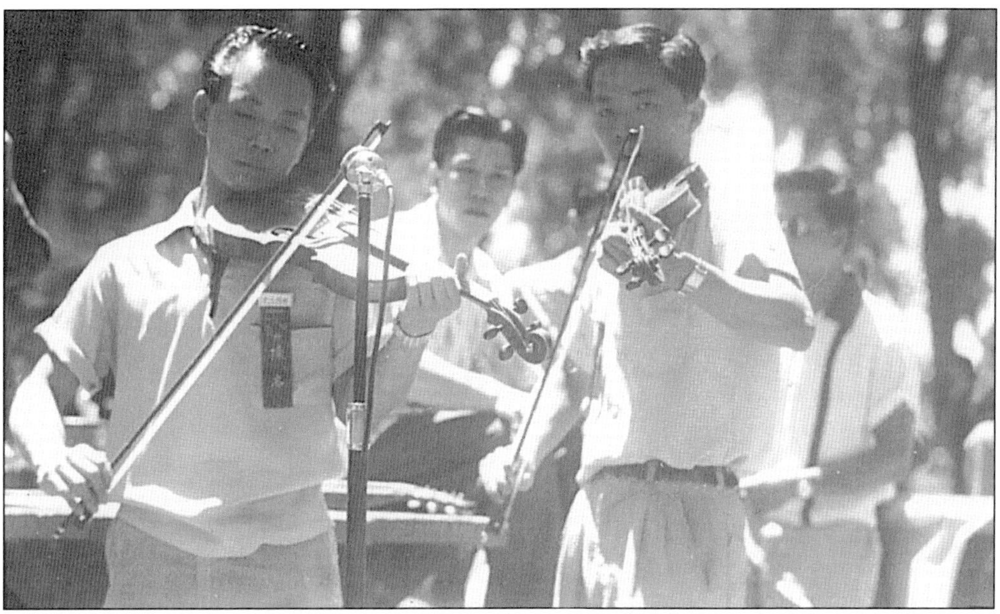

This is a 1952 picture of two local youngsters playing a violin-duet at the Chung Wah annual picnic. Bevin Hong (right) had recently come to Stockton. His career included working for the San Joaquin County Public Works Department. *(Courtesy of Wing Chan)*

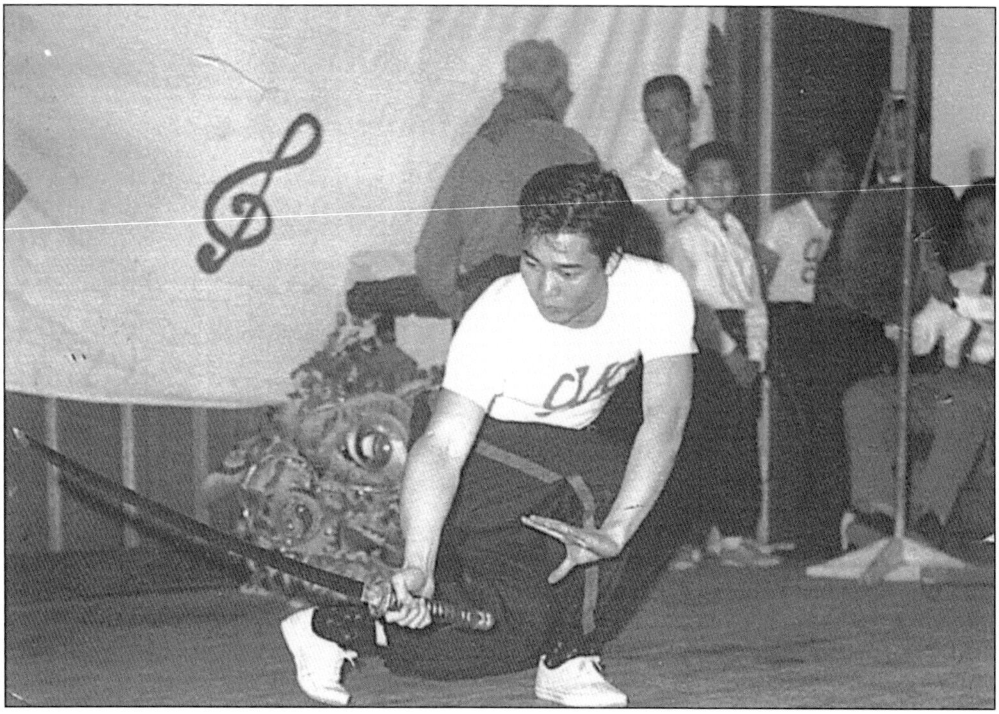

David Chin demonstrated his skills in a sword dance at the Chung Wah Christmas party in 1961. *(Courtesy of Margo Chin Mah)*

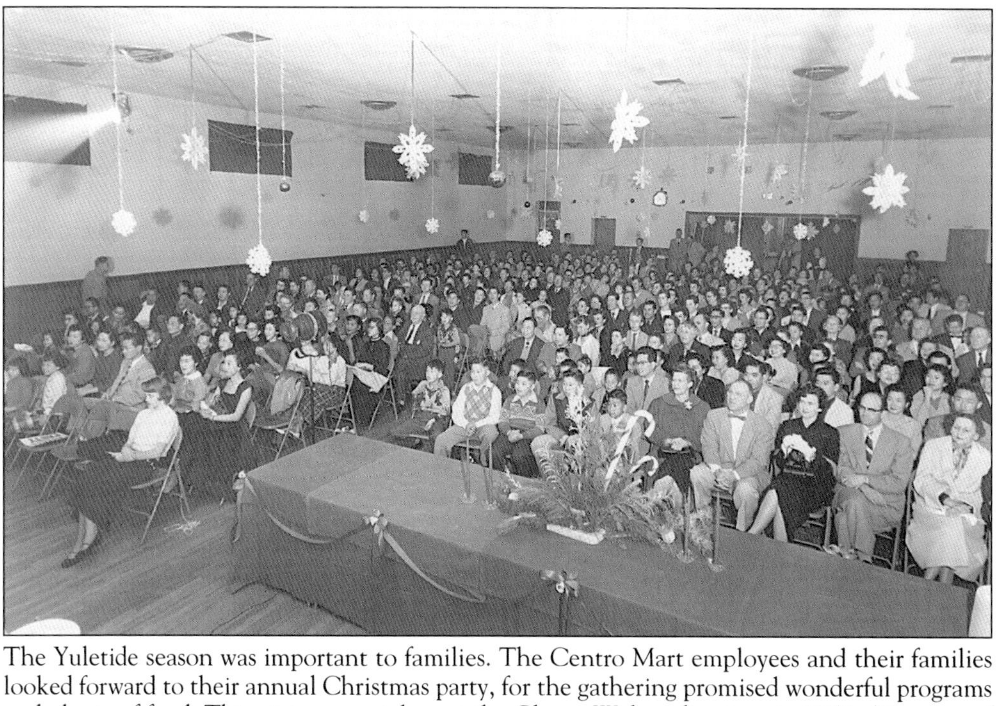

The Yuletide season was important to families. The Centro Mart employees and their families looked forward to their annual Christmas party, for the gathering promised wonderful programs and plenty of food. This picture was taken at the Chung Wah auditorium in 1954. *(Courtesy of Jimmy Lam)*

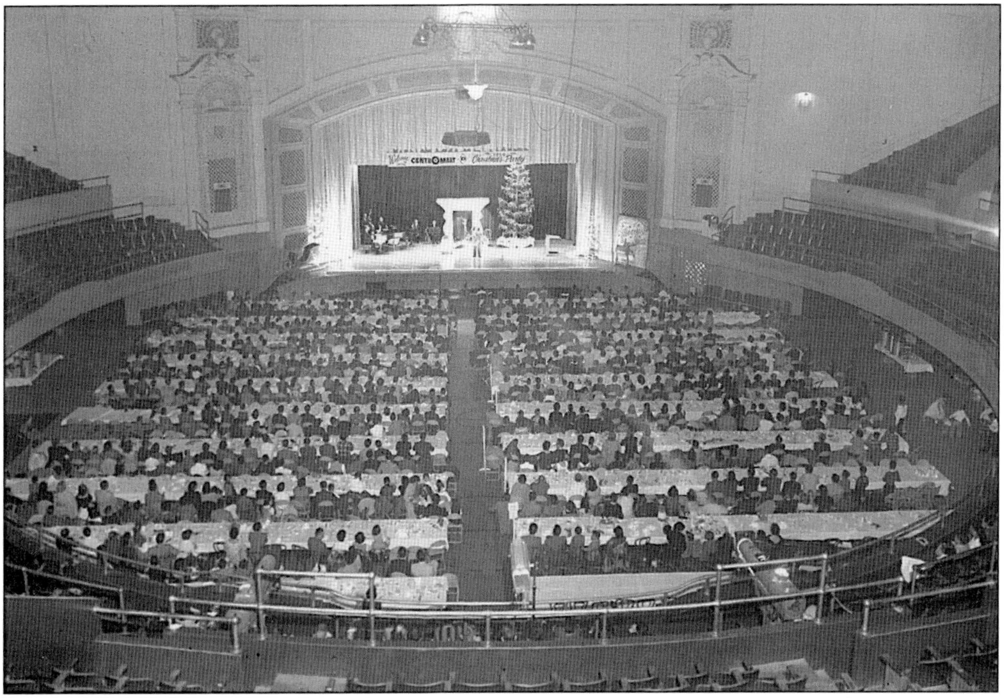

Realizing the old Chung Wah auditorium was not really large enough to handle all the Centro Mart employees, management decided to rent the Stockton Civic Auditorium for the 1959 Christmas party. There were enough people and tables to take up the whole bottom floor of the main auditorium. *(Courtesy of Jimmy Lam)*

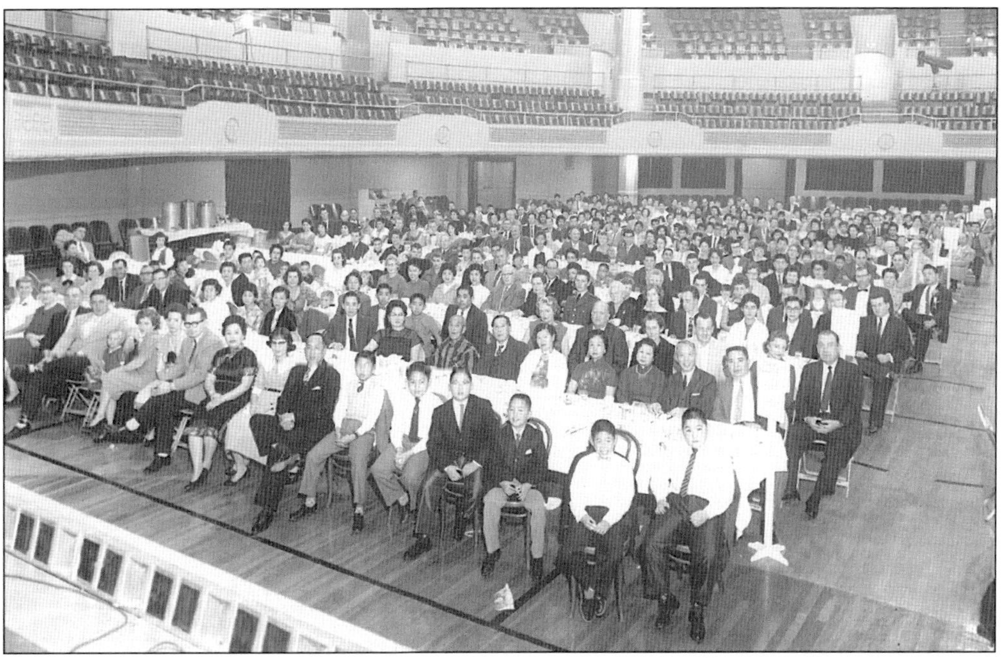

This picture shows only the left side of the room at the above Christmas party. *(Courtesy of Jimmy Lam)*

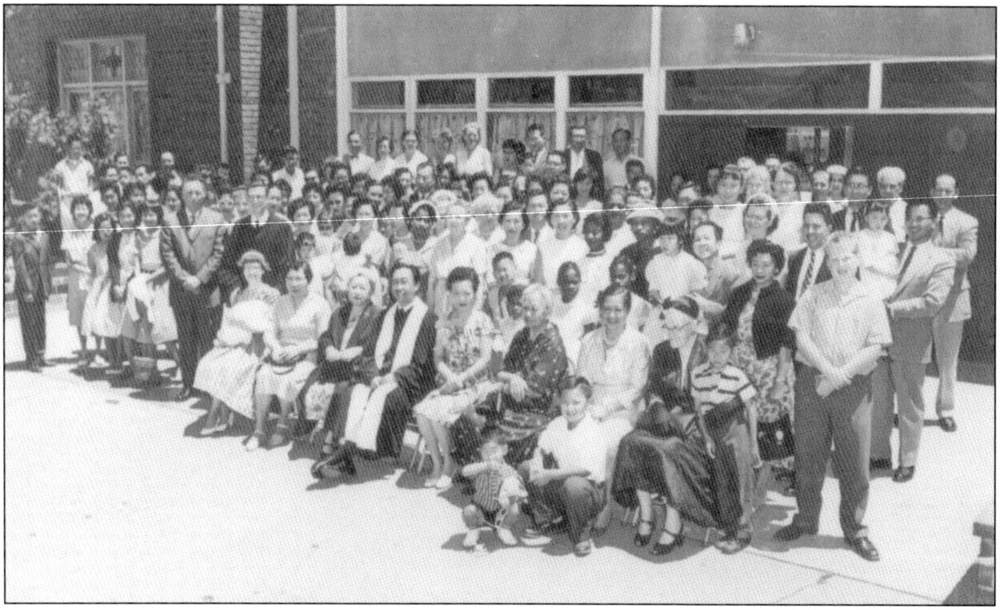

The Chinese Christian Center consolidated with the Clay Street Methodist Church on June 4, 1954. By 1956, St. Mark's Methodist Church became the official name for the combined church. This picture taken in the spring of 1957 shows Pastor Wilbur Choy (seated front center) who became the chaplain for the California State Legislature and later a bishop and a member of the Council of Bishops of the United Methodist Church before his retirement.

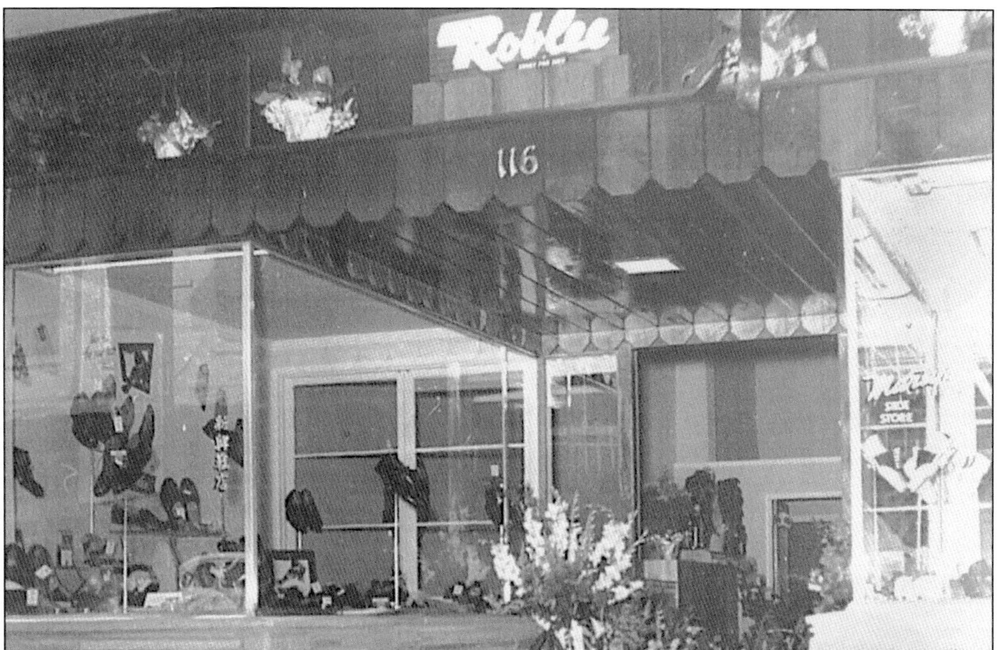

Marty's Shoes, a retail store, provided not only merchandise, but also had another attraction in that two new Chinese men's club held organization meetings there 20 years apart—the Cathay Club and the Yellow Seed. *(Courtesy of Rose Yip)*

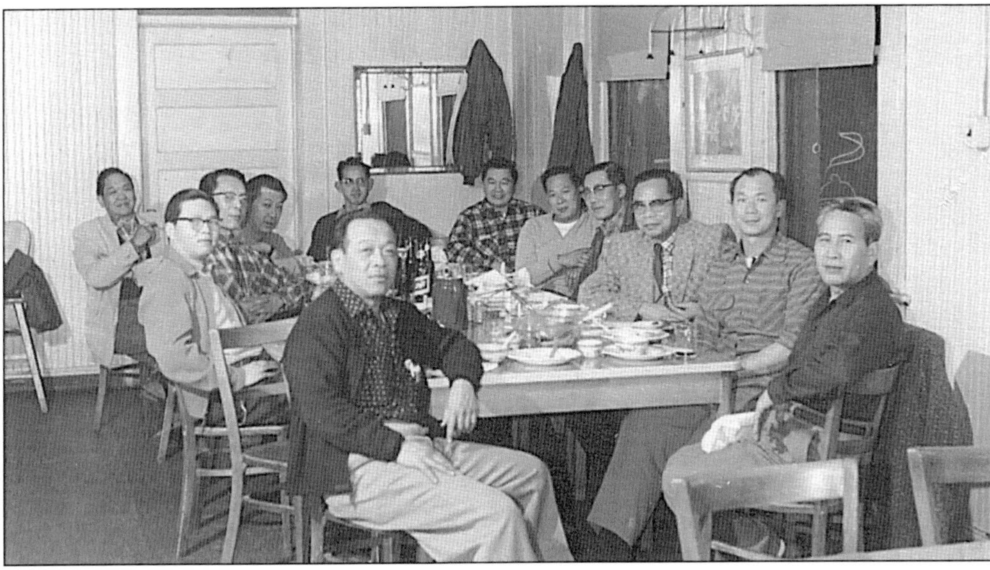

Cathay Club was organized initially as a social organization. The second and third generation and others who were working more closely with Caucasians found a comfort level straddling the two cultures in language, customs, and even food. Family and district associations remained traditional and rigid; all meetings were still conducted in the Chinese language. Cathay members were the Chinese Christian Center's youth coming of age and their interests had now included ball games, dances, picnics, and so forth. Originally an all-male club, it admitted women in the 1980s. This is an early picture of the club and many charter members taken at Canton Low.

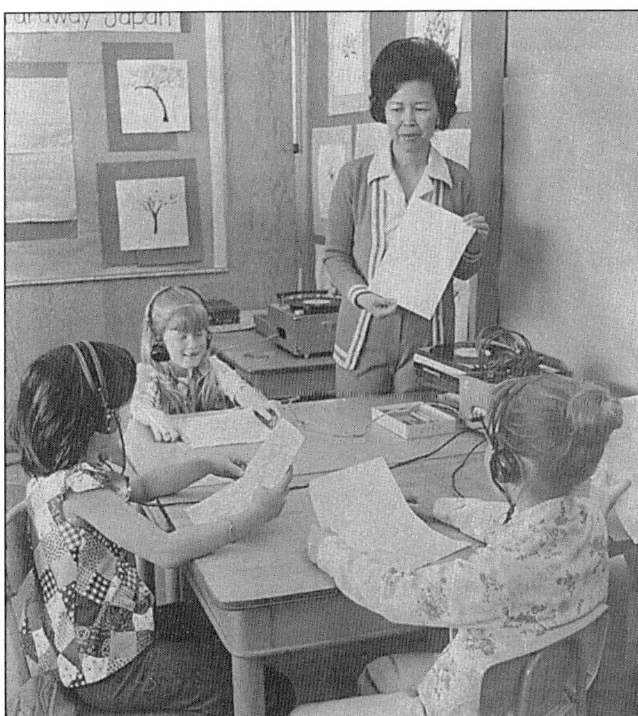

Esther Lee Fong, the first Asian teacher in the Stockton schools, began teaching at Monroe Elementary School in 1950. Being adaptable best summarized her pioneering effort. She married Ken Fong who founded the first and only Chinese Ad agency in Stockton. His contribution to Junior Achievement is legendary. When Ken died, Esther assumed the presidency of the agency until her retirement. Today, eldest son Les heads the agency. *(Courtesy of Esther Lee Fong)*

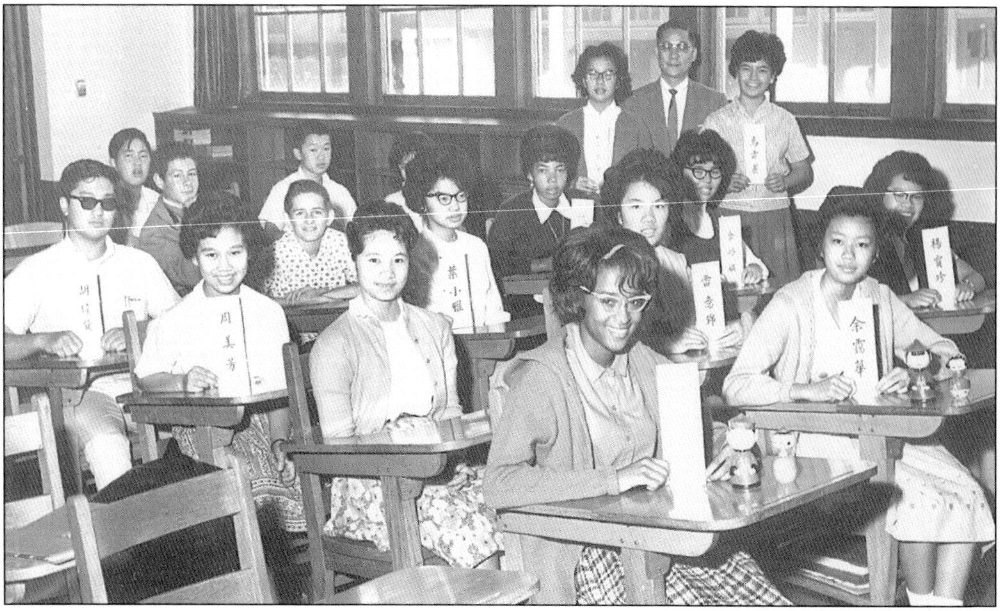

Edison High School students pose for this 1961 Mandarin Class taught by Harry Chin. Those who have actual Chinese names are holding up their placards. Harry Chin taught elementary school before moving to Edison where he also taught science courses. He later taught adult education. Harry was a past president of Chung Wah and the Gee How Oak Tin (Chan Family) for many years. Not only was he a teacher in the western sense but was also recognized in the Chinese community as a Chinese scholar. *(Courtesy of Margo Chin Mah)*

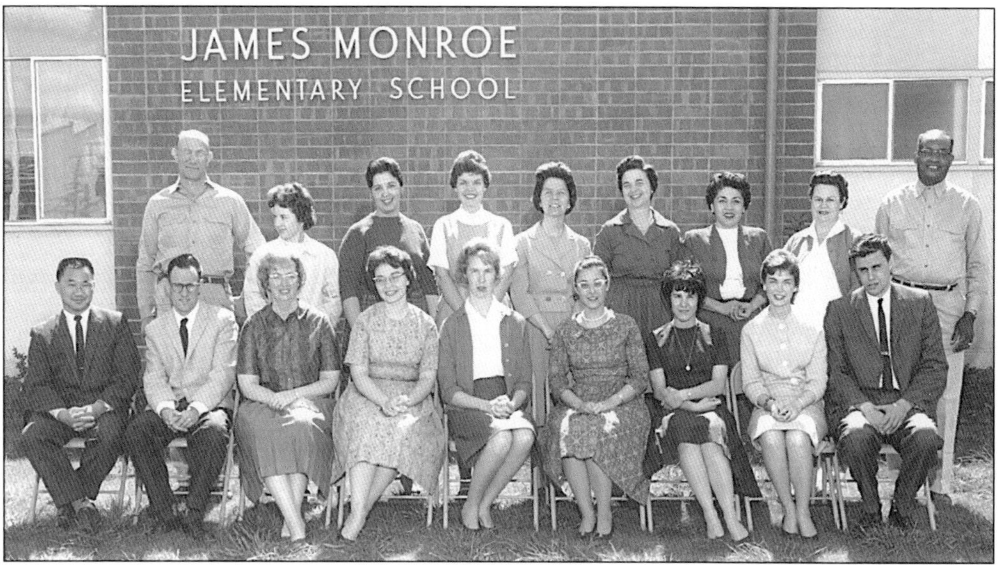

Keith Wong, another pioneer in the field of education, was the first Chinese principal for the school district. After serving in the Navy at Subic Bay, Philippines, Keith returned and completed his education including his masters at the University of the Pacific. In 1960 he became principal of the new James Monroe School. Seated on the far left with his faculty and staff, Keith also was principal at Hoover and Victory schools before retiring in 1987. *(Courtesy of the Keith Wong Collection)*

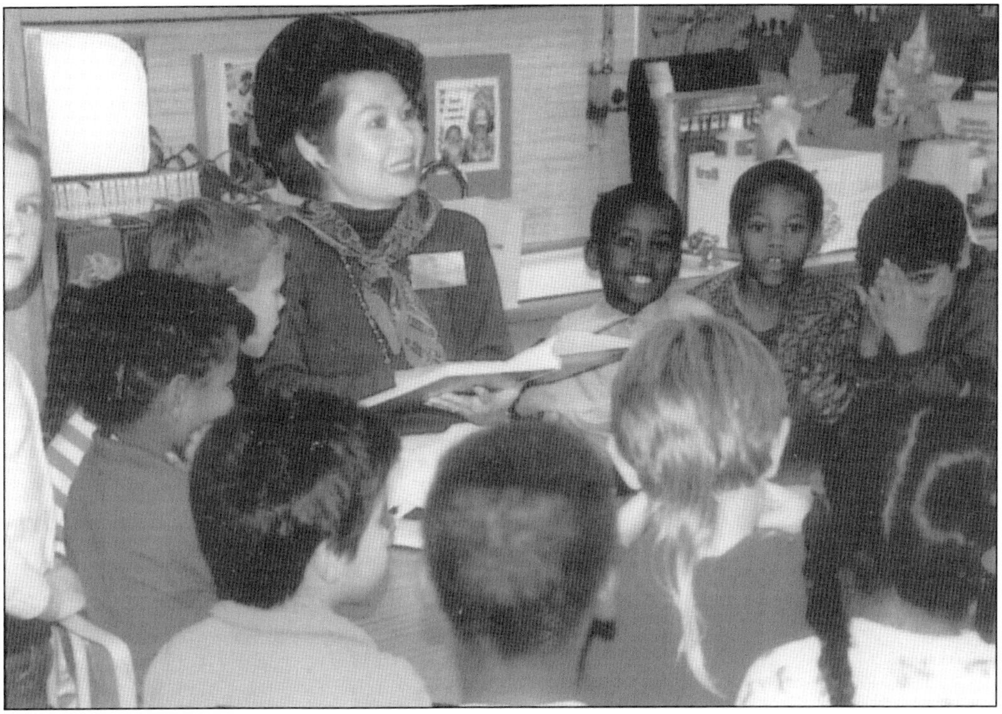

Dr. Elena Wong was Associate Superintendent of Stockton Unified School District until 1997. She previously held a high position in the California State Department of Education.

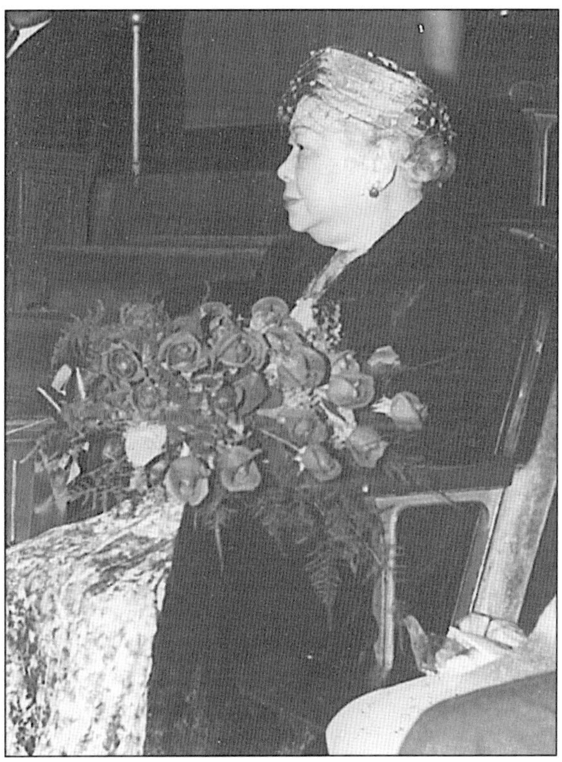

Mrs. Rose Ah Tye, pictured here in 1963 at age 75, was honored not once but twice as Chinese Community Leader of the Year, in 1963 and 1970. She was born in Red Bluff, California, and after her marriage to Dilly Ah Tye Sr. in 1907, they moved to Stockton in 1918. Rose Ah Tye was very committed to the Chinese Christian Center. The Ah Tyes had 15 children but that never deterred her from doing her part, particularly during World War II when she worked at the local Red Cross surgical dressing headquarters. Her later activities included helping the blind and elderly Chinese in Chinatown.

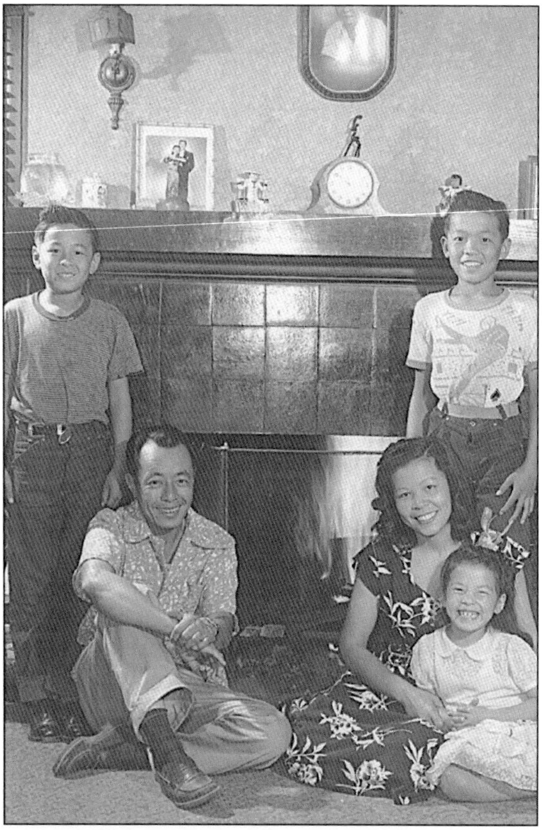

By the 1950s and '60s, there was affluence among the Stockton Chinese. Many had reached professional ranks in the medical, dental, engineering, and accounting fields to name a few. As with many other families, it was "peace in our time" at the Charles Wong's home. Pictured with Charles are his wife, Lola, and their three children, Derald, Chance, and Isis. *(Courtesy of Chance Wong)*

In the 1960s unrest and the civil rights movement swept the country. A few young Stockton activists felt they too needed self-expression. Formed in 1969, they called themselves "Bobbie Lew And the Raiders" but changed the name to the Yellow Seed. They met in the back room of Marty's Shoes. The rebellion stage was short lived, for they matriculated through the universities and entered the professional world. Bobbie Lew (center) became a space designer and others became educators. The camaraderie that existed then continues to this day. *(Courtesy of Bonnie Lew)*

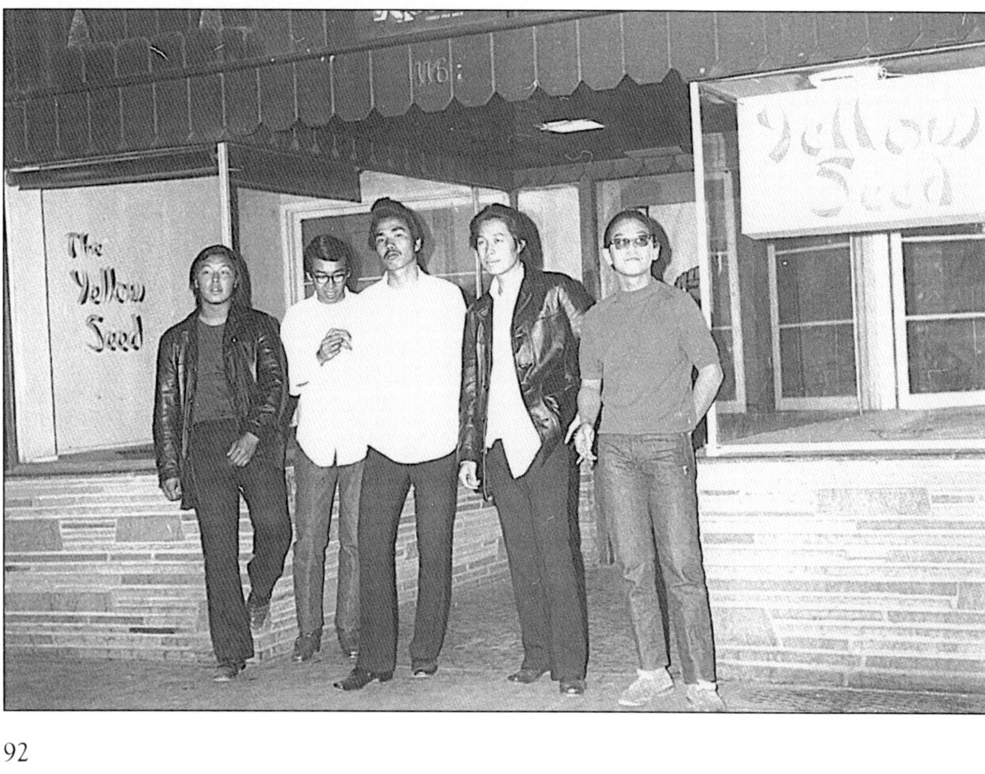

Five

SPIRITED RENEWALS

Often times when trauma hits and changes the normal course of life, one looks for meaning or even the lesson learned. In the early 1970s when the Chinatown buildings disappeared and the familiar sights and sounds were no longer evident, one would assume the community's heart and the spirit died. New buildings in the redevelopment area did not spring up overnight. Even today there are still a number of vacant lots, yet to be owned. The Stockton Chinese know it does take brick-and-mortar to make a Chinatown, but it does not take the same components to bond a Chinese community. Ethnic ties, a sense of face-saving, and a strong family commitment that includes bloodlines and clan affiliations helped the Stockton Chinese "get on" with life. And got on they did. The second and third generations made great personal strides in policy-making roles. Others born here but who followed their dreams elsewhere also succeeded nicely.

Truly, the Stockton Chinese did not just begin to lift the glass ceiling—they raised it high enough in preparation for the generations to follow.

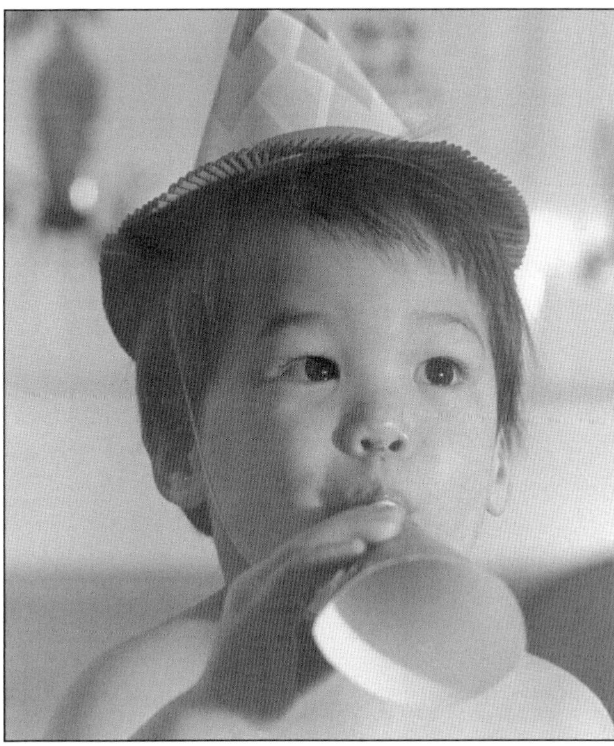

A poster child in 1970, Christian Kim heralds the beginning of 4668 in the Chinese calendar. Analogously it calls attention to the refocusing that took place within the Chinese community as they re-prioritized in the subsequent three decades. Many children had grown and sought higher education and careers elsewhere. Today, the Stockton Chinese community faces a brain drain. (*Courtesy of Pat Kim*)

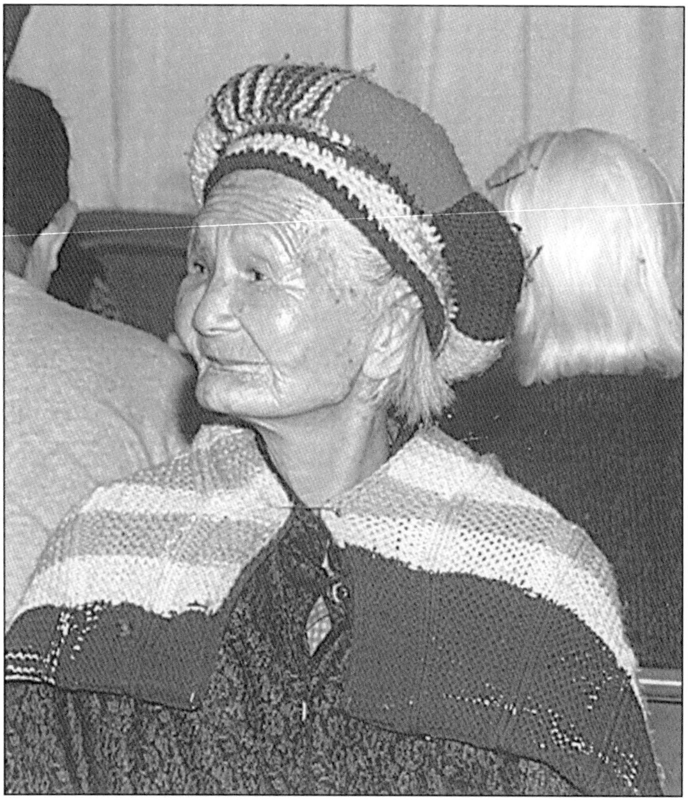

The Chinese population is aging, with the elderly outnumbering those under the age of 40. In larger numbers, new arrivals from Taiwan, Hong Kong, and Mainland China included a greater number of the aged and less affluent population. (*Courtesy of Jene Wah, Inc.*)

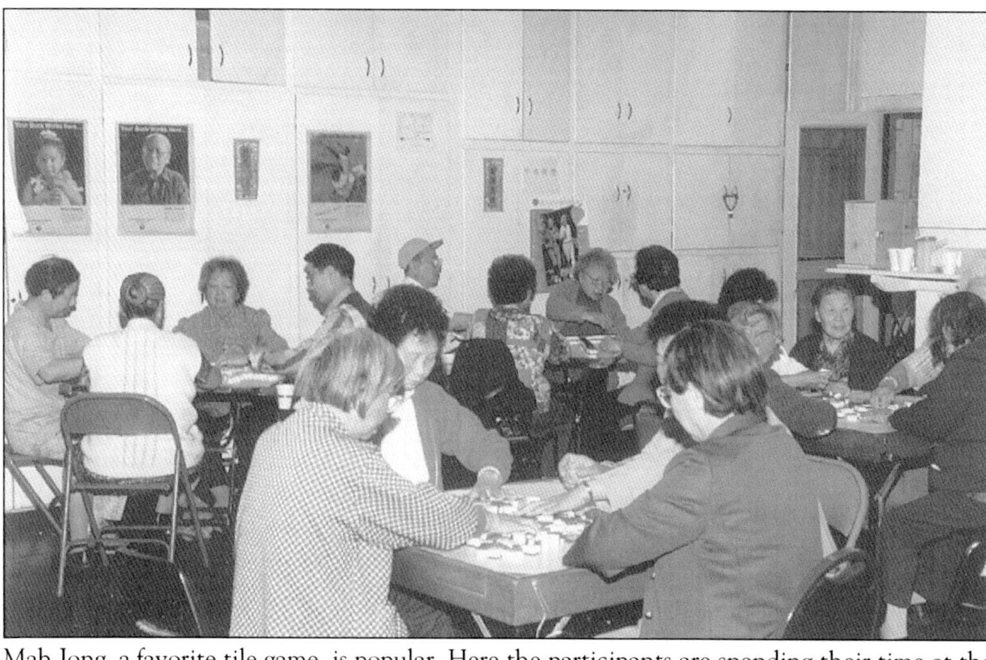

Mah Jong, a favorite tile game, is popular. Here the participants are spending their time at the Jene Wah Senior Center. (*Courtesy of Jene Wah, Inc.*)

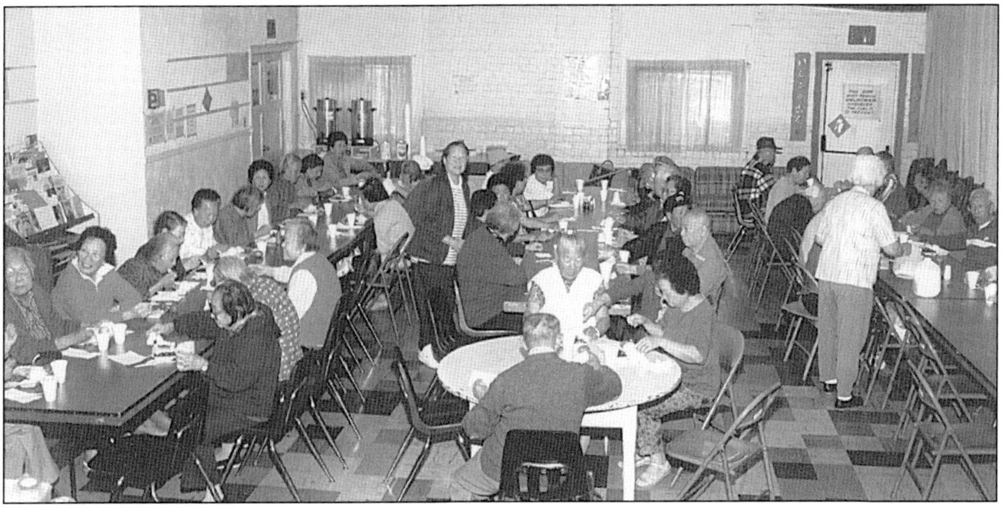

Jene Wah, a not-for-profit organization founded in 1975, is very dedicated to the Chinese seniors. Programs that are offered include assistance in obtaining social security benefits, health care, welfare assistance, transportation, housing assistance, and translation services. Under the auspices of the County Department of Aging it also runs a nutritional program and provides In-Home services and consumer services. This photo of the nutritional program was taken in 1983. (*Courtesy of Jene Wah, Inc.*)

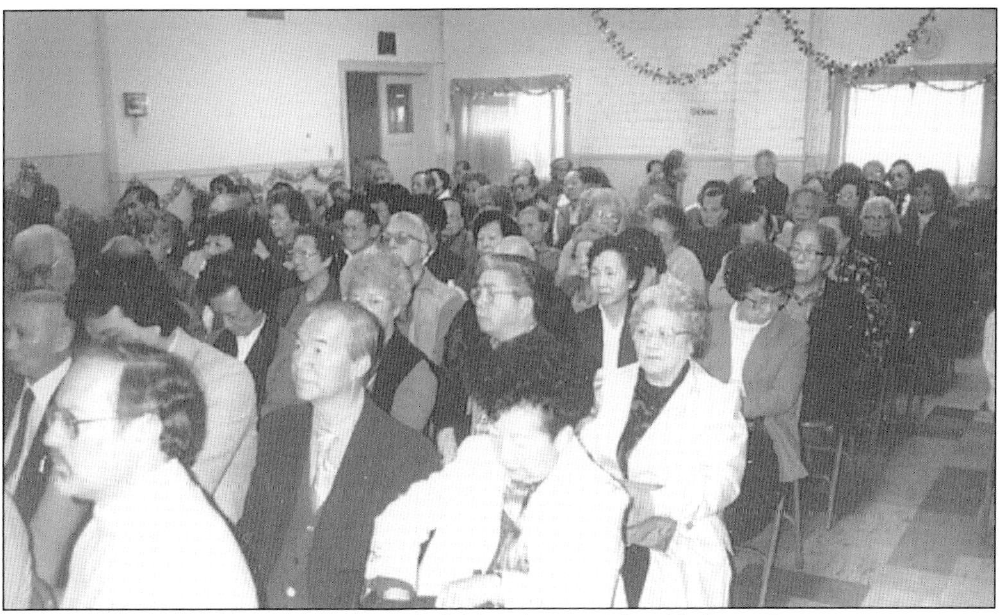

The annual Christmas program draws a faithful audience of the elderly. In this 1986 program, one of the most attentive was Paul K. Yee (looking forward on second row) sitting with his wife, Bessie. Paul Yee was a multi-professional. He was a licensed chiropractor, businessman, herbalist, and schoolteacher. Civically, Paul founded the Yee Family Association in 1946, served as the Chinese Language School principal for 15 years, and on the Board of Directors of Chung Wah for 47 years. He was a founder of the Chinese Cultural Society of Stockton. This photograph is very special for it pictures some of those who are no longer with us but who remain in our hearts. (*Courtesy of Jene Wah, Inc.*)

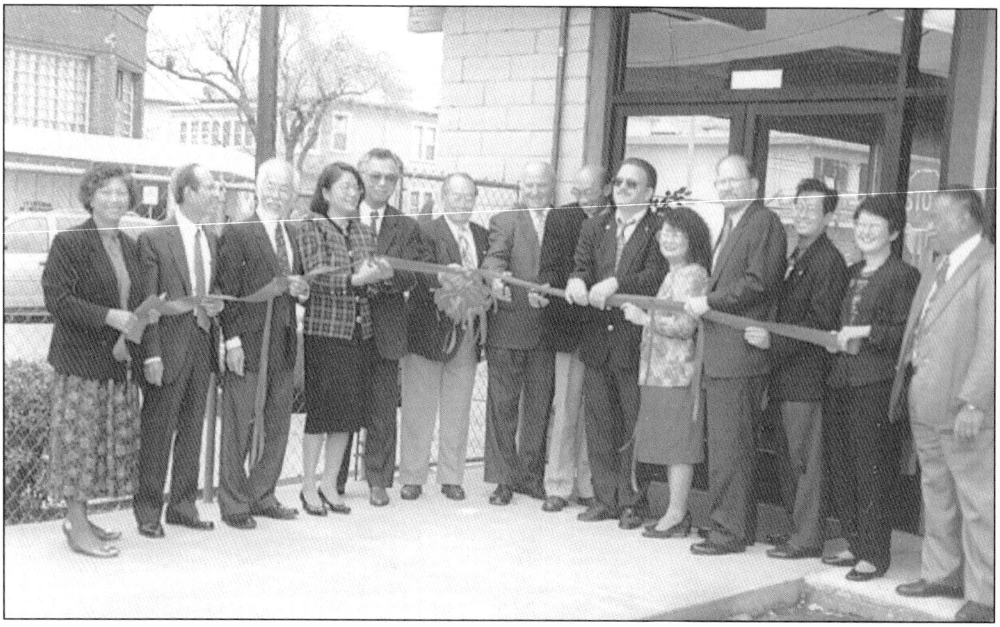

Jene Wah board members participate in a ribbon cutting to raise funds for a new kitchen. The organization initially housed at 236 E. Lafayette (in the original Chinese Christian Center building within Chung Wah's complex) realized it was time to find their own quarters. They moved two blocks away to 238 E. Church Street. Currently, there are seven paid staff and endless number of volunteers. (*Courtesy of Jene Wah, Inc.*)

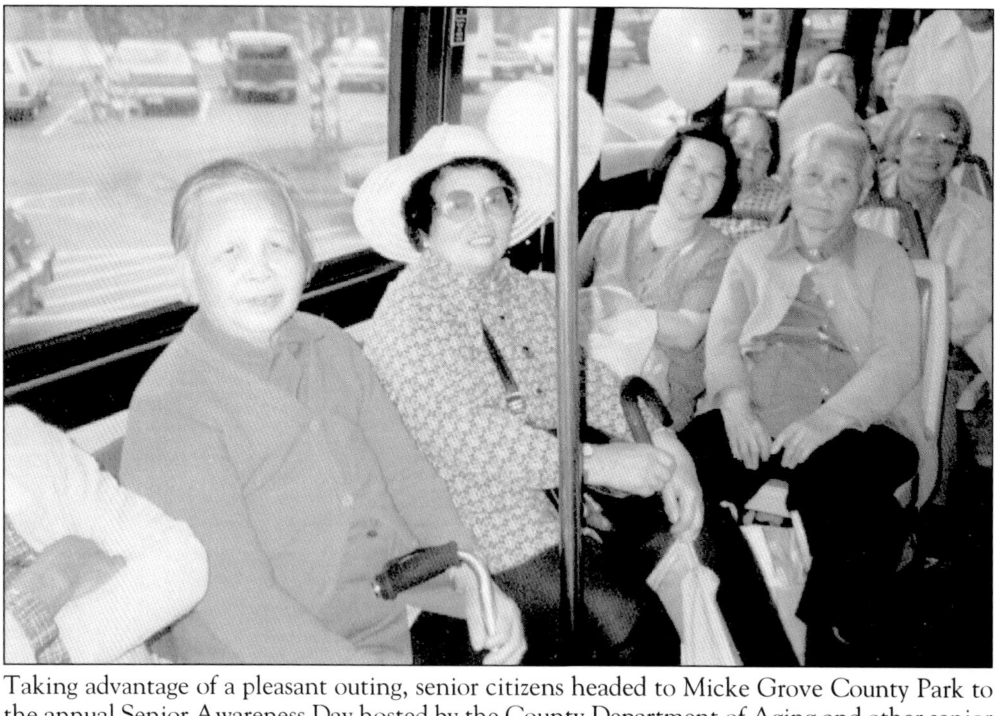

Taking advantage of a pleasant outing, senior citizens headed to Micke Grove County Park to the annual Senior Awareness Day hosted by the County Department of Aging and other senior organizations. (*Courtesy of Jene Wah, Inc.*)

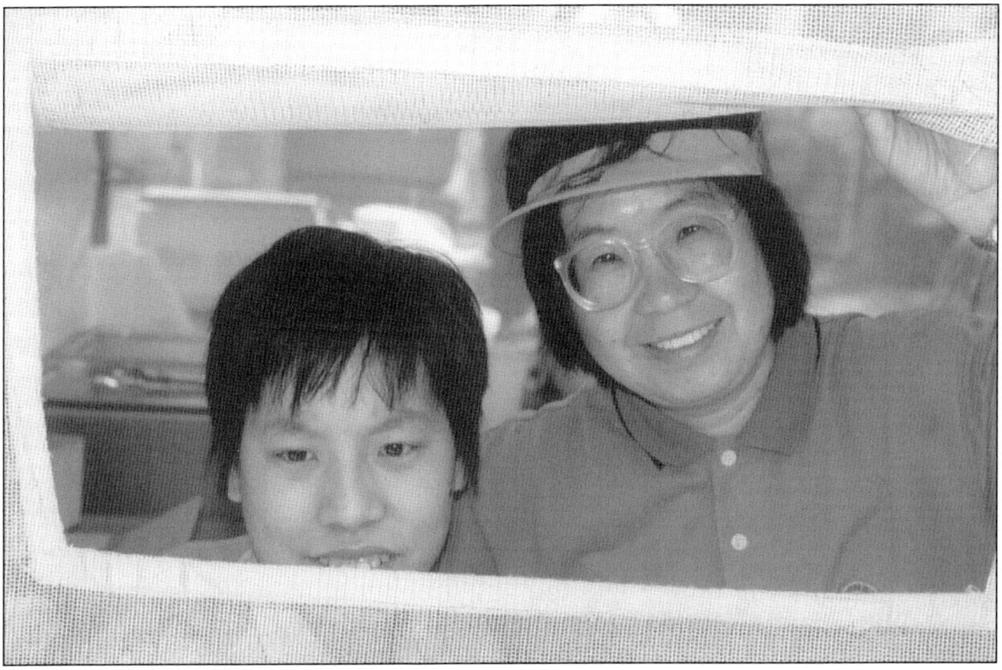

Lucia Miao and helper, a staffer at Jene Wah, Inc., stops for a moment to greet friends as she peeks through the serving area at the Senior Awareness Day. *(Courtesy of Jene Wah, Inc.)*

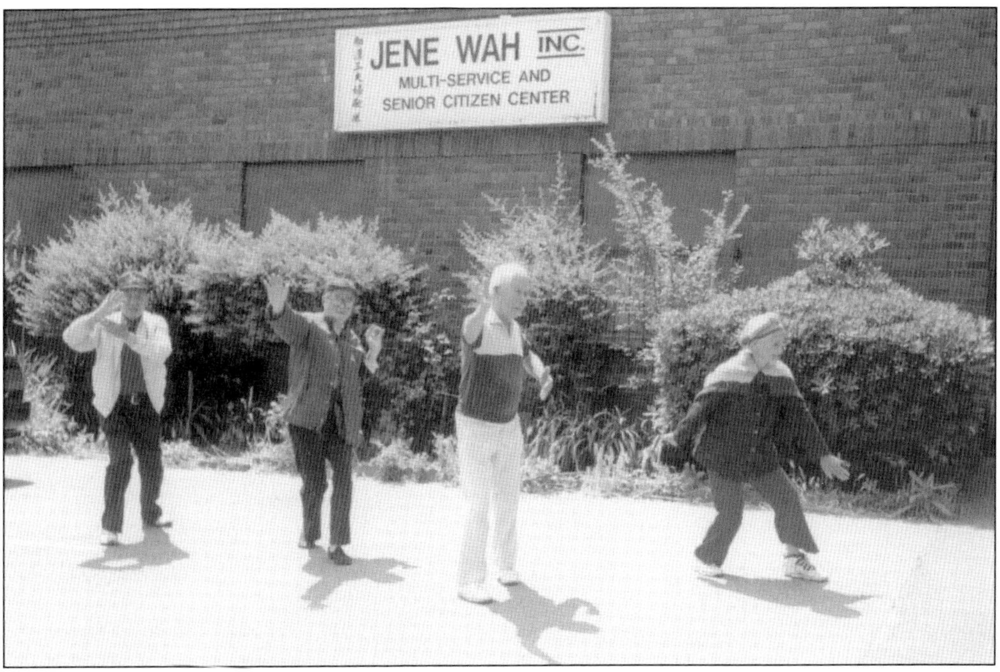

T'ai Chi Ch'uan is a solo exercise consisting of a slow, graceful, choreographed series of relaxed but alert natural movements. The art emphasizes the combination of mind and body in every motion with slow breathing combined with mental and visual concentration. *(Courtesy of Jene Wah, Inc.)*

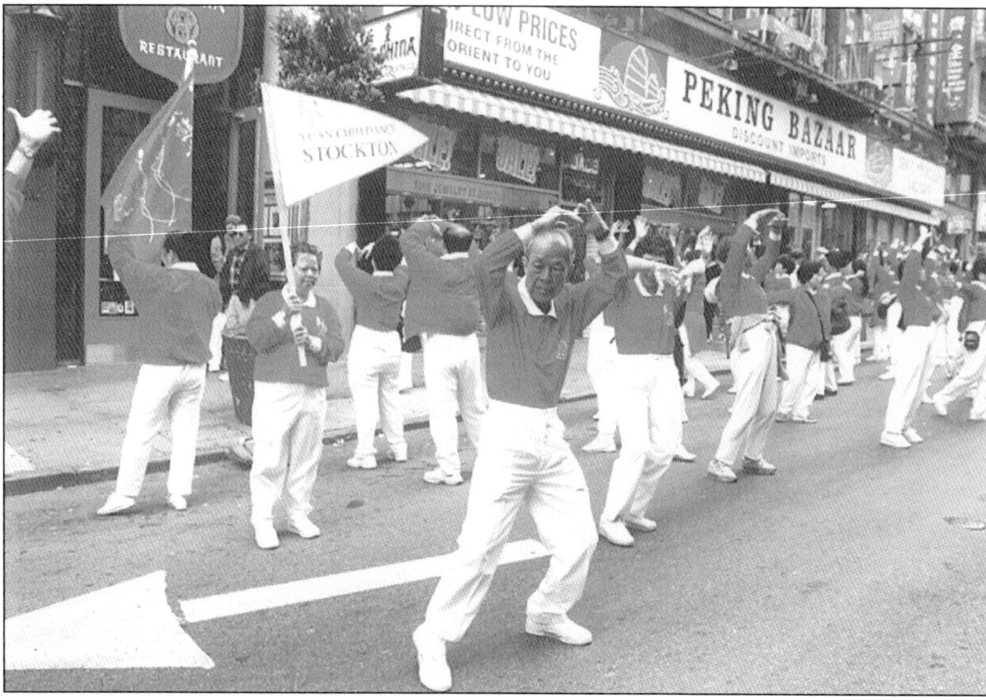

Yuan Chih, another exercise combining dance, martial art, physical therapy, and "chi" movements, has gained popularity. It has the traditional effect of Chinese massage, entertainment, bodybuilding, and health care. Stockton Yuan Chih dancers are performing on Grant Avenue in San Francisco Chinatown. (*Courtesy of the Norman Lew Collection*)

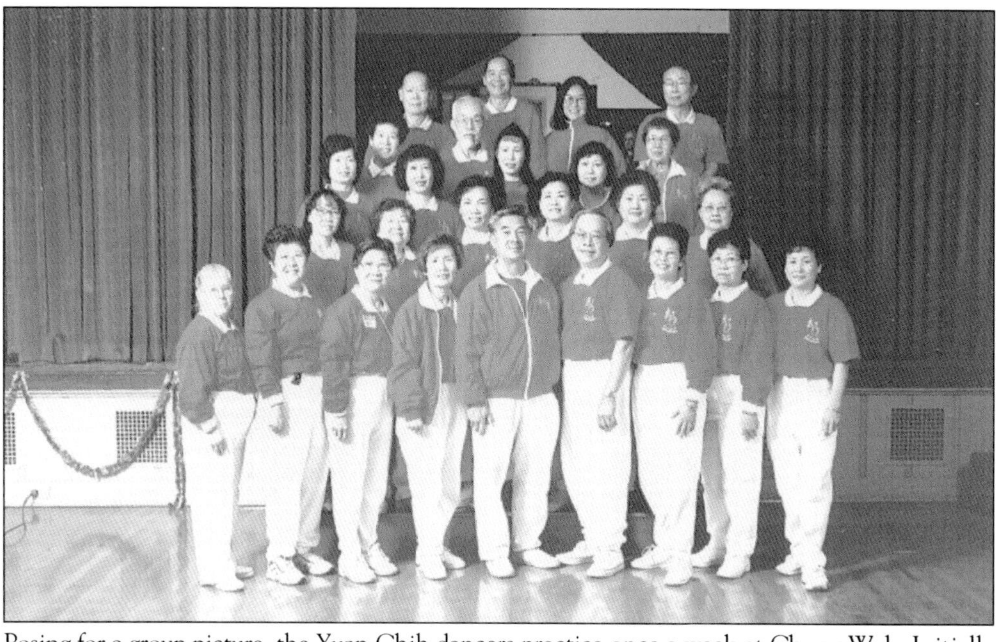

Posing for a group picture, the Yuan Chih dancers practice once a week at Chung Wah. Initially begun as a fun way to exercise, the group now gets bookings for their performances, including out-of-town appearances. (*Courtesy of the Norman Lew Collection*)

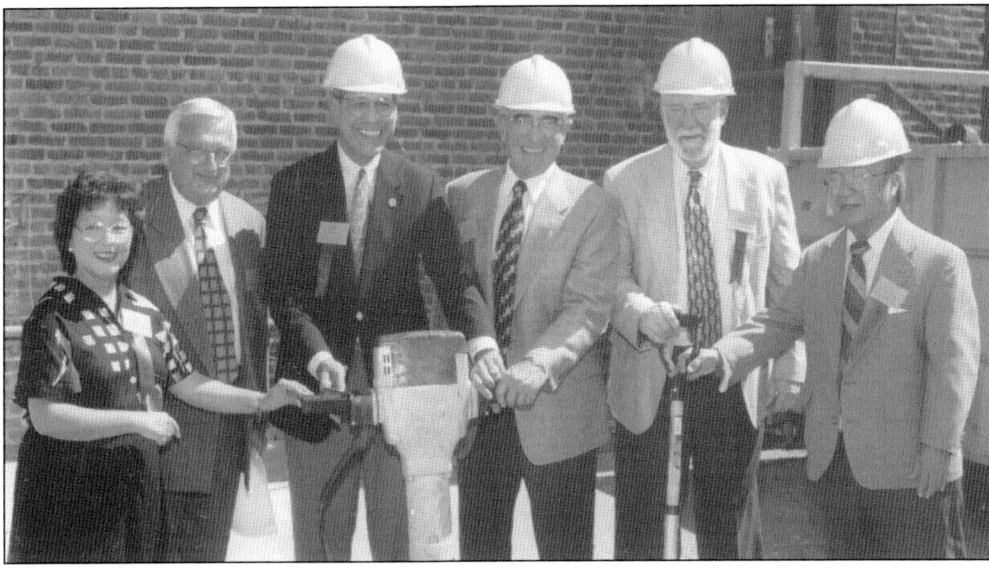

In the early 1970s, Chung Wah leaders purchased an old hotel, never maintained it, and by 1999, it deteriorated to the point that the organization faced 76 code violations and city officials threatened to demolish the building. Under new leadership the building was renovated, seismically tied, and ADA (American Disability Act) retrofitted into a 20-unit, low-income senior apartment building with financing through a $1.2 million in tax credit and a $900,000 city loan. The building's title was transferred to the Quan Ying Foundation, a non-profit organization. The picture is at the groundbreaking on May 5, 2000.

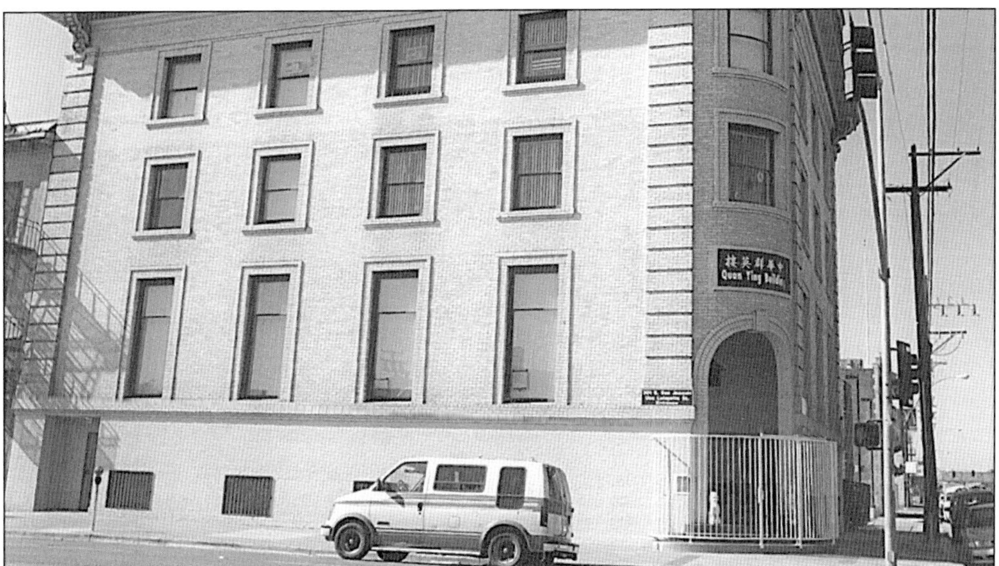

The term *Quan Ying* translates to "a gathering of good people." The Salvation Army built the building in 1911 and is listed now as historic in city records. The terra cotta buff brick building is accented with emerald green trim and touches of Chinese red at the doors. Adding to Chinese tradition, *foo dogs* within the wrought iron fence protect the corner alcove. Since its completion, the building received the Award of Excellence from the City Planning Commission and the Glen Allen Award from the Cultural Heritage Board.

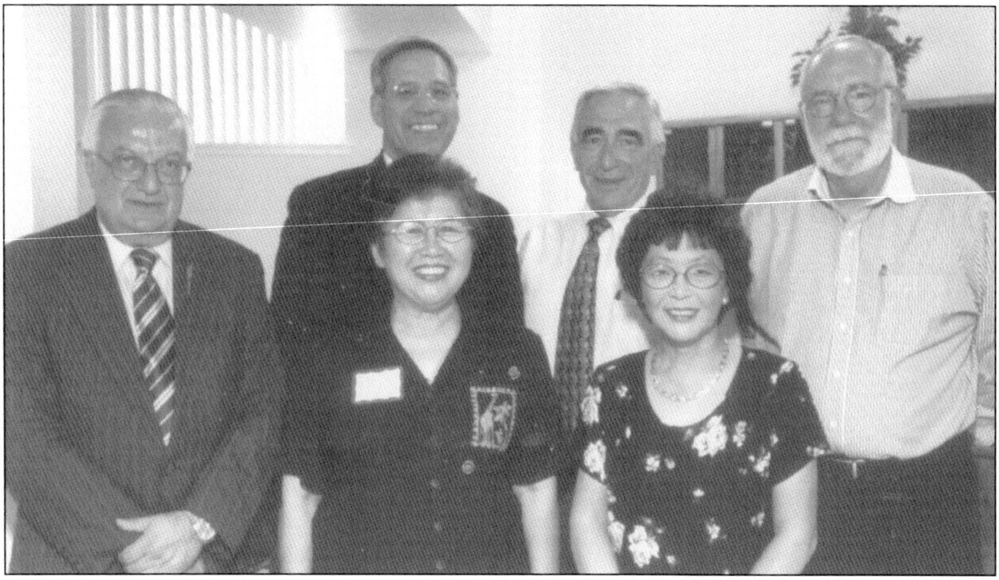

The one-year anniversary of the Quan Ying building became a reunion for those who put the project together. From left to right: (back row) Cyrus Youssefi, developer/contractor; Walter Liang, Asst. State Treasurer, chief of California Tax Credit Dept.; Mayor Gary Podesto; D. Donald Geiger, President of Downtown Alliance and Quan Ying Foundation secretary; (front row) Judy Hong, manager; and Sylvia Minnick, President of Quan Ying Foundation. (*Courtesy of the Norman Lew Collection*)

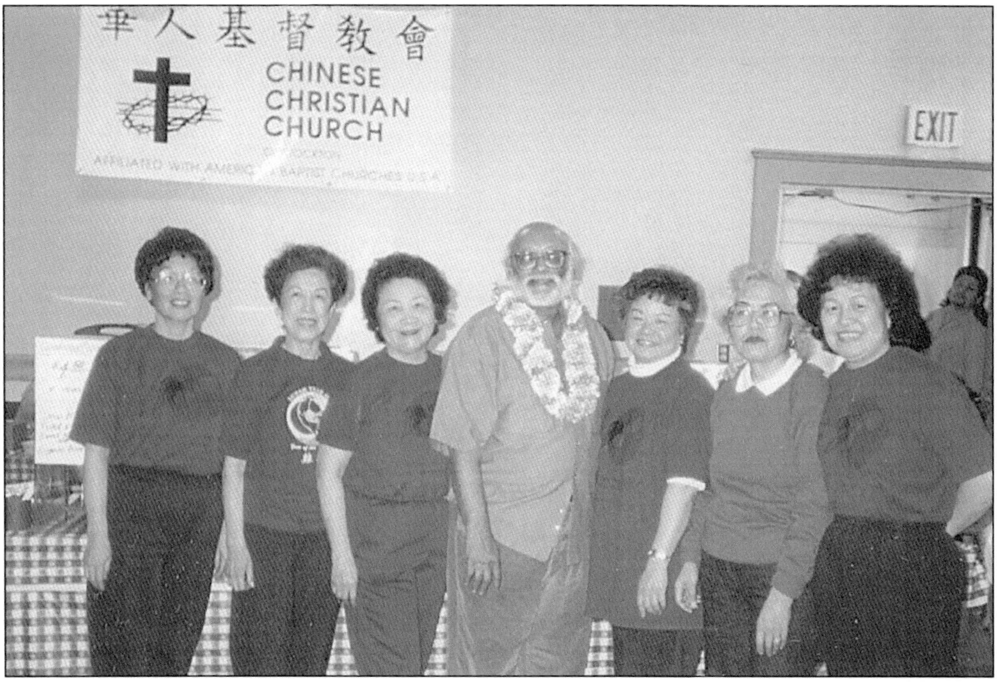

The ladies of the Chinese Christian Church participate at the International Friendship Day Festival in 1992. In the center is Raj Ramaya of the American Friends Service. (*Courtesy of Leona Wong*)

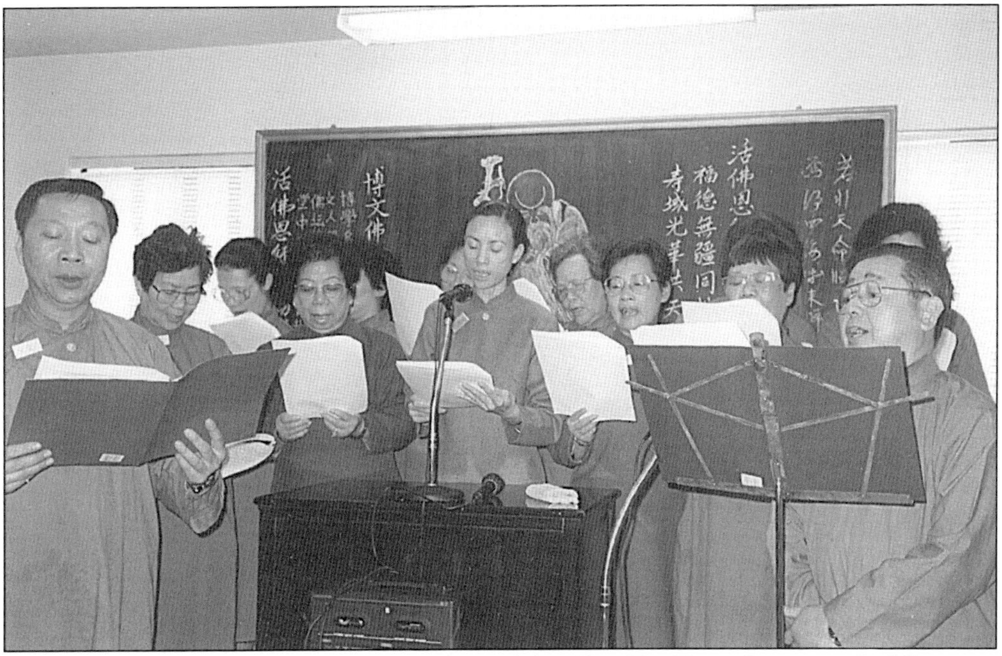

Practicing for their own service are members of the Shin Yat Tong Society, a Buddhist sect established in North Stockton in 1990. (*Courtesy of Wing Chan*)

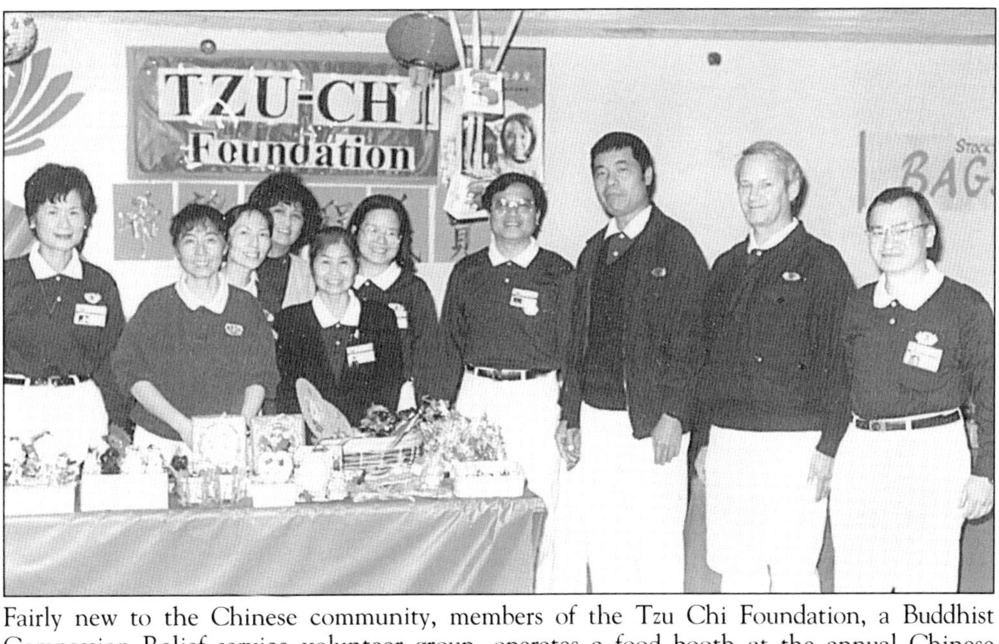

Fairly new to the Chinese community, members of the Tzu Chi Foundation, a Buddhist Compassion Relief service volunteer group, operates a food booth at the annual Chinese New Year Festival. The organization's missions are charity, medicine, education, and culture. (*Courtesy of Sulin Duan*)

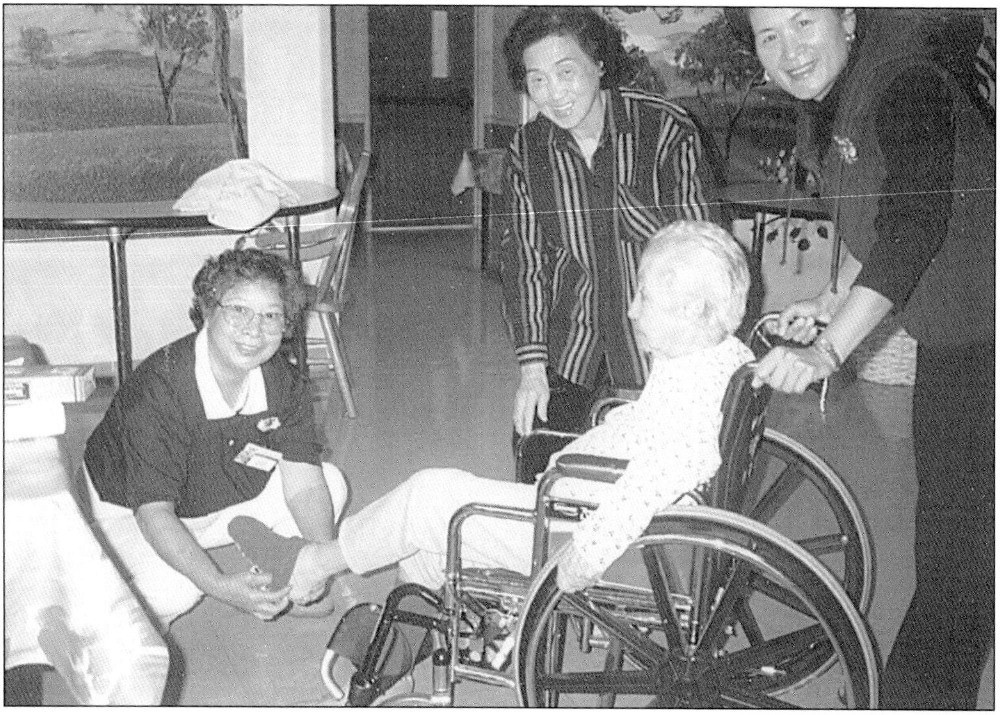

The Tzu Chi members provide emergency relief in a variety of ways. They also visit convalescent homes (as seen here when members visited Wagner Heights, a senior complex) and gives seminars on health care. (*Courtesy of Sulin Duan*)

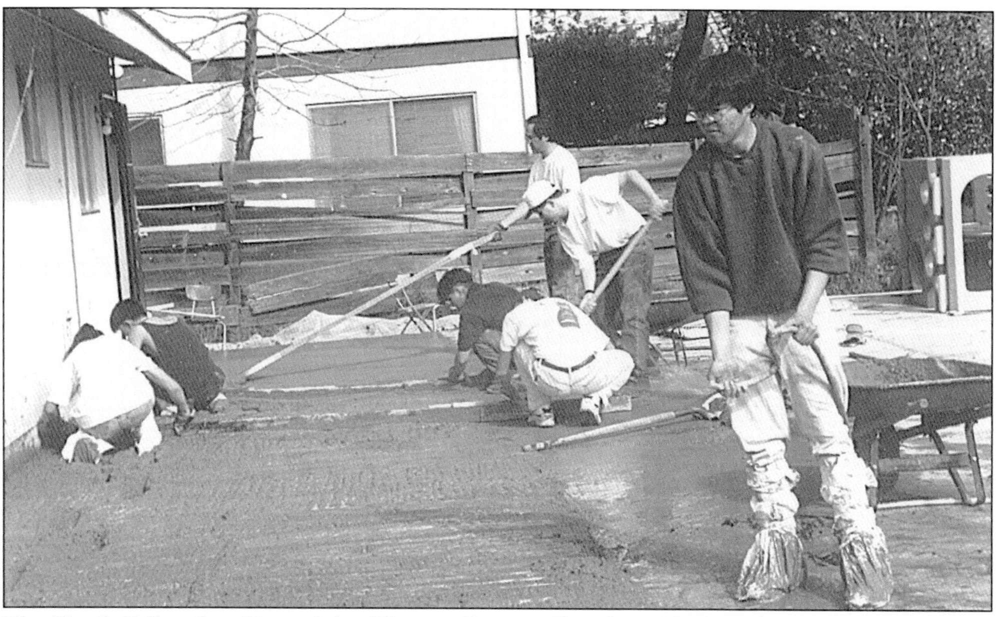

The Youth Fellowship Unit of the Chinese Baptist Church at 2315 Carlton Avenue rolled up their sleeves to build a foundation for a children's play area within their church complex. Aside from the activities of St. Mark's United Methodist Church, the oldest among the Stockton Chinese, other Christian sects now have sizeable congregations. (*Courtesy of Esther Chan*)

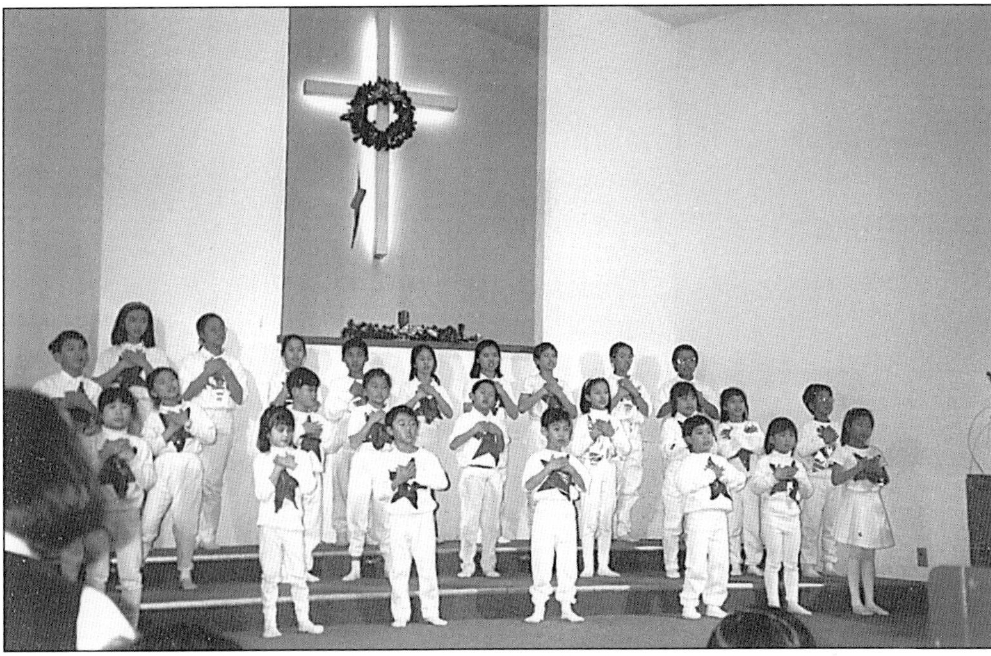

Activities at the Chinese Baptist Church include English classes for new immigrants, tutorial services for school children, and a language school. The school, with an enrollment of just under a hundred, operates on Saturdays. At the end of the semester the school holds a graduation night program as seen here in which the students are the main participants. (*Courtesy of Esther Chan*)

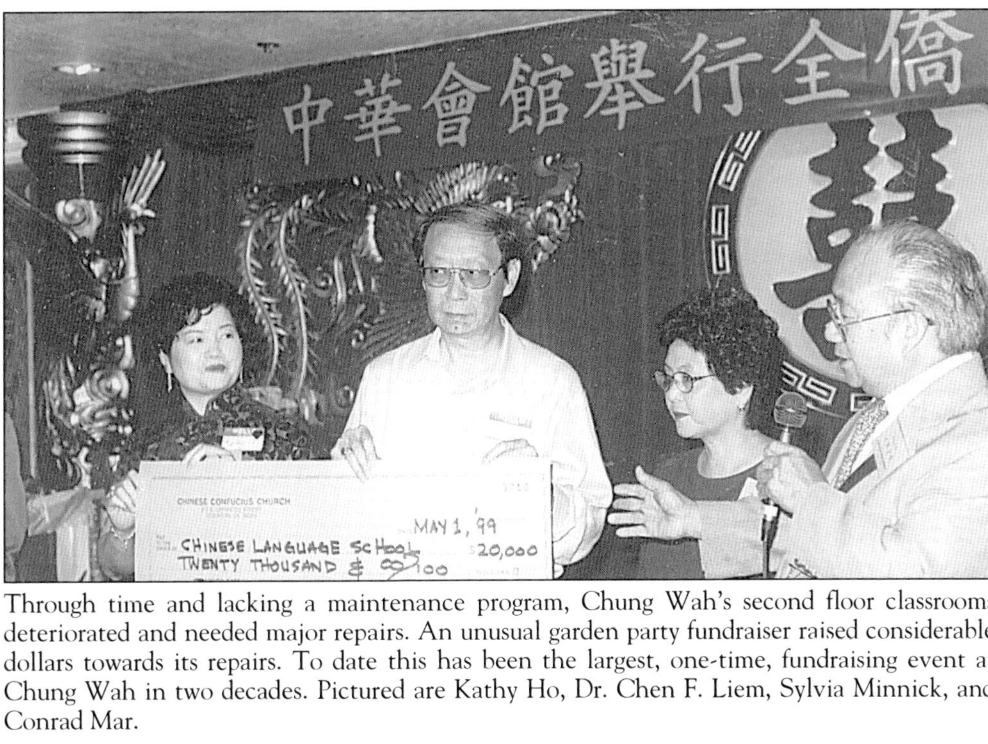

Through time and lacking a maintenance program, Chung Wah's second floor classrooms deteriorated and needed major repairs. An unusual garden party fundraiser raised considerable dollars towards its repairs. To date this has been the largest, one-time, fundraising event at Chung Wah in two decades. Pictured are Kathy Ho, Dr. Chen F. Liem, Sylvia Minnick, and Conrad Mar.

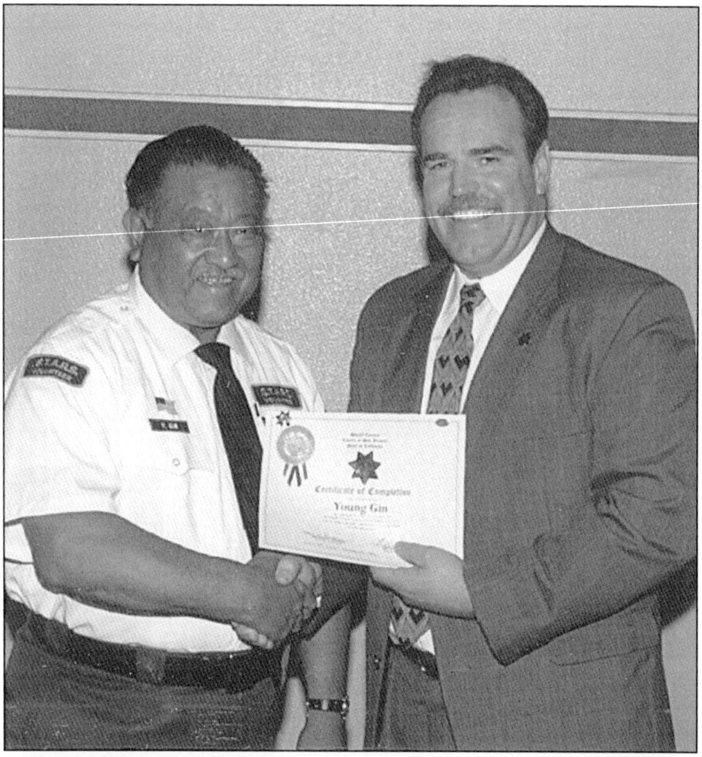

Volunteerism is very strong among the active retirees. Wanting to help beyond the Chinese community, Young K. Gin became a member of STARS, (Sheriff's Team of Active Retired Seniors) and is shown receiving a certificate of appreciation from County Sheriff Baxter Dunn. Nicknamed "Muscles," Young attended school at Fort Huachuca, Arizona. During the Korean War he joined the Merchant Marines and upon retirement went to work at the County Jail teaching inmates cooking. (*Courtesy of Young K. Gin*)

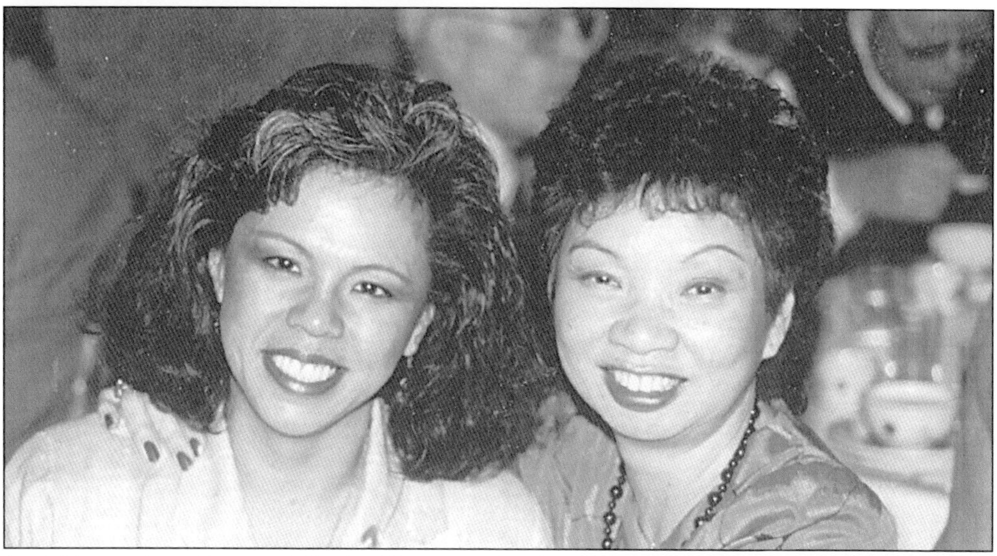

Both Bonnie Lew (left) and Shirley Ng are credited with reviving Chinese folk dance. Shirley Ng, while on the county spring Festival Committee in 1975, noticed that other ethnic groups' promoted native dance. Shirley, as founder, and Bonnie, as artistic director, assembled a troupe under the auspices of the Chinese Cultural Society of Stockton (CCSS) in 1970. Shirley was a bookkeeper and office manager and Bonnie, a native of Mississippi, is a supervising librarian at the Public Library. Shirley, formerly on the Stockton Arts Commission, was a nominee for the Susan B. Anthony Award and cited as the Chinese Outstanding Citizen of 2001. (*Courtesy of Bonnie Lew*)

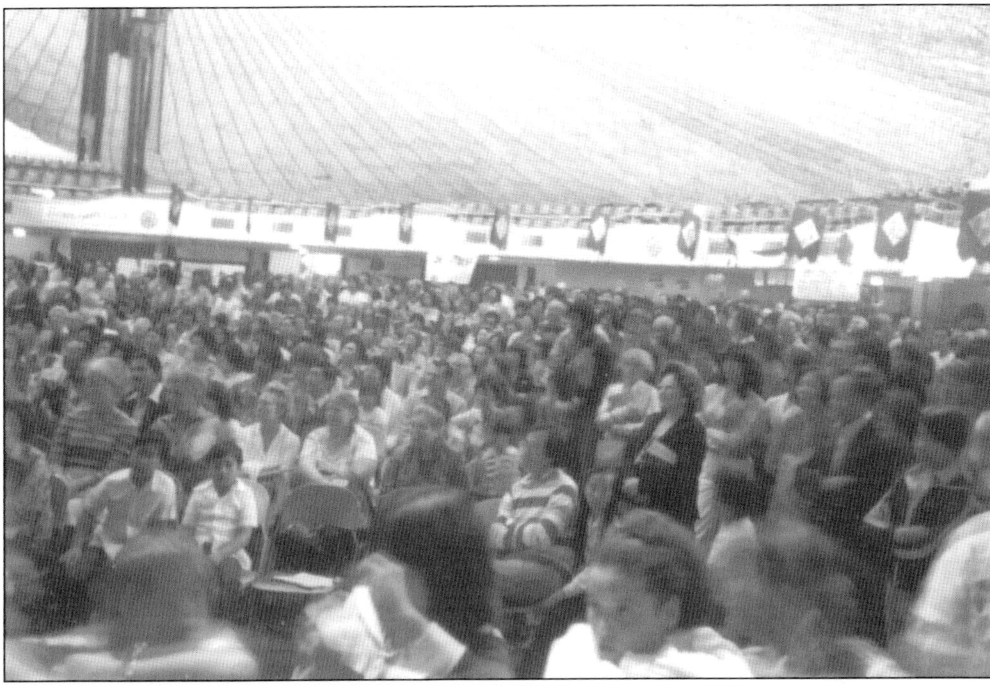

The Chinese Cultural Society of Stockton (CCSS), organized in 1978, promotes appreciation of Chinese culture and sponsors the Chinese Year Festival at the Civic Auditorium. The annual event attracts as many as 8,000 people with all-day entertainment, food booths, calligraphy, sale items, cooking demonstrations, and a large assortment of exhibits. At the organization's annual Spring Banquet three perpetual scholarships are awarded and a Chinese Citizen of the Year is honored. (*Courtesy of Bonnie Lew*)

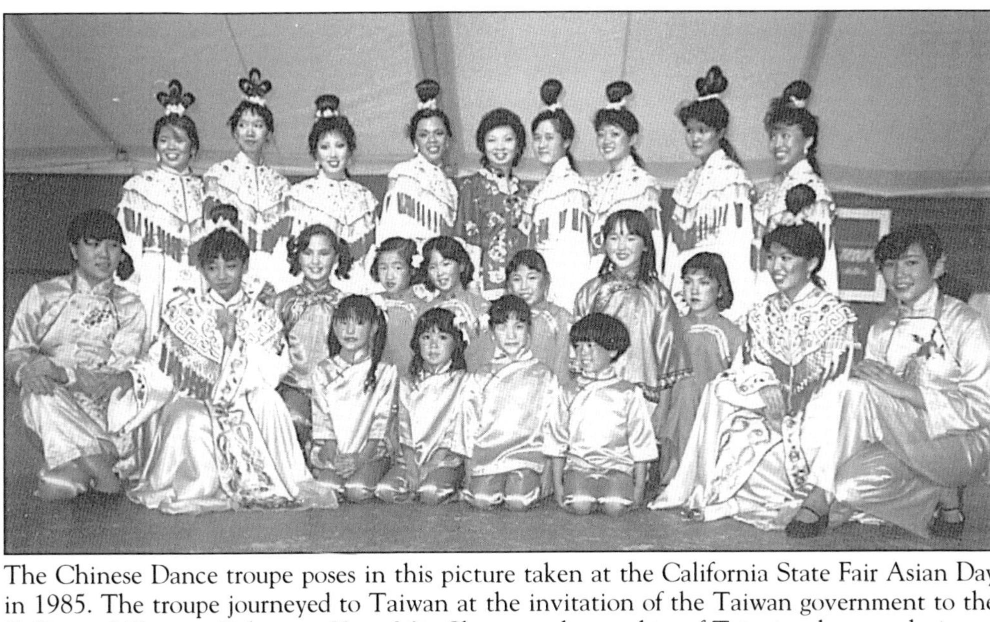

The Chinese Dance troupe poses in this picture taken at the California State Fair Asian Day in 1985. The troupe journeyed to Taiwan at the invitation of the Taiwan government to the College of Chinese Culture at Yang Min Shan, on the outskirt of Taipei to learn techniques. The dance troupe ceased performing in 1998. (*Courtesy of Bonnie Lew*)

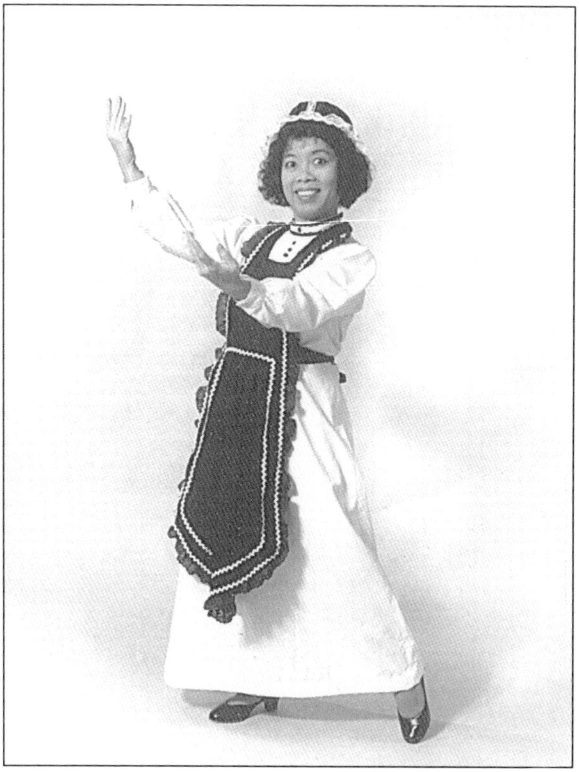

Valerie Lee Acoba organized the Asian Repertory Theatre in 1990. Its mission is to provide a forum for Asian Americans to display talents in dramatic arts and educate and increase the public's knowledge of Asian culture through live theatre. As a theatre group, they have performed in various venues. Valerie, a member of the Stockton Arts Commission, is seen here in a ballet performance of the *Nutcracker Suite* in 1989. By profession, she teaches middle and high school drama and dance. (*Courtesy of Valerie Lee Acoba*)

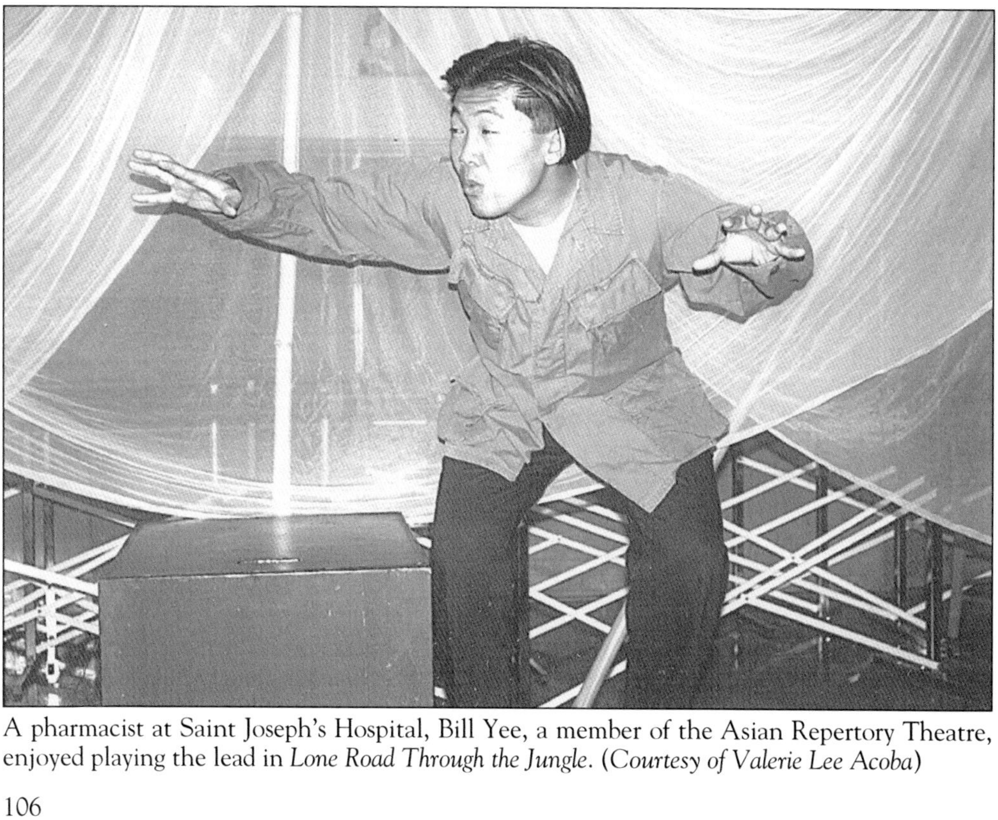

A pharmacist at Saint Joseph's Hospital, Bill Yee, a member of the Asian Repertory Theatre, enjoyed playing the lead in *Lone Road Through the Jungle*. (*Courtesy of Valerie Lee Acoba*)

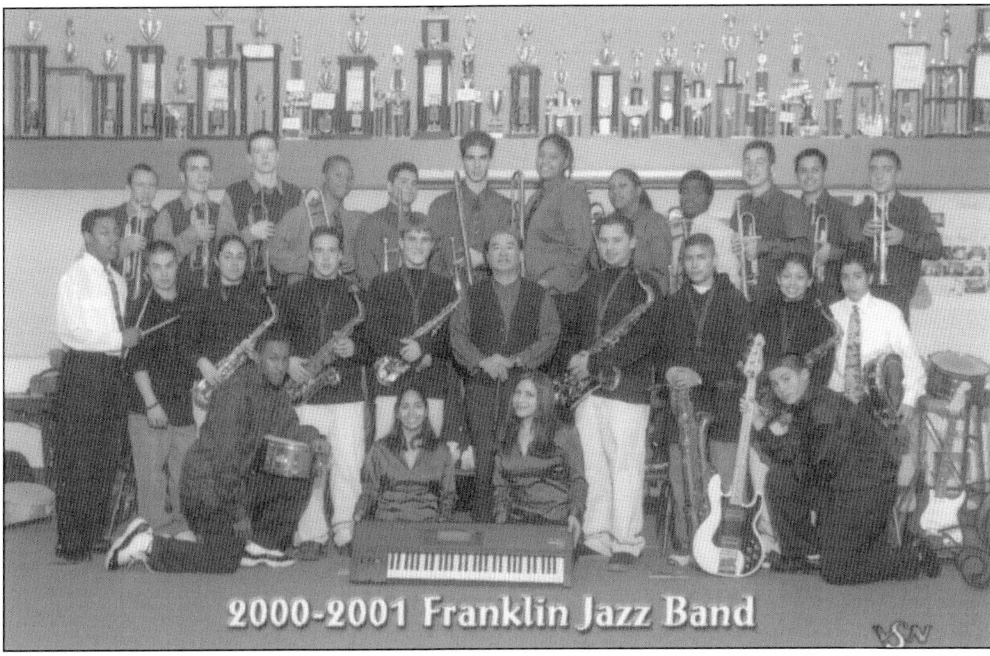

A comment in the Editorial Page of the *The Record*, "... leaves Legacy of Excellence at Franklin," imparts a complimentary phrase about Mel Won and his renowned jazz band at Franklin High School. For the over 200-plus awards amassed from 1974 to 2001, the school district trustees named the music room in his honor. A soft-spoken but dry-humored trombonist teacher, Mel Won taught over 2,000 students in his 33-year teaching career. (*Courtesy of Leona Wong*)

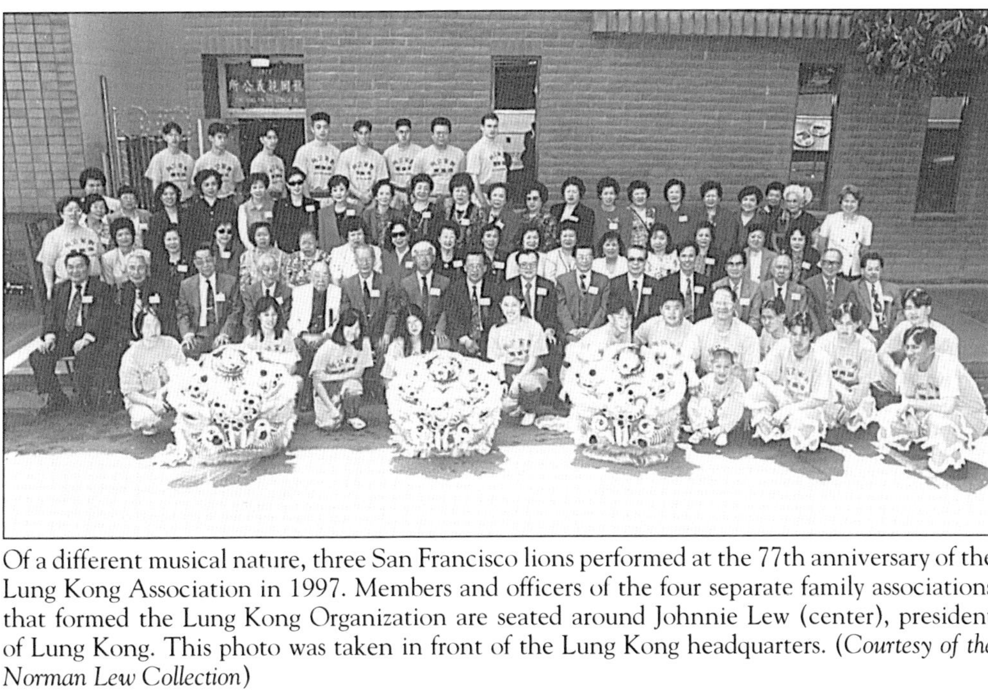

Of a different musical nature, three San Francisco lions performed at the 77th anniversary of the Lung Kong Association in 1997. Members and officers of the four separate family associations that formed the Lung Kong Organization are seated around Johnnie Lew (center), president of Lung Kong. This photo was taken in front of the Lung Kong headquarters. (*Courtesy of the Norman Lew Collection*)

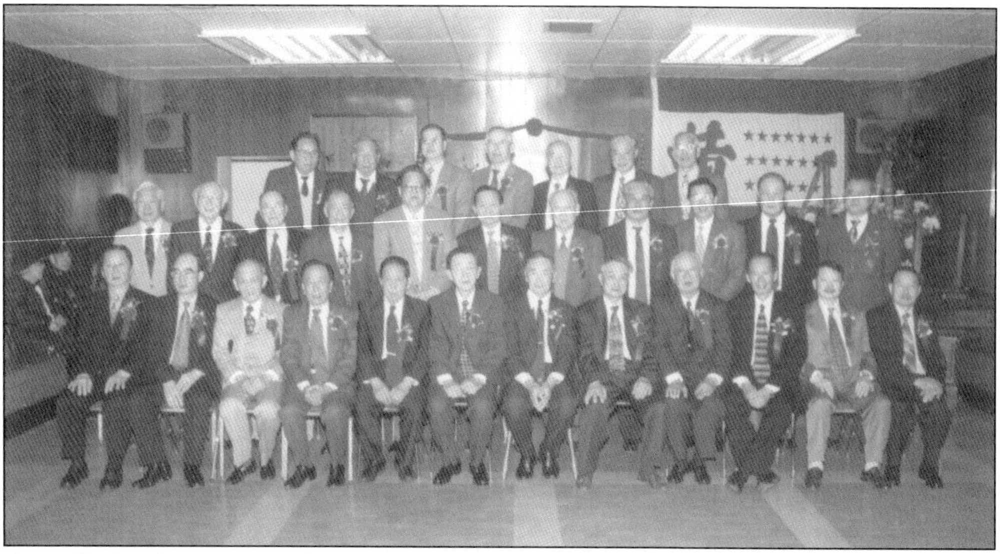

Annually family association boards, officers, and delegates pose for the record. These are the Wong Family officers in 1994 taken within their headquarters. To the far right is the Wong family banner with 21 stars representing the legendary 21 sons from which the Wongs believed as their ancestors. (*Courtesy of Leona Wong*)

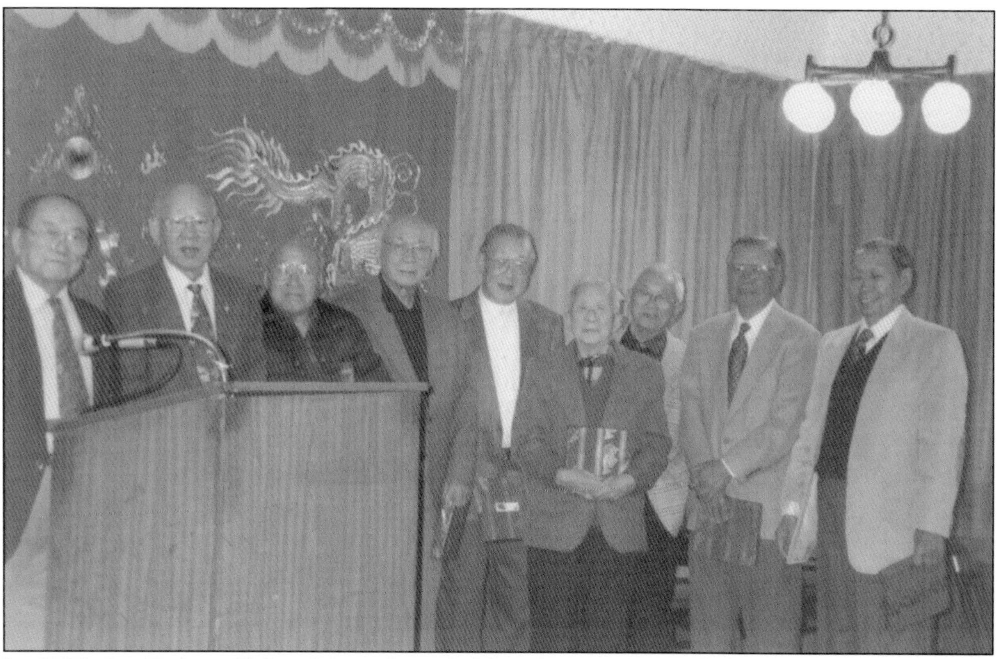

In 1996 the Cathay Club celebrated its Golden Anniversary and this photo honored some of the charter members. Of the original 14 charter members, those present were: Jack Wah Wong (actually not a charter member), Ed Ah Tye, Dilly Ah Tye, John Wong, Bill Foo Wong, Vincent Yim, Dun Fong, Al Foo Wong, and King Lee. (*Courtesy of Leona Wong*)

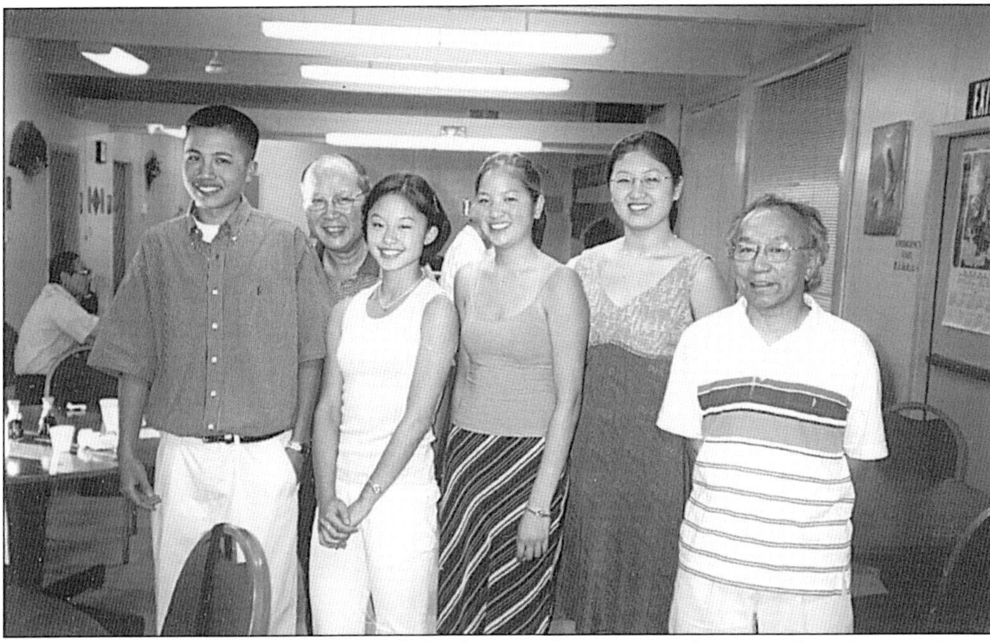

Cathay Club annually awards four scholarships to deserving students. In this photograph are recent recipients, from left to right: Kevin Low (Creighton University); Dr. Eugene Low, chairman of Scholarship Committee; Jamie Funamura (Stanford University); Jennifer Huey (CSU-Long Beach); Ning Ma (U.C.-Berkeley); and Harry Low, president. (*Courtesy of Jun Wang*)

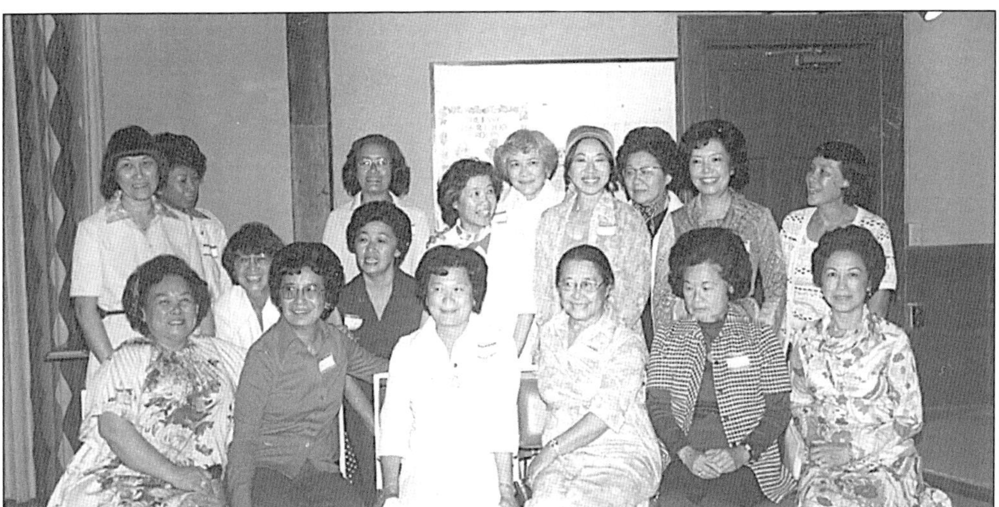

Dora Lee organized the Tau Lamda at the Chinese Christian Center in 1938. As the first service club for girls, it focused primarily on helping with programs centered on the church. This photo is of their 40th reunion in 1977. Hence, the group organizes reunions every five years. (*Courtesy of the Keith Wong Collection*)

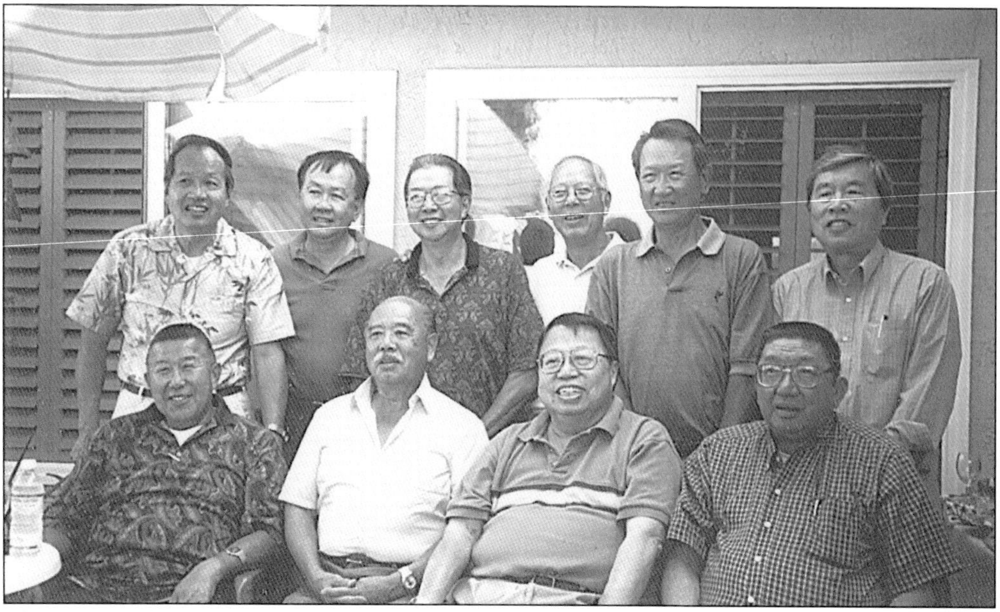

This recent photo of a 55th year reunion shows that camaraderie still exists for the Chi Y basketball team. Pictured, left to right, are (top row) Johnny Low, Johnny Kao, Bob Lee, Charlie Chan, Gordon Mar, and Raymond Chan. Seated are Henry Wong, Willard Moore, Gilbert Lan, and Genson Wong. (*Courtesy of Violet Chan*)

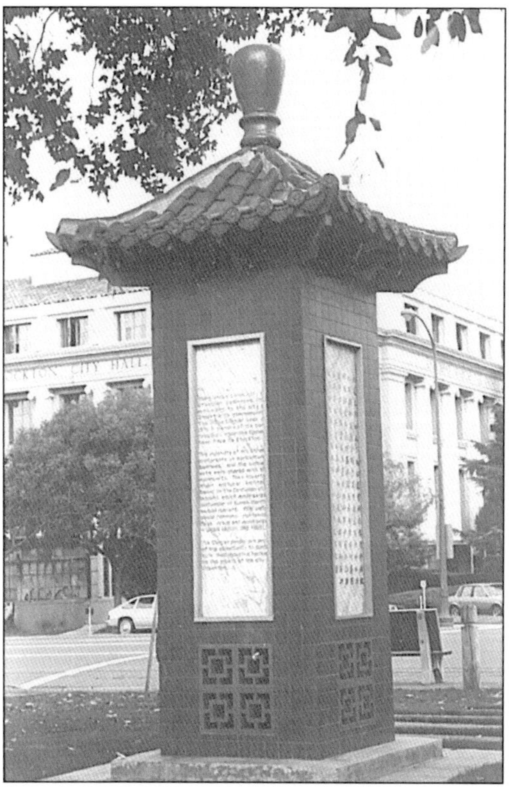

To commemorate the bi-centennial of the U.S., the Chinese community donated this Confucius monument to the city of Stockton. Located within sight of City Hall the gift suggests the Chinese presence in the long history of the city.

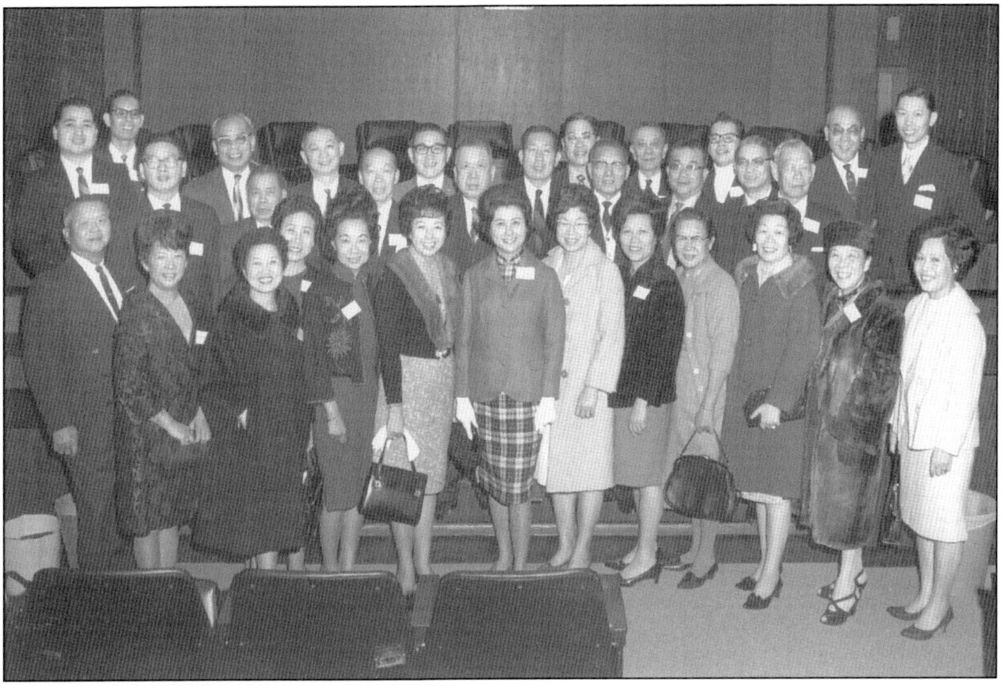

In 1967 a group of Stockton Chinese leaders and their wives gathered at the California State Capitol for a tour as guests of then Speaker of the Assembly Robert Monagan. (*Courtesy of Frank Kim*)

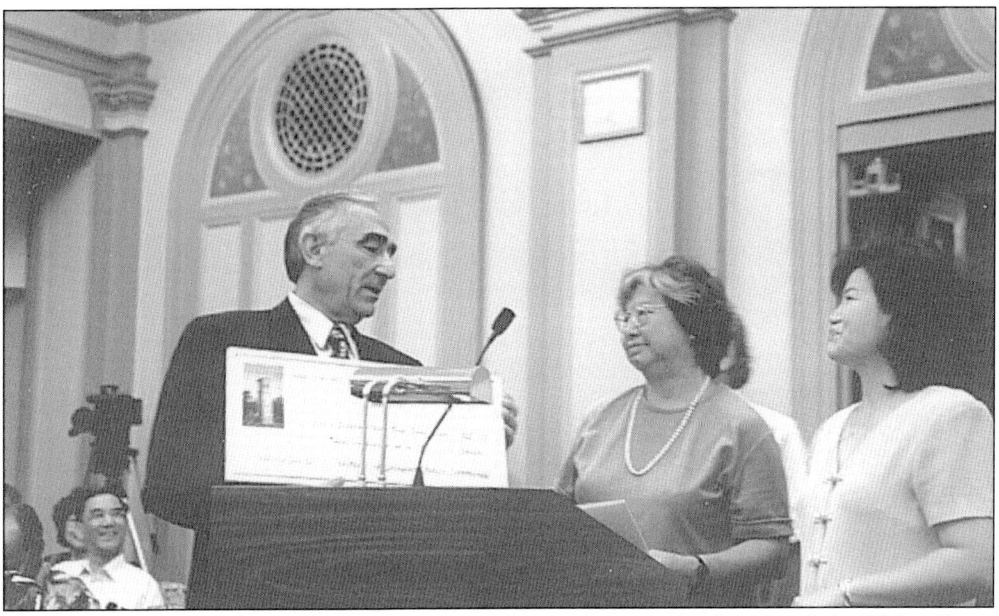

City Hall invited the general public to match public and private funds to build the Weber Point Plaza. The Chinese community stepped forward and funded the cost of the entry gate. In this 1999 photo, Gladys Ikeda (center) and Kathy Ho presented a check to Mayor Gary Podesto. The community itself raised $25,000 and Dr. Wyman Chan, on behalf of his family, donated the other $25,000. (*Courtesy of the Norman Lew Collection*)

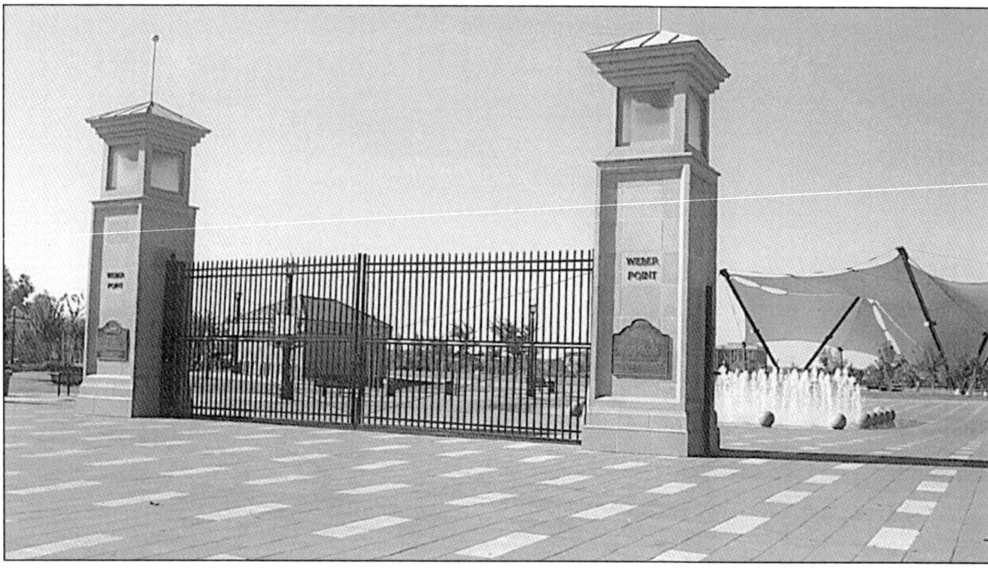

Weber Point was the original site of Capt. Charles Weber's home at the mouth of the Stockton Channel. The gate is the third major public gift from the Chinese.

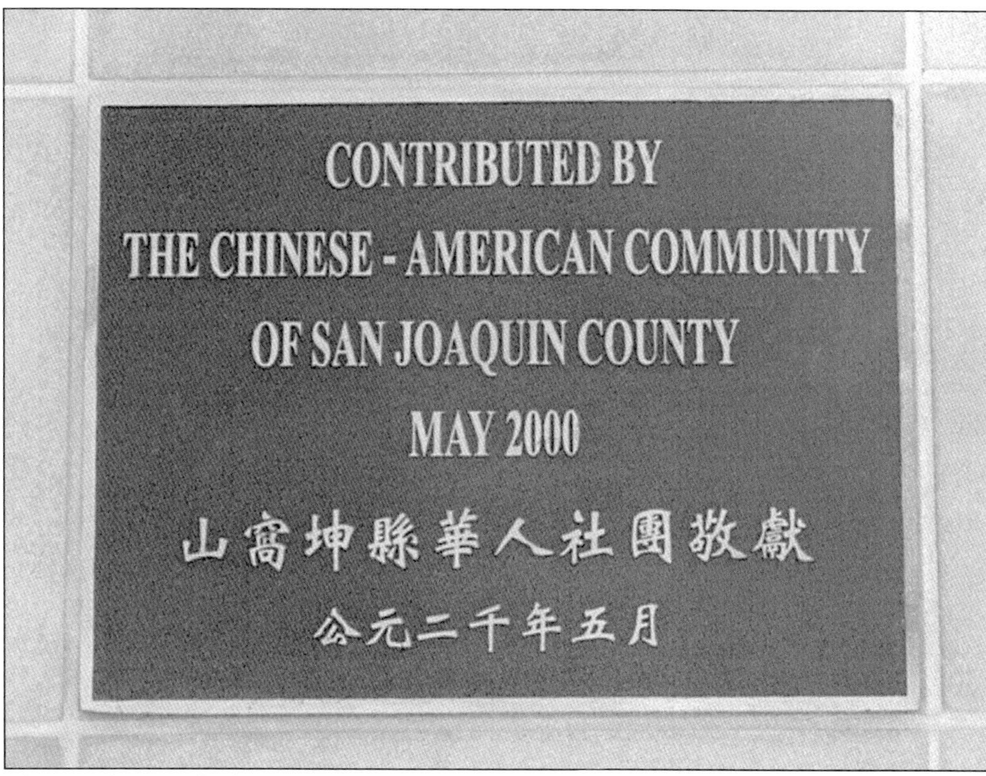

The translation of Chinese to English is exactly as written. This plaque is affixed to the backside of the entry gate north column and the south column notes the contribution by Dr. Wyman Chan.

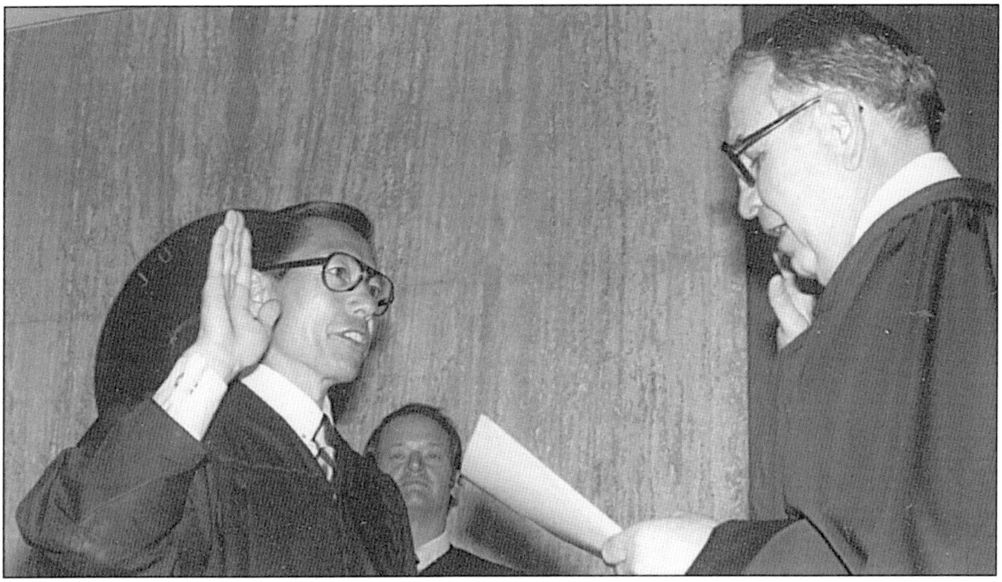

On March 9, 1971, the Honorable Frank Kim was sworn in as a Judge of the Municipal Court. Judge Kim, born in Marysville, was taken to China at age 7 months. He returned at age 8. His memories included shining shoes at the age of 10, and picking fruit in the orchards and crops in the fields. He served in the U.S. Army during the Korean War and later graduated from U.C. Hastings School of Law. After passing the bar in 1959, he moved to Stockton with his family in 1960 and began a career, first in the District Attorney's Office, and then in private practice before his appointment. His grandfather came to California in 1867. Judge Kim was elevated to the Superior Court and sworn into that office on March 9, 1979. He is now retired. (*Courtesy of Frank Kim*)

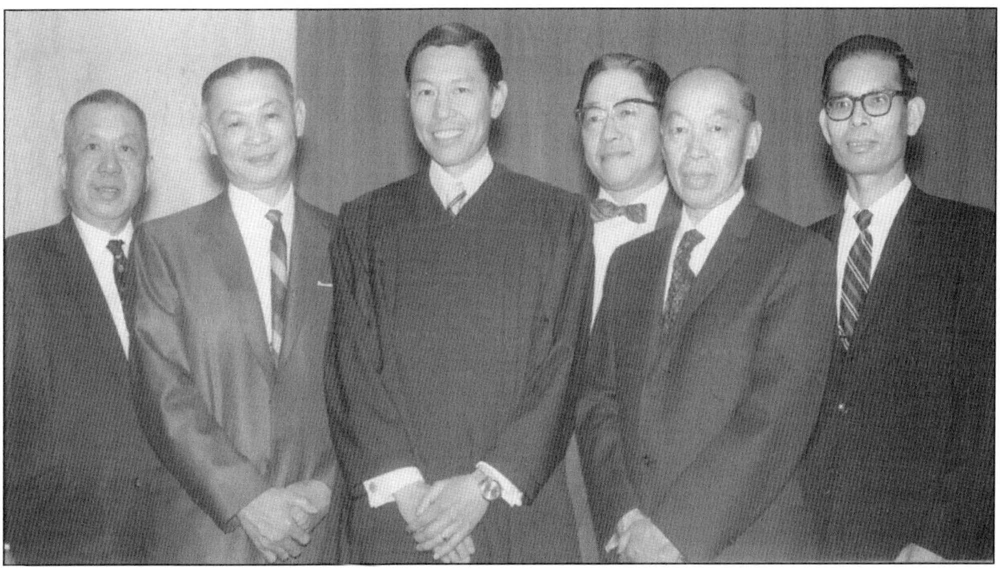

Community pride is evident as officers of Chung Wah flank Judge Frank Kim following a swearing in ceremony in 1971. Pictured, starting from the left, are S.L. Fong, past president; Doon G. Wong, president; Ray Wong Quen, English secretary; Lyman Mow, vice president; and Henry Yip, secretary. (*Courtesy of Frank Kim*)

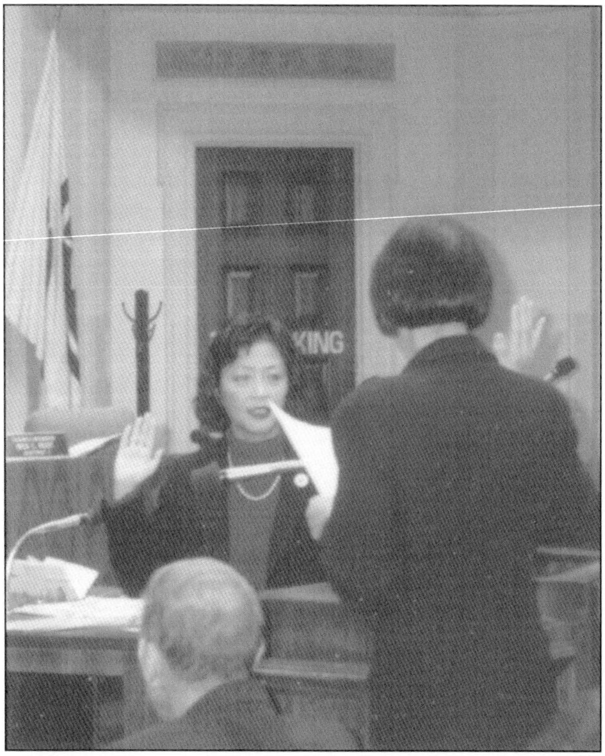

Frances Hong, city clerk, swears in Sylvia Sun Minnick to her second term as a city council member in 1991.

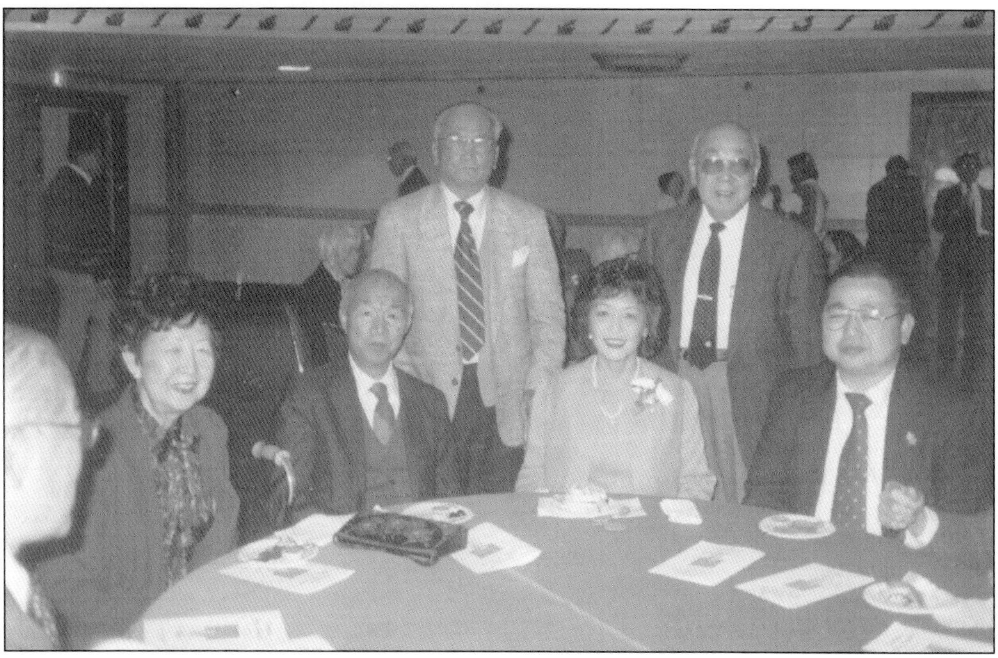

Chung Wah leaders in 1990 enjoyed the reception immediately following the swearing in of the first Asian to the city council, member Sylvia Minnick. Pictured are (standing) Dr. Lee Kwong Wah (left) and Johnnie Chang; (seated) Harry Chin (left), Bessie Yee, Dr. Paul K. Yee, Minnick, and Wing Chan. (*Courtesy of the Freeman Chang Collection*)

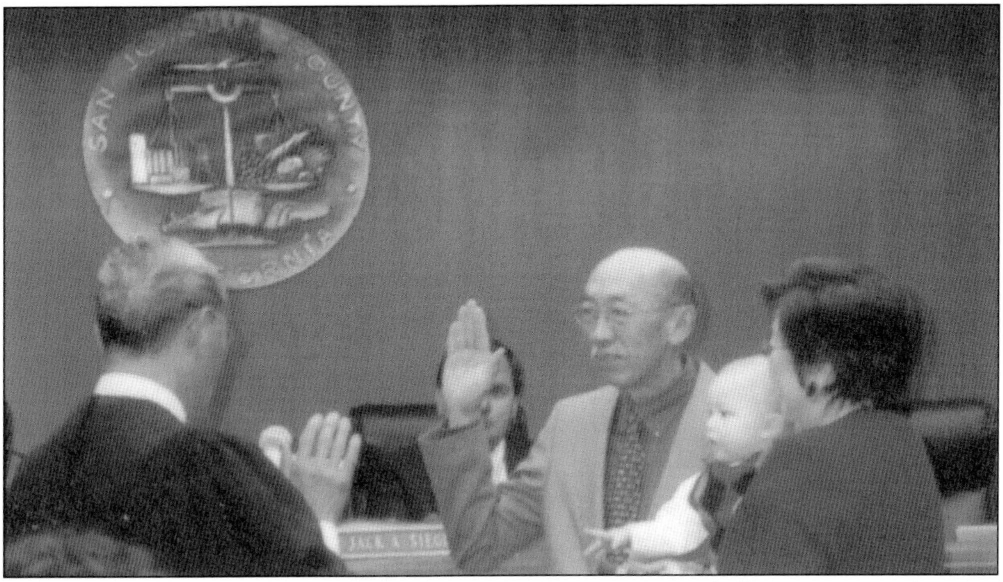

In 2001, Judge Frank Kim swore in Victor Mow to the County Board of Supervisors in this 2000 picture. Victor, formerly city council member and vice mayor, is the first Chinese to serve on the Board of Supervisors. Victor attended local schools, received an MBA from CSU-Stanislaus, and began a career at the San Joaquin County General Hospital. He served in the U.S. Army Medical Corps during the Viet Nam War. In the Chinese community he has been on the Jene Wah Board of Directors and CCSS. Also in this photo are his wife, Carolyn Sue, a Stockton public school teacher and the Mows' first grandson.

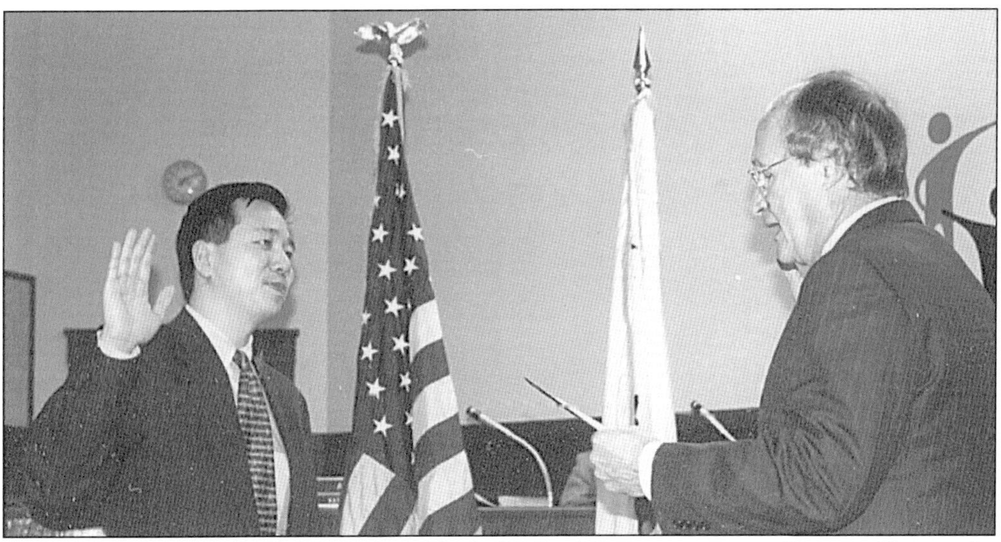

Charles Bloch, chairman of the Stockton Unified School District, swears in Clarence Chan to the Board of Trustees. Clarence attended local schools and graduated from Yale University and U.C. Hastings College of Law. A local attorney with political experience, he was a field representative to Senator Patrick Johnston. He is active in the Chinese Baptist Church and the American Lung Association. Other Chinese involved as trustees of school boards are Dr. Everett Low, current member of the Lincoln Unified School District Board of Trustees, and Dr. Norman Wong, former member of Stockton Unified School District Board of Trustees.

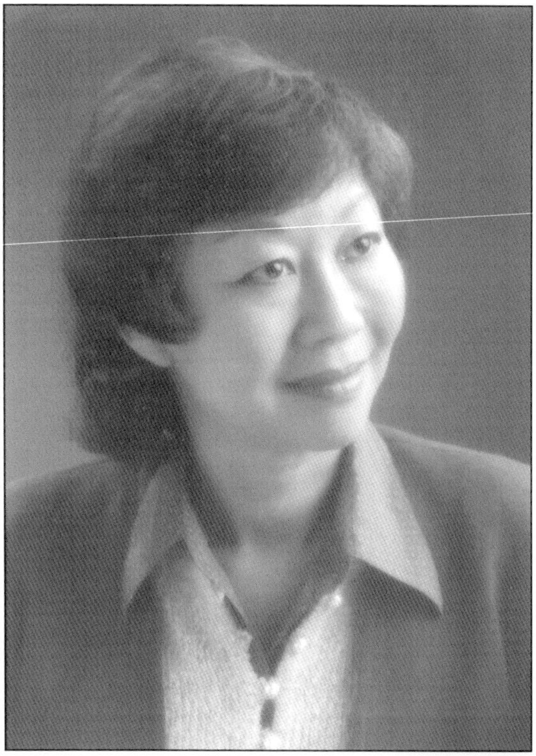

Frances Hong helped raised the "glass ceiling" in city hall as the first Asian city clerk. Frances, a native of Watsonville, began her career with the city in 1956. She became the Executive Assistant to the Assistant City Manager in 1981 and the city council appointed her to the city clerk position in 1984. She retired in 1996, ending a 39-year career in increasingly responsible roles including initiating modern techniques to systematically archive City Council minutes. (Courtesy of the Stockton City Clerk's Office)

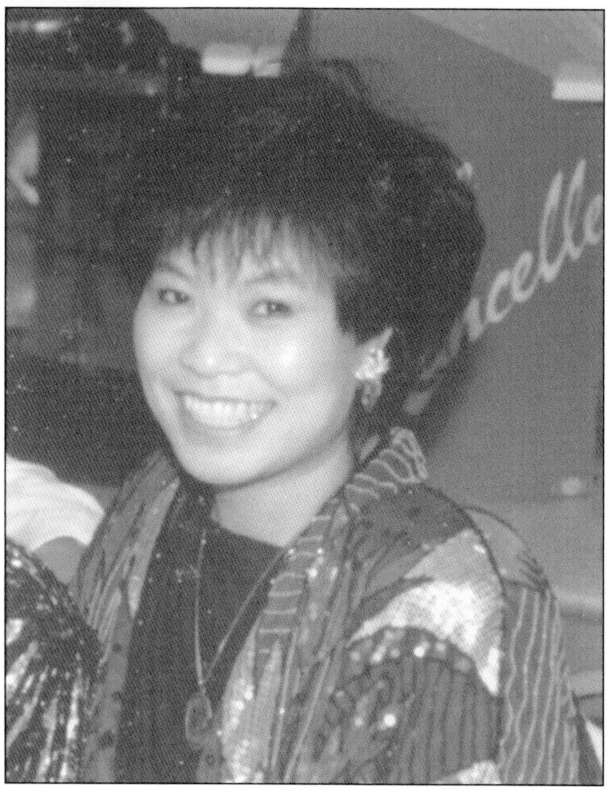

When Frances Hong retired, Kathy Gong Meissner was appointed her successor in 1996. Kathy, daughter of the Gong Lees, joined the clerk's office in 1985 after a stint as a court reporter in San Francisco. She brought her division into the technological age. (*Courtesy of Kathy Meissner*)

Gladys Lee Ikeda, a native of Canton but raised in Phoenix, Arizona, was a senior consultant in the California State Senate and served for former Insurance Commissioner John Garamendi as the Assistant Insurance Commissioner until her retirement in 1995. She was a probation officer in Alameda County before moving to Stockton. Another community activist, Gladys is the president of the CCSS and spearheaded the Weber Point Plaza gate fund drive.

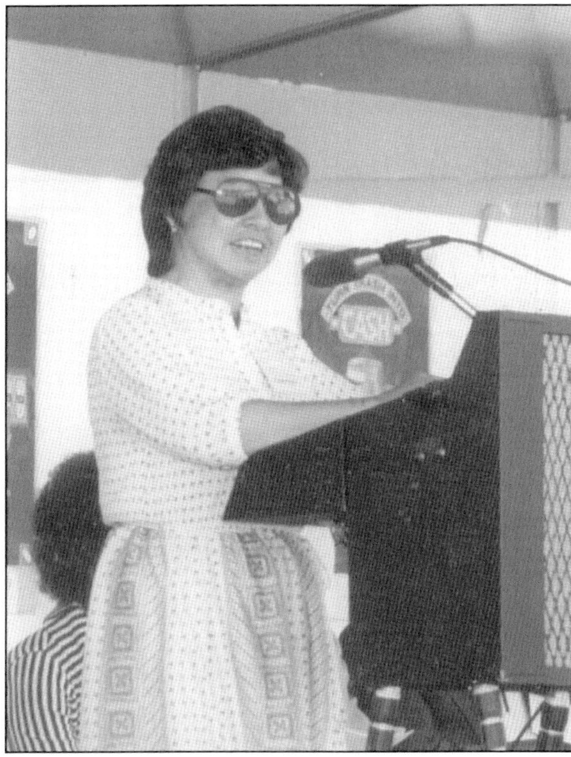

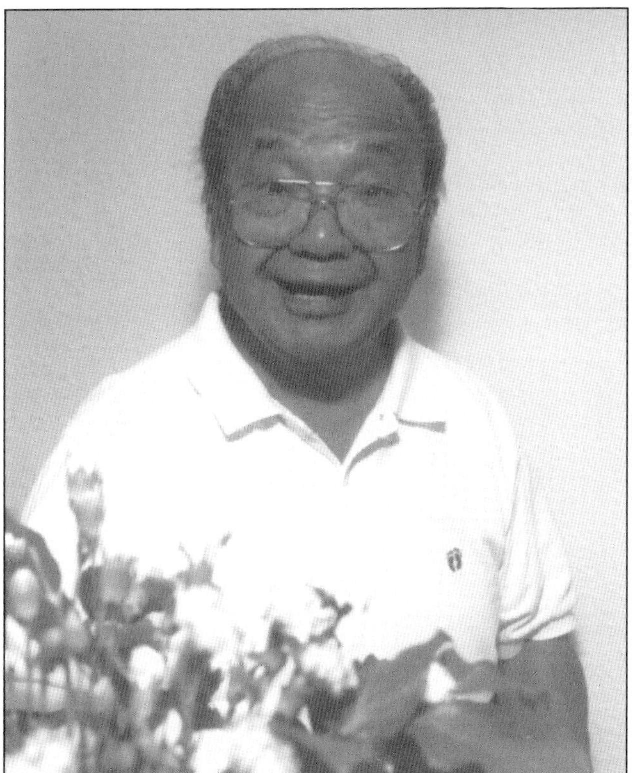

Conrad Mar came from Canton at the age of 5 and was washing dishes in a restaurant at age 10. He spent 35 years working up the career ladder in the California Department of Corrections, later becoming a Deputy Commissioner on the California State Board of Prison Terms. Involved in many Chinese organizations and churches, he also has served as president of Chung Wah multiple times. (*Courtesy of the Norman Lew Collection*)

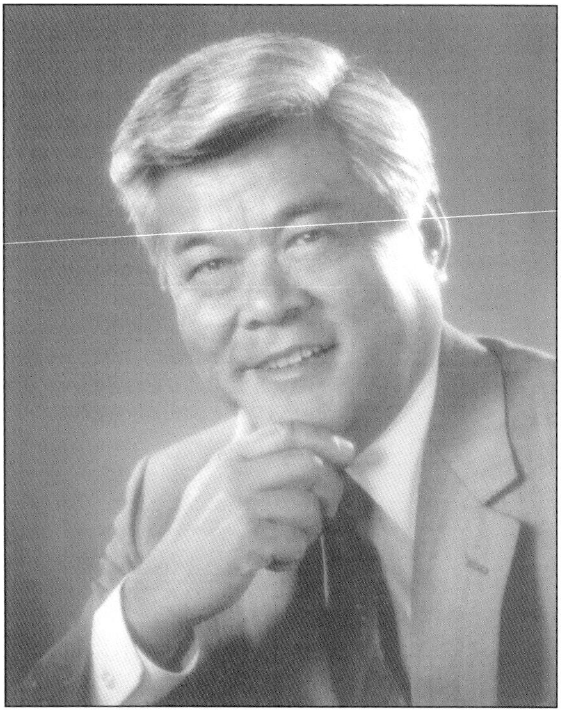

Jimmy Lam, native of San Francisco, began working for Centro-Mart in 1948 in the small town of Brentwood. At age 21 he became a store manager and by age 42 the Chief Executive Officer/Chairman of the Board of the Centro-Mart Co-op. Today there are eight stores in the company. He received numerous awards and recognitions, including those from Cathay Club–1979, CCSS–1991, and was also named Grocer of the Year in 1987 by the Stockton Quality Travelers' Club. He married Mary Ng, an elementary school teacher and they have three children. An avid 49'er fan, Jimmy is an annual volunteer in the beer and soda booth at the yearly Chinese New Year Festival.

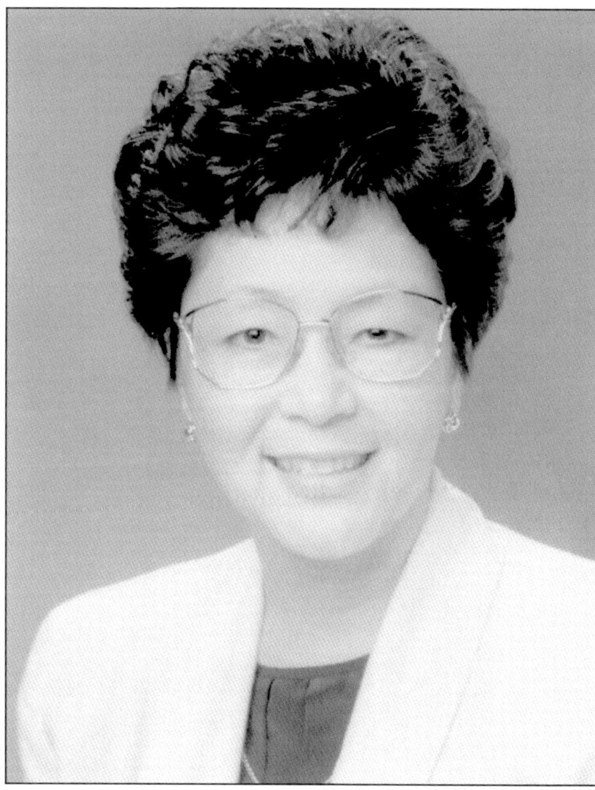

Sylvia Sun Minnick, born in Kuala Lumpur, Malaysia, came to American in 1950 and to Stockton in 1961. A multi-career person, Sylvia is a research historian, author of *SAMFOW: The San Joaquin Chinese Legacy* (1988), founder and publisher of Heritage West Books, and became a Deputy Assistant Director and then Assistant Director for various California State departments before retiring. Civically, she was the first Asian on the Stockton City Council, the first woman president of Chung Wah, and spearheaded the effort to finance and renovate the Quan Ying Senior Apartments. She has received numerous awards and recognitions at local, state, and international levels.

Dr. Elizabeth Yip Blanchard began her career at San Joaquin Delta College in 1964. Born in Hong Kong, "Liz," a psychologist and counselor at the junior college, worked also for the University of the Pacific and counseled a number of campus clubs. She is the first Chinese to be elected to head a college teachers' association. Civically, she is politically active and chaired the City Planning Commission and served as president of Chung Wah among other organizations. A winner of multiple awards, her greatest pride lies in her three children and their accomplishments. (*Courtesy of Gladys Ikeda*)

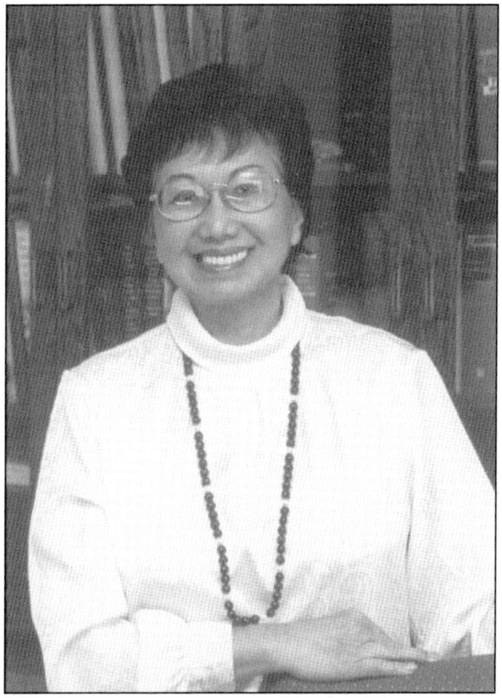

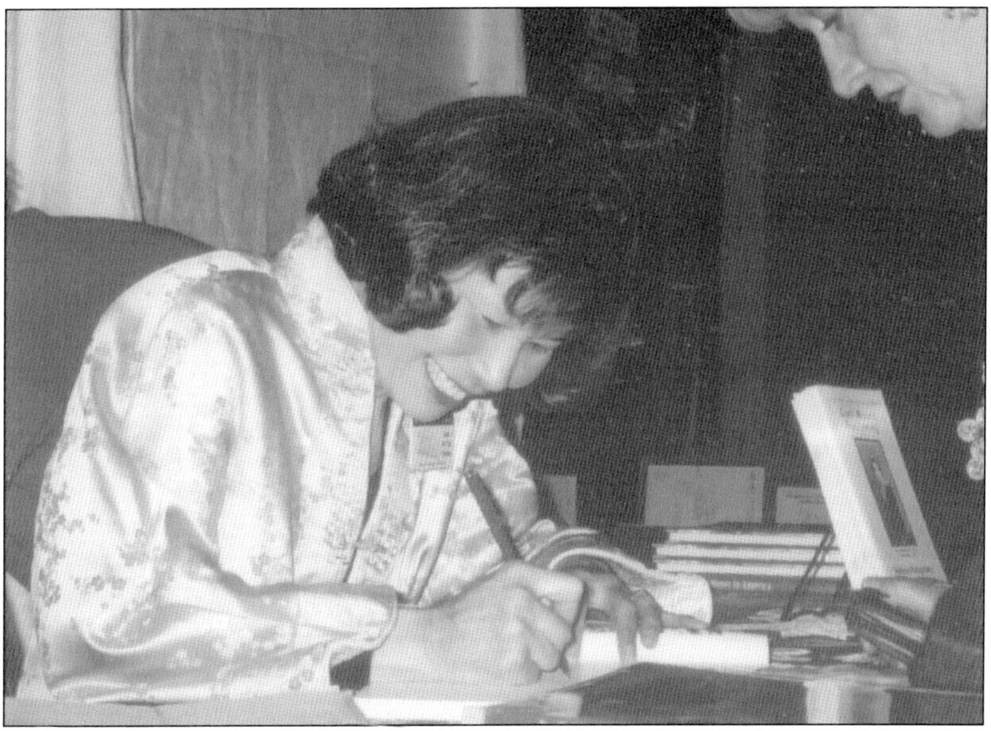

A fourth-generation, Stockton-born elementary school teacher, Lani Ah Tye Farkas recently authored *Bury My Bones in America: The Saga of a Chinese Family in California 1852–1996*. Her research into her great-grandfather's life and times in California history enhances researchers' cache of California's Chinese-American history. (*Photo by Kim Wood*)

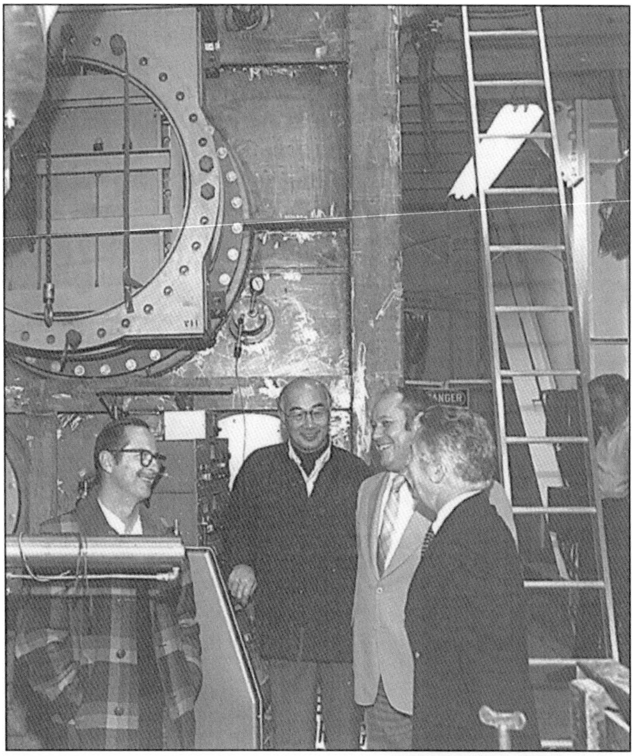

The Regents of the University of California conferred the title of Staff Senior Scientist Emeritus on Kenou Lou, an alumni of the original Tri-C (Chinese Christian Center). Kenou's work at the UC-Lawrence Laboratory in Berkeley concentrated on high energy physics, engineering, and fusion energy, and he later worked on the Keck telescope on top of Mauna Kea on the island of Hawaii. Kenou and his staff built the Neutral Beam Injector, a $12 million project to develop a prototype system designed to deliver ions with no electrical charges through the magnetic field of the Princeton Tokamak Fusion Test Reactor (TFTR). The neutral ions heated plasma up to 100 million degrees Celsius.

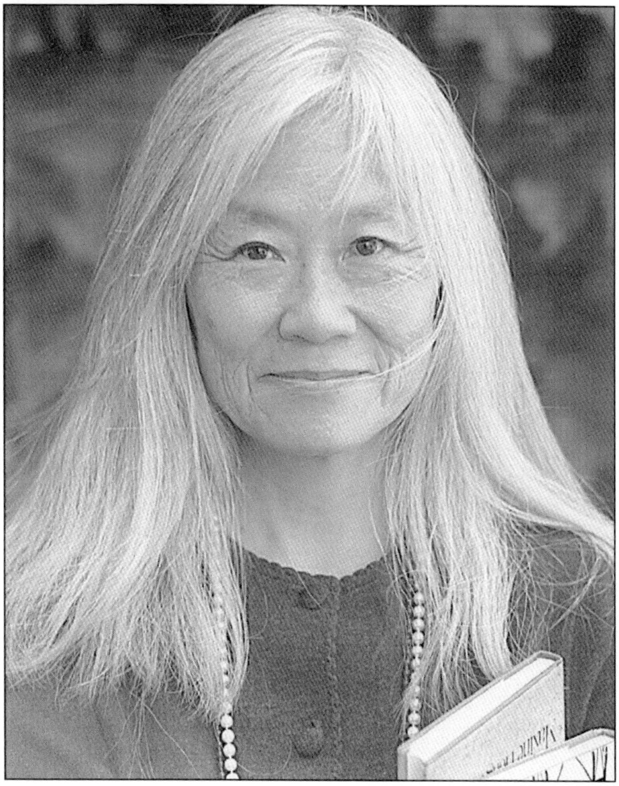

In 1980 author Maxine Hong Kingston received the very first Career Achievement Award from the Stockton Arts Commission. A graduate of local schools and the University of California-Berkeley, she was recognized for *The Woman Warrior* and *China Men*, which had received numerous awards and national acclaim. (*Photo by Glenn Williams, courtesy of Stockton Arts Commission*)

In her youth, Beulah Ong Quo was an extremely active youth leader at the Chinese Christian Center. Beulah captured a long and distinguished career as a movie, stage, and television actress. She is the first Asian American to receive an Emmy Award as producer of a television documentary of Oscar-winning cinematographer James Howe Wong. She founded the East-West Players, the first Asian-American theatrical group in the nation. As a California Sesquicentennial Commissioner, Beulah spearheaded and raised funds for *Heading East*, the musical production focusing on Asian Americans in California's history. The California State Assembly recognized her as the Woman of the Year in 1998.

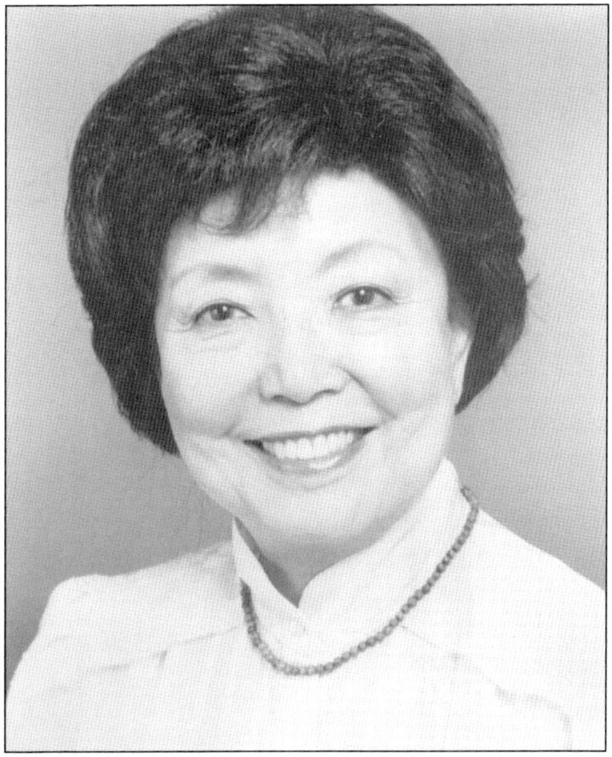

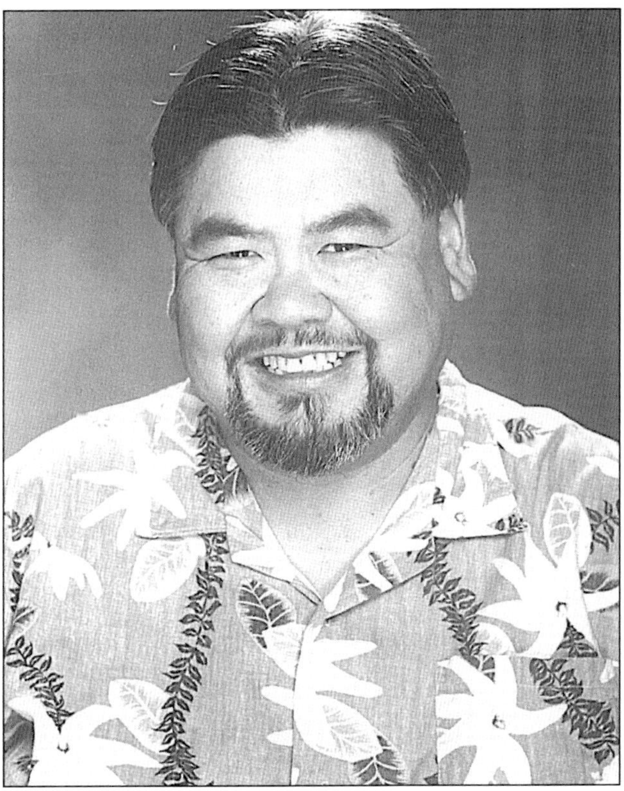

Glen Chin, son of William Chin (Quong Wah Yuen, sausage factory), has multiple credits as a director, producer, and actor on the screen, stage, and television media and commercials. In addition to theater, Glen also is a talented musician and graduated from the Conservatory of Music at the University of the Pacific. He was a bass player in the Stockton Symphony for 12 years, sings baritone, and conducts musicals.

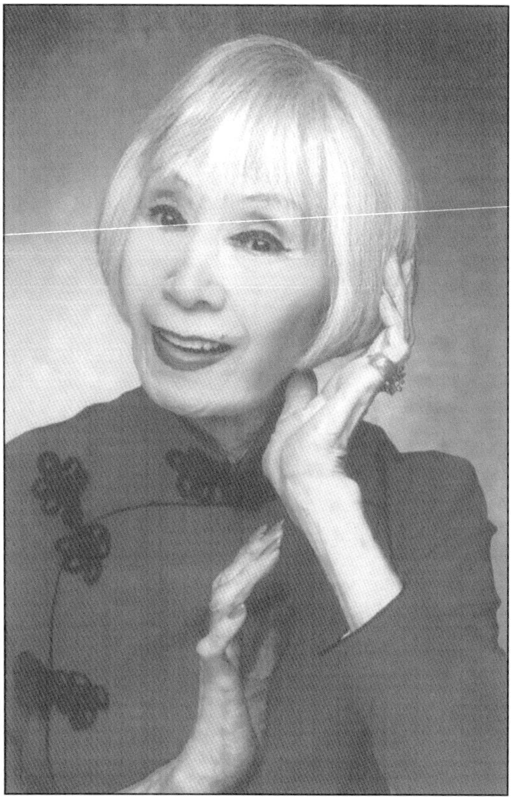

Jadin Wong is another multi-talented Stocktonian with many credits to her name. Formerly a dancer at Forbidden City in San Francisco, she did comedy for 20 years. During World War II she logged in more than 3,000 hours entertaining the troops. She played such a crucial role as a proponent of Asian-American performers that both the Lincoln Center for the Performing Arts and the Public History Museum have established collections of her life's work. Today, she is a high-powered, New York theatrical agent who represents over 700 Asian-American performers.

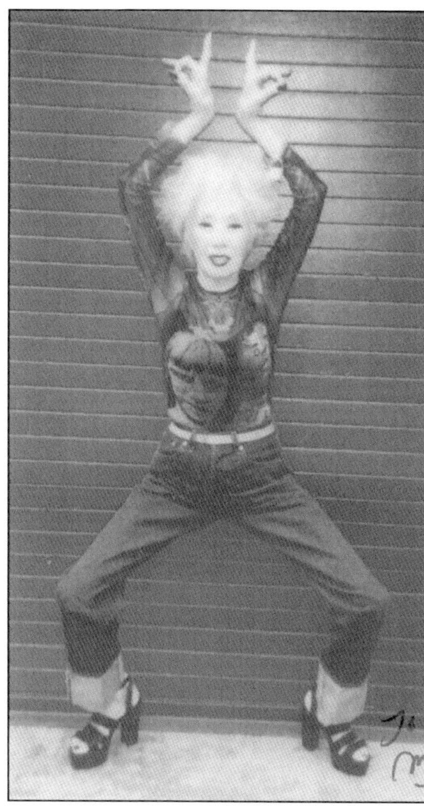

Jadin Wong still works. In 1997, at age 83, she modeled for a Levi commercial that was placed on a website. She appeared on the cover of *Life* in 1940 and also was featured in *Look* and other magazines. Jadin is the sister of the late Charles Wong, the county public works director.

Sandra Gin, raised in Stockton and a University of California-Berkeley graduate, became a newscaster first in Sacramento and then Hollywood, and now works for Channel 11 in Houston, Texas. Her sister, Janice, also went into the communication field and spent several years in Washington D.C. before settling in the Bay Area and working for Channel 2 in Oakland.

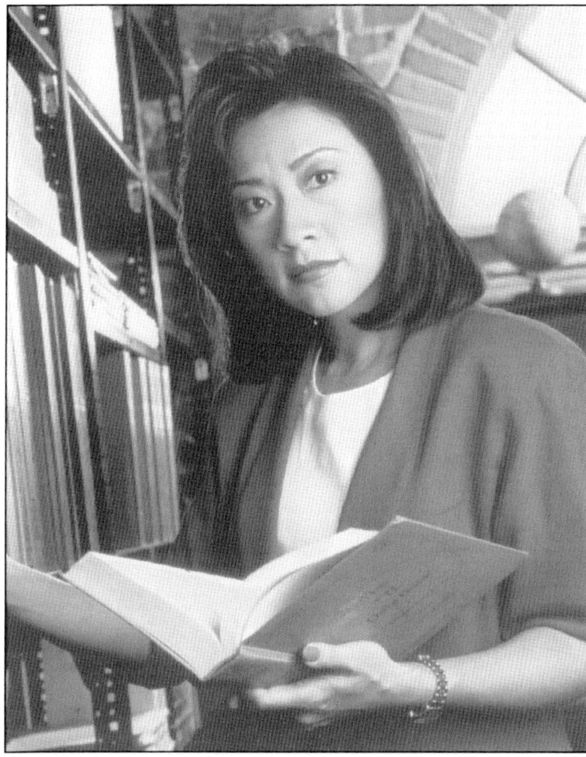

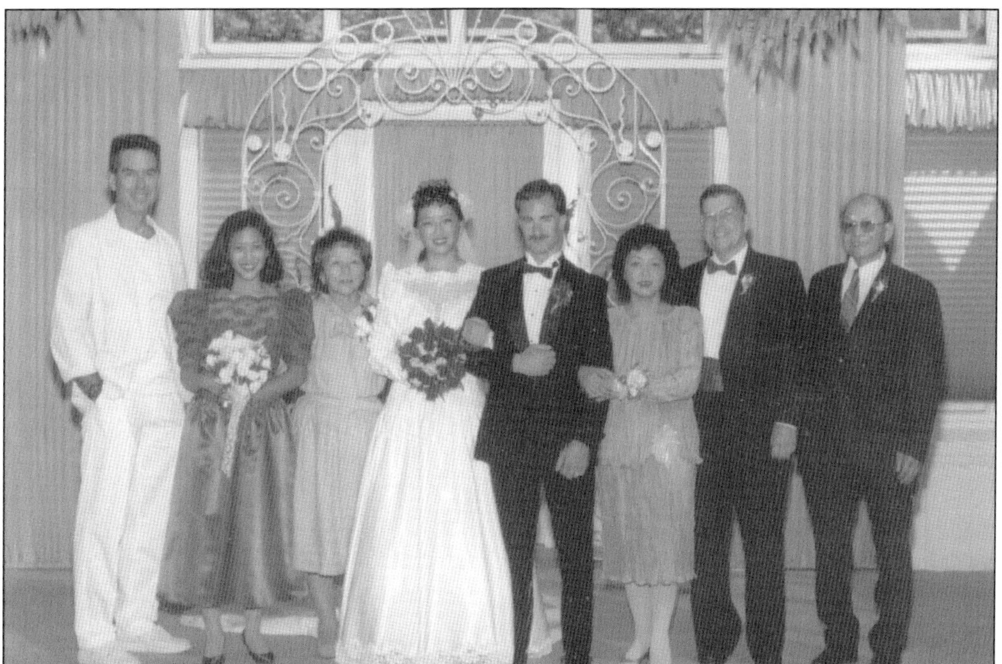

The repeal of California's Miscegenation Law in 1948 benefited the third and fourth generation Chinese Americans. As this 1989 wedding photo of Michael Forsch and Donna Chan shows, interracial marriages became very accepted in many Chinese-American families.

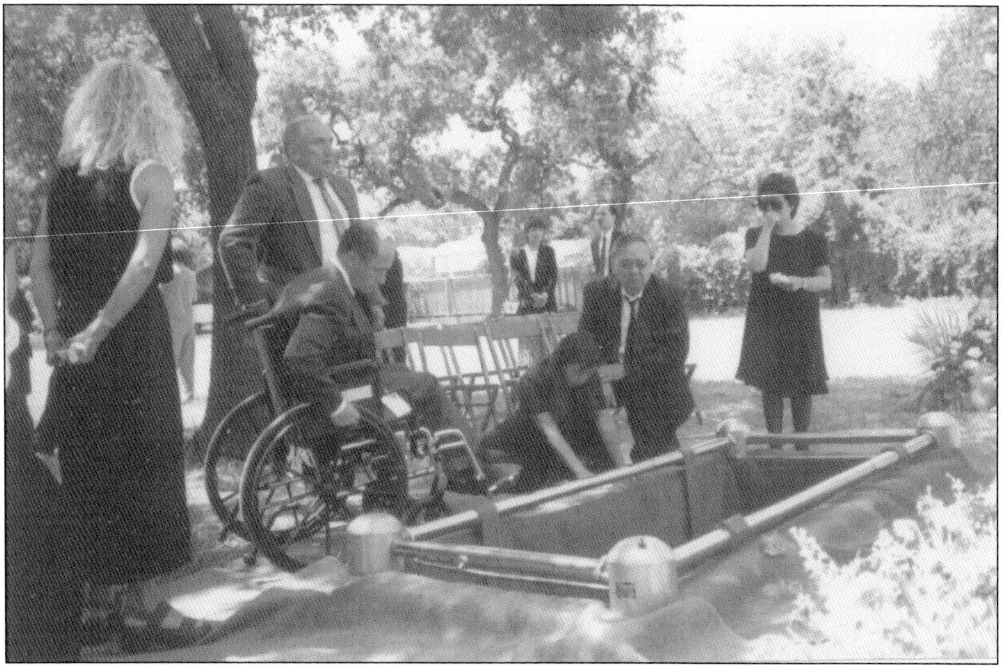

The Stockton Chinese expect to have a full life cycle, as does everyone. Tragedy does strike, however, and not only do families mourn, but so does the community. This was taken in 1999 at the burial of Donna Chan Forsch who was killed by a rockslide while vacationing at Sacred Falls in Hawaii. The Forschs were celebrating their 10th anniversary.

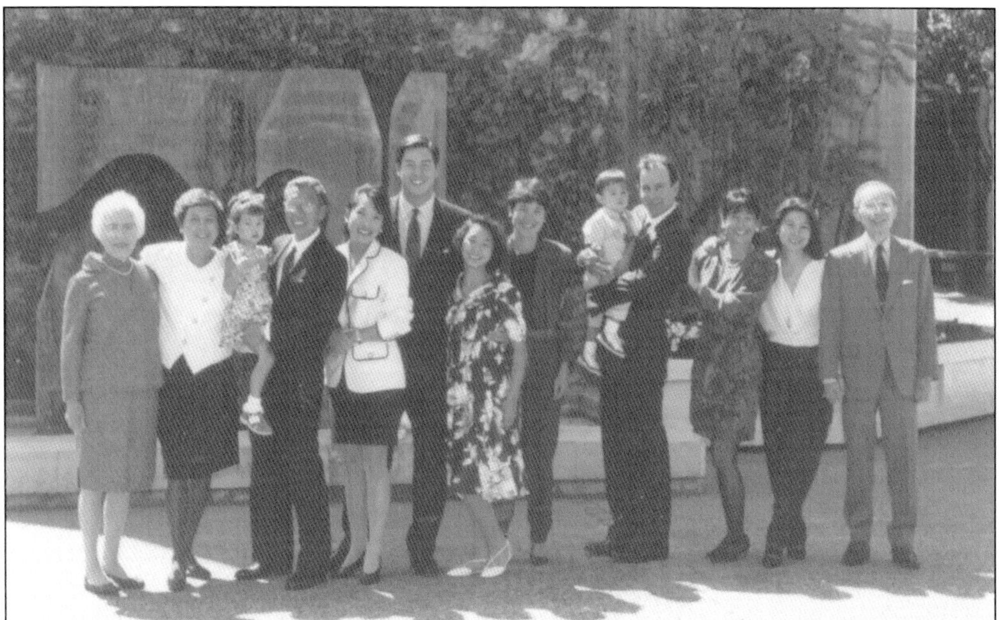

This photo of the Frank Kim family taken in 1992 is one of four generations. While the children now have families of their own and live in other parts of the country, family reunions are very meaningful. (*Courtesy of Leona Wong*)

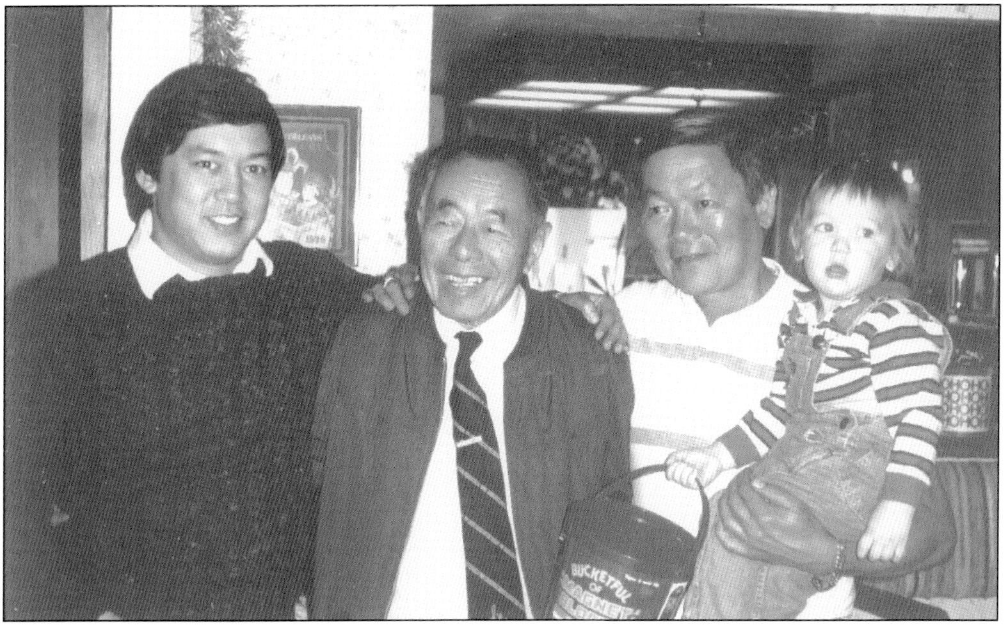

Charles Wong beamed in this family photo of the four generations taken in 1989. Pictured are Zachary (president of Wong Engineering), Charles, Chance (founder of Wong Engineering), and Wesley (aka "Bubba") at age two. (*Courtesy of Chance Wong*)

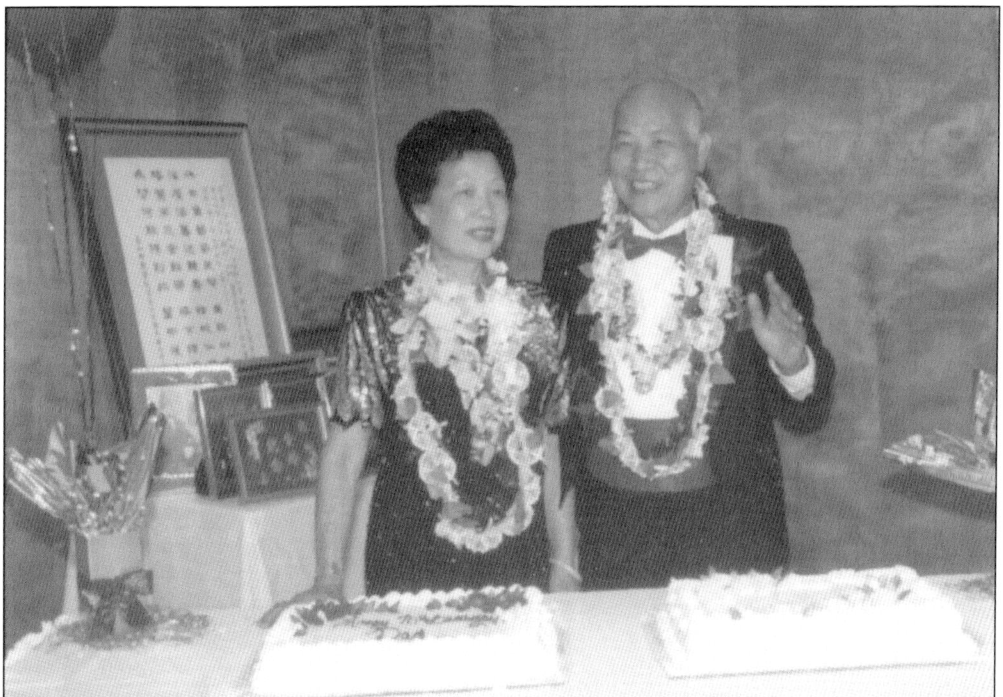

The Gong Lees celebrated their Golden Anniversary at Saint Basil, the Greek Orthodox Church in August of 1990. The devoted couple, wearing money leis, displays their gold-engraved, congratulatory plaques. (*Courtesy of Kathy Meissner*)

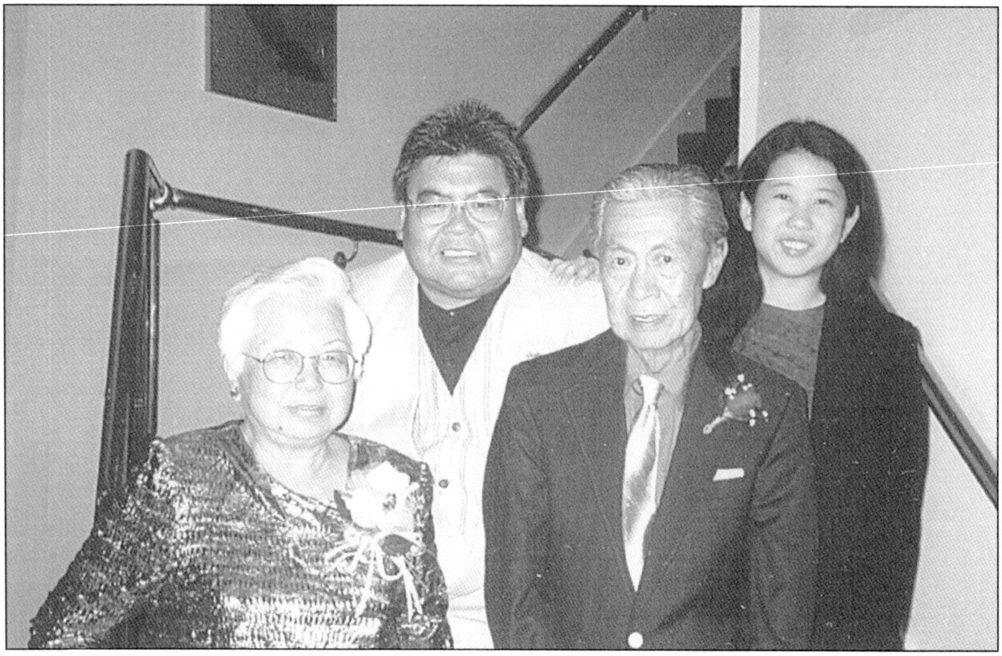

At their 50th Anniversary, Lily and William Chin (Quong Wah Yuen store) counted their many blessings—8 children, 14 grandchildren, and 1 great-grandchild. This photo taken in 1997 included son Glen and daughter-in-law Roberta. (*Courtesy of Gail Chin Tucker*)

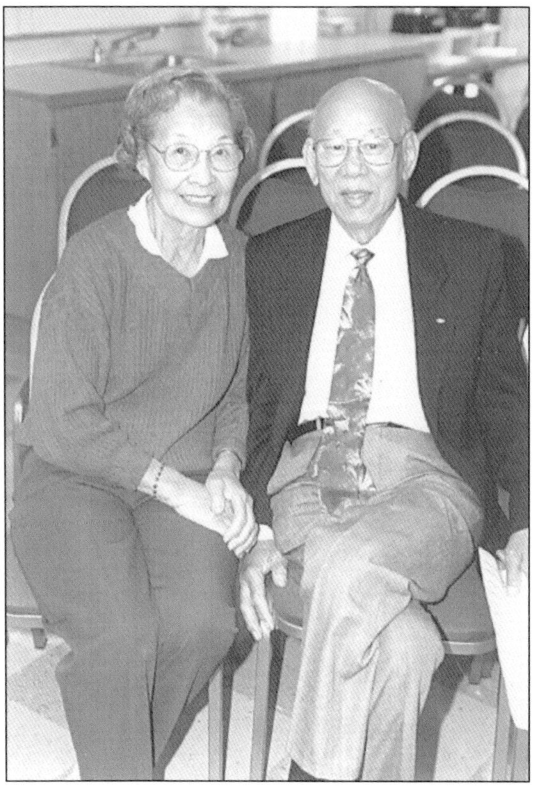

Married now for over 60 years, Edward and Blanche Chin Ah Tye continue to be active at Jene Wah, Cathay Club, and St. Mark's Church. Together the couple coordinated, printed, and sold over 9,000 copies of a cookbook to raise funds for St. Mark's. (*Courtesy of Jene Wah, Inc.*)

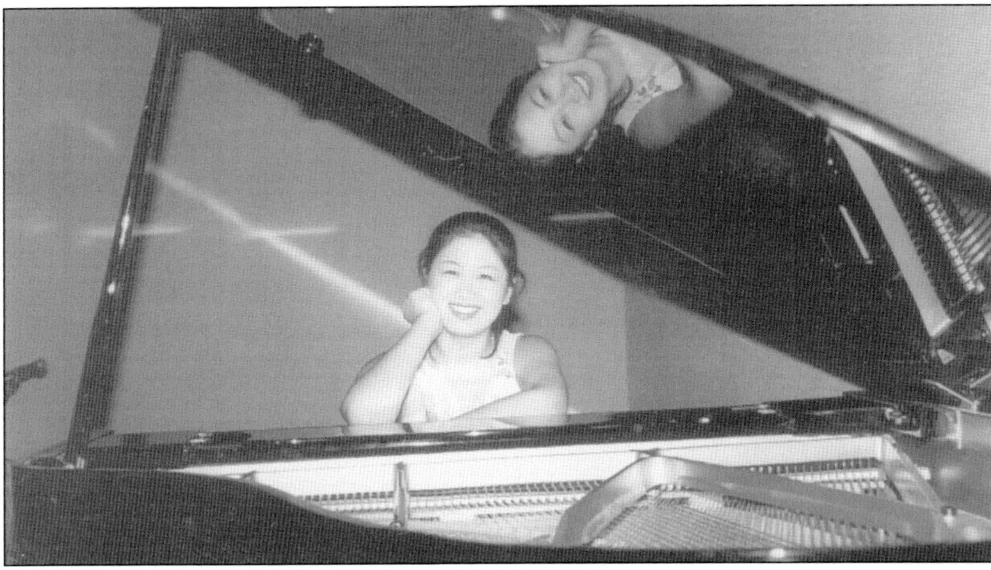

As a member of the up-and-coming generation, Ning Ma won a 1st in competition at age seven and continued to do so at numerous local and regional competitions in the Midwest, New York, and California. Now at University of California-Berkeley concentrating on biochemistry, this young accomplished pianist was the Lincoln High School editor-in-chief of the school newspaper. She received multiple scholarships upon graduation.

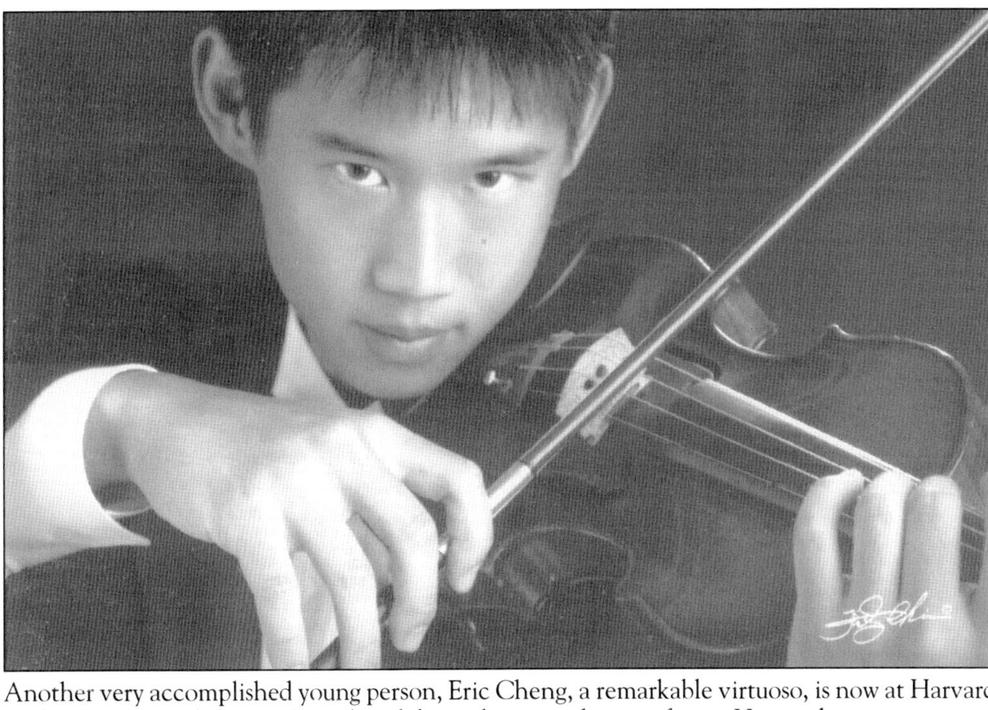

Another very accomplished young person, Eric Cheng, a remarkable virtuoso, is now at Harvard studying music and physics. Eric played the violin since the age of nine. He was the concertmaster of the Lincoln High School symphony and became the principal 2nd violinist of CMEA, All-state Honor Orchestra. Well-rounded on the varsity tennis team, cross-country team, and ice hockey team, Eric was the valedictorian of his class.

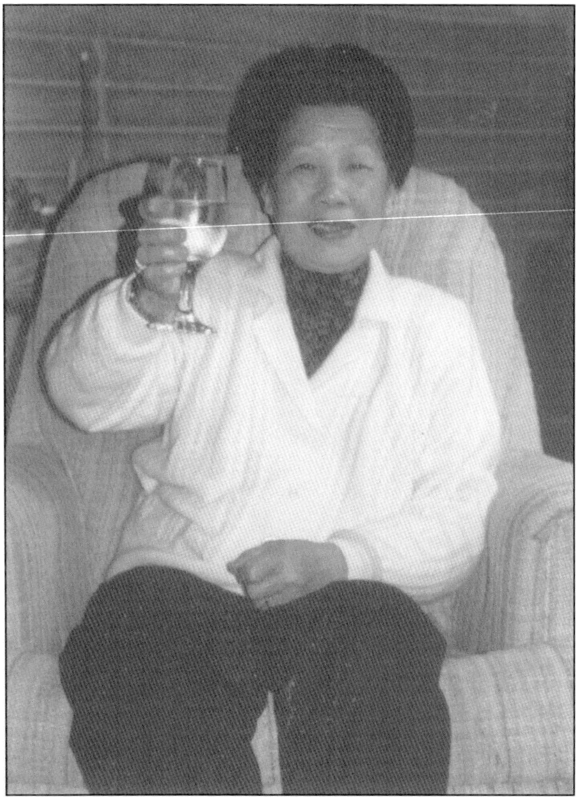

Toy Lee reflects—work for over 60 years, success in the restaurant business, wonderful husband and father, good children, smart grandchildren, retired, and healthy. Salute! (*Courtesy of Kathy Meissner*)

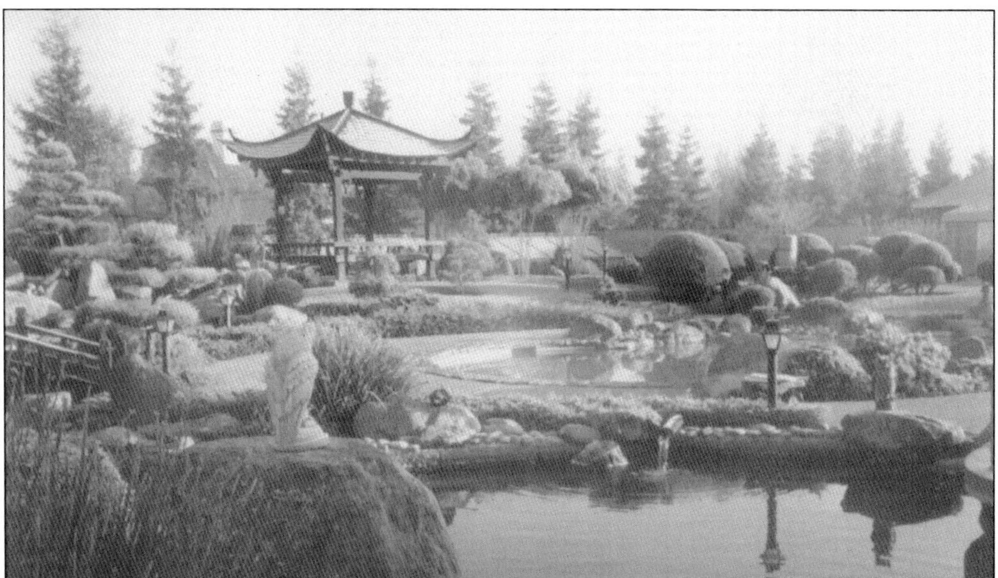

This park-like setting with reflecting pool and pavilion replicates the peace and tranquility sought by many, Stockton Chinese not withstanding. Located in North Stockton, the garden at the home of a Chinese couple brings much contentment in their retirement years.